PREPOSTEROUS REVELATIONS

The Bible in the Modern World, 39

Series Editors
J. Cheryl Exum, Jorunn Økland and Stephen D. Moore

Editorial Board
Alison Jasper, Tat-siong Benny Liew,
Caroline Vander Stichele

PREPOSTEROUS REVELATIONS

VISIONS OF APOCALYPSE AND MARTYRDOM IN HOLLYWOOD CINEMA 1980–2000

Laura Copier

SHEFFIELD PHOENIX PRESS

2012

Copyright © 2012 Sheffield Phoenix Press

Published by Sheffield Phoenix Press
Department of Biblical Studies, University of Sheffield,
45 Victoria Street, Sheffield S3 7QB
UK

www.sheffieldphoenix.com

A CIP catalogue record for this book
is available from the British Library

Typeset by ISB Typesetting
Printed on acid-free paper by Lightning Source UK Ltd, Milton Keynes

ISBN 978-1-907534-24-9 (hardback)

ISSN 1747-9630

CONTENTS

INTRODUCTION

Don't wait for the last judgment—it takes place every day.
>   Albert Camus, *The Fall* (Camus 1956: 111)[1]

> As the twentieth century's secularism hypothesis sits irrelevantly in the
> wings, 'religion' returns to center stage. The martyr, meanwhile, is one of
> this drama's most contentious yet riveting stars, the one who packs the
> house for every performance.
>   Elizabeth A. Castelli (Castelli 2004: 9)

This project focuses on the recycling of Biblical images and stories of the
Apocalypse, particularly its conceptions of martyrdom and self-sacrifice, in
contemporary Hollywood cinema. I examine to what extent representations
of martyrs and self-sacrifice are informed by traditional notions, and also
how these are transformed and redirected in the process of transmission.
Hollywood cinema can be regarded as a site of re-interpretation of Christian
and non-Christian visual and discursive traditions. However, these
adaptations are performed by a secular, not (explicitly) religious system.

Hollywood may recycle only certain elements of the original texts; yet,
the discourse of the precedent text still exerts its power in the new one.
Once the historical source is traced, I analyze in what ways the new text
is also an active intervention in the earlier material. Finally, I attempt
to define the transfer of meaning from past to present and from present
to past. This implies a rethinking of Hollywood as a mere duplicator or
recycler of original images and narratives. Instead of that standard view,
one can perceive the original to function as an aftereffect caused by the
images of Hollywood cinema. Thus, the leading notion of this study is the
reconfiguration of the relationship of the present to the past and vice versa.

In what follows, I elaborate on the key concepts and themes that
figure throughout this study. Mieke Bal's notion of preposterous history
and the concept of quotation are outlined first. This study attempts to be
interdisciplinary. Therefore, my two fields of interest, religion and cinema,
are addressed even though, given my corpus, cinema will certainly be
more prominent. The idea of genre as a means to cross the divide between
religion and film is persistent in my study. I address genre in Hollywood

---

1. 'N'attendez pas le jugement dernier. Il a lieu tous les jours', Albert Camus, *La
Chute*.

cinema, specifically the genre of the disaster film, and in both biblical and cinematic narratives of the Apocalypse.

The first major theme of this study is the Apocalypse. In addition to looking at the definition of this theme in terms of biblical genre and common usage, as well as an entrenched notion in American popular culture, I use narrative theory and philosophy on the topic of the Apocalypse. The second theme is martyrdom and the figure of the martyr. I discuss these contested terms in the Judeo-Christian and, to a lesser extent, the Islamic context. The apocalyptic narrative of the Book of Revelation is the key text in this respect. Finally, the two themes of Apocalypse and martyrdom are read through a critical gender approach. I find this approach indispensable, given the misogynistic nature of both the Book of Revelation and the films I analyze. Apocalyptic stories and their concomitant imagery of martyrdom are underpinned by assumptions about masculinity and femininity, the former's superiority over the latter. A critical gender approach not only signals these suppositions, but also, in combination with my main reading method, preposterous history, allows for these assumptions to be challenged.

Preposterous History

In *Quoting Caravaggio: Contemporary Art, Preposterous History*, Mieke Bal addresses a key question with regard to representation in art. She states that art is inevitably engaged with what came before it, and that that engagement is an active reworking. The question is, 'Who illuminates— helps us understand—whom?' (Bal 1999: 3). One may adopt the traditional view, which regards ancient art as the source, a foundational influence on everything that follows in its wake. However, as Bal contends, 'The problem with this view is that we can only see what we already know, or think we know' (Bal 1999: 3). This conception of the relationship between source and adaptation is based on recognition. To escape this deadlock between past and present, specifically the dominating influence of the past (what came first) over the present (what came later or after), Bal proposes the term 'preposterous history'. Preposterous history is 'the reversal of what came chronologically first ("pre-") as an aftereffect behind ("post") its later recycling' (Bal 1999: 7).

Bal takes her cue from T.S. Eliot's 1919 essay 'Tradition and the Individual Talent'. In this essay, Eliot acknowledges the indispensability of tradition; the influence predecessors have on artists. But he also states that new art can alter the meaning, or perception, of the art of the past. In the crucial passage of the essay, which Bal uses as an epigraph to her book, Eliot states: 'Whoever has approved this idea of order [...] will not find it preposterous that the past should be altered by the present as much as the present is directed by the past' (Eliot 1950: 50). Each work of art to some extent changes what came earlier, what Eliot describes as 'existing monuments': 'For order to persist after the supervention of novelty, the whole existing order must be, if ever so slightly, altered; and so the relations, proportions, values of each work of art toward the whole are readjusted; and this is conformity between the old and the new' (Eliot 1950: 50).

In Eliot's conception, past and present art form a simultaneous order. This order is in constant flux or tension, since it incorporates both order and change. The simultaneity or synchronicity of Eliot's notion of tradition suggests a new way of thinking about the relation between the past and present. The past should not be understood as a bound, coherent point of departure or origin, against which all later forms are to be evaluated. Rather, past and present engage in a dialogue, which brings about transformations between them.

Quotation

To set up such a dialogue between contemporary culture, in this case Hollywood cinema, and the art of the past, biblical images and stories, quotation can function as a mediator. Quotation can be defined as the recasting of past images, which is not only important to contemporary art, but in turn also affects the original source of the images for which it, in turn, becomes a source. In the practice of quotation we see preposterous history at work.

Quotation encompasses both iconography and intertextuality. Both concepts are relevant for preposterous history. The work of art historian Erwin Panofsky offers a systematic definition of iconography. Panofsky distinguishes between the traditional definition of *iconography*, a pictorial representation of a subject through a figure, and *iconology*, a larger understanding of iconic representations. Within iconology, Panofsky outlines three specific levels. The first level is the *pre-iconological* level of description. This concerns the natural subject matter, the 'motifs' or 'pure forms' that are carriers of primary and natural meanings (Panofsky 1967: 5). These motifs define for Panofsky a 'history of style', a controlling principle of interpretation. The history of style gives 'insight into the manner in which, under varying historical conditions, objects and events were expressed by forms' (Panofsky 1967: 15). The second is the *iconographic* level that recognizes the conventionality of images and their themes, demanding certain knowledge of the literary and textual sources. This defines for Panofsky a 'history of types', which concerns itself with the expression of themes and concepts by certain objects and events (Panofsky 1967: 15-16). Finally, Panofsky distinguishes the *iconological* level, defined by a 'history of cultural symptoms or 'symbols'.' This level discloses what he considers the 'intrinsic meaning' or symbolical values of a work, and should give the art historian insight into essential tendencies of the human mind and into the ways in which these tendencies are expressed by specific themes and concepts.

Panofsky's theory provides a practical method that moves from description to analysis and finally to interpretation, a progression that presupposes the separateness of these three activities. I use iconography in a somewhat different sense. As is clear from Panofsky's model, the historical precedent is viewed as source. This precedent then more or less dictates to the artist what forms can be used. Bal attempts to escape from this passivity inherent in the traditional view of iconography. The work of the later artists should be considered an active intervention in the material that is handed down to them. Furthermore, iconography frequently avoids interpreting the meaning of the borrowed, or quoted, signs in their new context; the reconceptualization of meaning is neglected. Bal proposes to trace the process of meaning-production over time, and crucially in this respect, in both directions: from past to present and from present to past. Finally, Panofsky's model, in particular its most frequently practiced element, iconography, tends to refer back visual motifs to written texts. Bal's methodology not only takes the textual nature of precedents seriously as a visual textuality, but also includes the visuality of the precedent text. By recycling forms taken from earlier works, an artist brings along the text from which the borrowed element has been taken, while at the same time constructing a new text with the debris. The new image-as-'text' is 'contaminated' by the discourse of the precedent (Bal 1999: 8-9). This is the concept of quotation I will employ in this study.

The second concept is a complicated one, since it is as often used as it is misused. Julia Kristeva originally introduced the concept of intertextuality. Her reading of the Russian critic Mikhail Bakhtin inspired her to elaborate on his concepts of dialogism and interaction. Kristeva refers to texts in terms of two axes: a horizontal axis connecting the author and reader of a text (what Bakhtin calls dialogism), and a vertical axis, which connects the text to other texts (what Bakhtin calls interaction). From this, Kristeva posits that texts engender texts: 'Any text is constructed as a mosaic of quotations; any text is the absorption and transformation of another' (Kristeva 1980: 66).

Intertextuality, defined by Jonathan Culler in his book *The Pursuit of Signs: Semiotics, Literature, Deconstruction*, is the idea that 'works are to be considered not as autonomous entities, "organic wholes", but as intertextual constructs: sequences which have meaning in relation to other texts which they take up, cite, parody, refute, or generally transform' (Culler 2002: 38). Culler asserts that texts can only be read in relation to other texts. He elaborates on intertextuality by highlighting a common misapprehension, namely that the study of intertextuality is the investigation of sources and influences: of the work's relation to particular prior texts. This would entail that, once the 'original source' is located, a definite meaning can be established, closing the process of signification. The opposite is the case with intertextuality. In its nature lies the paradox of discursivity:

> If one attempts to identify an utterance or text as a moment of origin, one finds that they depend upon prior codes. A codification, one might say, can only originate or be originated if it is already encoded in a prior code; more simply, it is the nature of codes to be always already in existence, to have lost origins (Culler 2002: 103).

As a consequence, Culler writes in his earlier *On Deconstruction*, 'texts are multi-dimensional spaces in which a large range of different writings blend and clash' (Culler 1982: 32-33). Who then is to make or assign meaning to them? According to Culler, following Roland Barthes, it is inevitably the reader (as a function, not so much as a person), and not the author of a text who inscribes the quotations that make up writing. As Barthes puts it, 'a text's unity lies not in its origin but in its destination' (Barthes 1977: 146-48).

If one agrees on these two basic traits of intertextuality, the non-autonomous status of the text and the absence or impossibility of origin, another problem arises: how to recognize intertextuality, or claim with some assurance that one is dealing with a case of it? Culler speaks of the 'dangers that beset the notion of intertextuality'. One of those lies in the assumption of the intractability of possible sources of origin: there is a 'vast and undefined discursive space it designates' (Culler 2002: 109). A possible solution is to narrow this vast space, which runs the risk of falling into a positivistic approach. Alternatively, for convenience's sake, particular texts can be designated as 'pre-texts'. A pre-text is understood as what comes before, but not fully determines, the later text. The pre-text is often used negatively as alibi, or pretext, to submit the later text to a definite source, or to claim the prestige of the source for the later reworking. The pre-text can also be understood in a constructive way. It can function as a source for the later text, because, for instance, there are thematic similarities. In that case, the pre-text will initially signal recognition, but more importantly, this will be followed by the observation of differences between the two texts. The pre-text then functions not so much as a model, but as a, possibly negative, counterpart.

Another possible way to limit intertextuality analytically is to concentrate on genre. Culler suggests relating a work of art to a whole series of other works, treating them not as sources, but as constituents of a genre. The next step, then, is to infer the conventions of that genre. The focus should be on the conventions that, for instance, direct the production and interpretation of character, plot structure, and thematic synthesis.

The issue of genre is at stake in both the cinematic texts and the Bible text I have selected. Hollywood cinema and the apocalyptically themed films in this study consist of a mixture of genres. In Bible and religious studies, much attention has been paid to the delineation of an apocalyptic genre. The traits of this genre are significant for my analysis of cinematic renderings of the Apocalypse, since the Bible functions as a pre-text for Hollywood films. The interconnectedness of these two fields, Bible and film, calls for an interdisciplinary approach.

Interdisciplinarity: Religion and Film

This study endeavors to set up a dialogue between past and present through secular cinematic representations as well as religious biblical representations of apocalypse and martyrdom. Hence, it is interdisciplinary by nature. Interdisciplinarity is not a simple encounter between two disciplines. It involves more than the extension of the subject matter of the respective fields or the use of tools and concepts of the other discipline. In my initial survey of the encounter between religion and film, I came across a number of recurrent issues that thwart a productive dialogue between film studies and religious studies.[2]

In their introduction to *Screening the Sacred: Religion, Myth, and Ideology in Popular American Film*, Joel Martin and Conrad Ostwalt examine film and religion as independent, yet connected objects of study. As Martin remarks, the relationship between religion and film is largely overlooked in the work of film scholars. Film studies has gained immensely from interdisciplinary encounters with disciplines such as literary studies, linguistics, and psychology; yet, religion studies remains absent. It appears, Martin argues, that 'film studies has little to learn from religious studies' (Martin 1995: 2). Religious scholars feel that film scholars do not take them seriously. Vice versa, religion scholars have largely neglected the effect of film and film studies. Martin's critique points to the mutual misrecognition between film studies and religious studies.

Some religion scholars have begun to venture into the field of film. These ventures, Martin argues, are not unproblematic. Much work of religion scholars reveals a politics of taste and prejudice with regard to film, namely that 'only a highbrow film can be truly religious' (Martin 1995: 3). Only

---

2.   The long overdue estimation of the relevance of the study of religion and film is signaled by the publication of the first anthology on the subject. *The Religion and Film Reader* (2007), edited by Jolyon Mitchell and S. Brent Plate, is the first book that attempts to address the depth and width of the field. For an older survey of the theological engagement with film, see Steve Nolan, 'The Books of the Films: Trends in Religious Film Analysis'.

the films of established artists or auteurs have been the subject of interest in religious studies.[3] This assumption is confirmed by Melanie Wright's observation that religion scholars 'regard the study of mass cultural forms as simply the hors d'oeuvre before the 'real work' of theology and religious studies begins' (Wright 2007: 439).[4] Since religion itself is just as much a mass-culture phenomenon, this attitude is unproductive for a sustained encounter between the two disciplines.

Most encounters between religion and film are characterized by a lack of engagement, not just with the larger field of film studies, but also with the *medium* of film. The analysis of film as an audio-visual entity is absent, resulting, as Wright puts it, in the 'tendency to elide film meaning into narrative' (Wright 2007: 438). Contrary to that neglect of the medium, I use the kind of film analysis that extends beyond themes and motifs. Instead, the visual aspect of film is given prominence. Each of my chapters consists of a detailed shot analysis of one or several sequences of the film under discussion. The analysis offers the possibility of examining the shot-by-shot dynamics of a given sequence. Moreover, in each chapter, I engage closely with aspects of film studies, ranging from the notion of the star text to the influence of DVD technology on film analysis.

3.   See for example, Joseph Cunneen's article 'Film and the Sacred', or his book on the work of director Robert Bresson (Cunneen 2003).

4.   Unfortunately, also within film studies itself, a certain kind of condescension persists with regard to contemporary, commercial cinema. As José Arroyo argues in the introduction to *Action/Spectacle: A Sight and Sound Reader*, the contemporary blockbuster is often critically evaluated as 'mass culture at its most crudely capitalistic' (Arroyo 2000: ix). This 'contempt for the contemporary' (Arroyo 2000: viii), as Arroyo phrases it, is also the subject of Yvonne Tasker's monograph of action cinema, to which I will refer several times in this study. Tasker's study underscores film studies' previous neglect of the aesthetic and political credibility of action cinema. Too often, the premise is accepted that there is nothing to be said about this type of cinema 'other than to signal the genre's ideological complicity with the operations of patriarchal capitalism' (Tasker 1993: 8). Questions of 'bad' ideology put aside, the issue of 'taste' and what constitutes 'good' or 'bad' taste seems always implicitly present in the discussion and reviews of the types of films I am discussing here. It seems as though one has to apologize for their choice of topic, or even dismiss it all together. For instance, in an article published in the online Journal of Religion and Film entitled 'Armageddon at the Millennial Dawn', Conrad Ostwalt, who has written extensively on apocalyptically themed films, is negative about the cinematic representations of the Apocalypse as produced by Hollywood. He concludes his article by stating: 'Thus, Hollywood's apocalypse might not spell the end of the world as we know it—only the end of culture and good taste' (Ostwalt 2000). I am not arguing for an uncritical stance toward the ideology blockbuster film, as my chapter on *Armageddon* will show. Yet, I think the least analysts can do is engage with their chosen object, without dismissing it, either in advance or afterward.

Hollywood Cinema and the Question of Genre

This study analyzes contemporary Hollywood blockbuster cinema. Above, I have proposed that genre, as a field of intertextuality, can function as mediator between biblical and cinematic representations. Genre functions as a mediator between producers and audiences, and is a device that works to contain possibilities of reading. Genre guides the reader in the direction of a preferred reading and blocks other, non-preferred readings. Its rules constitute a necessary code for a 'correct' (preferred) interpretation of a work. The ability to identify a text as belonging to a particular genre enables the viewer to see that text in the frame of a group of similar texts. Understanding the approximation of a text to a particular genre is an intertextual process. It involves experience with other texts; from that experience emerges expectation. Genre limits the number of readings that are possible, and provides a border in which intertextuality is captured; it sacrifices an infinite number of readings in favor of one, or at least to a limited number of readings.

Within film theory, much work has been dedicated to the question of film genre. Genre is an important marketing tool of popular cinema. Both audiences and filmmakers categorize films by genre. The act of designating genre may seem fairly unproblematic, since most viewers have sufficient knowledge of dominant genres. However, once one attempts to produce a definition of a particular genre, one encounters problems. As David Bordwell and Kristin Thompson in *Film Art* put it, 'A genre is easier to recognize than to define' (Bordwell and Thompson 1997: 51). Stumbling blocks are manifold. For instance, an attempt to define genre by subject matter and theme produces confusion rather than clarity, as Bordwell effectively shows:

> A Western seems identified primarily by its setting, a science-fiction film by its technology, a musical by its manner of presentation (song and dance). Thus one could have a science-fiction musical, in which Martians visit Billy the Kid and everyone puts on a show (Of course, this could also turn out to be a comedy, but how is *that* genre defined?) (Bordwell 1989: 147).

An historical approach to genre, Bordwell continues, also has its shortcomings, 'since many currently accepted genres, such as melodrama and film noir, did not exist as categories for audiences or filmmakers of the 1930s and 1940s' (Bordwell 1989: 147).

Despite many efforts, attempts to construct a coherent map of genres have been unsuccessful. Genre is nevertheless important for this study. Genre serves as way to limit the potentially unlimited semiosis of intertextual relations. Because genres cross media borders, they serve as a guiding principle through which interdisciplinary studies can be undertaken.

The film *End of Days* (USA: Peter Hyams, 1999) introduces the generic status of the group of films in this study. Following Bordwell's line of argument, it is easy to recognize the genres at work in *End of Days*. The film is an example of the hybridity of contemporary Hollywood cinema in that it carefully mixes several genres. I can easily identify a handful of genres, or subgenres, in *End of Days*: the action genre, the disaster genre, the horror genre, and perhaps, the apocalyptic genre. There is a particular strategy to Hollywood's genre mixing. As Rick Altman argues, the designation of genre is a practice mostly carried out by film critics. The Hollywood studios, on the other hand, try to draw the largest possible audiences. Declaring a film to belong to a particular genre, Altman continues, 'always risks alienating potential spectators who avoid that genre, Hollywood studios prefer instead to imply generic affiliation rather than actually to name any specific genre' (Altman 1999: 128).

Hollywood targets its films at the widest possible audience groups (differentiated by age, sex, race, ethnicity, class, education, preferred activities, geographical location and income), which results in making films that consist of 'a mix of as many genres as called for by the targeted audience' (Altman 1999: 129). Altman also argues that genre mixing is not a postmodern practice. Instead, he claims, genre mixing has long been a standard Hollywood practice. Contemporary forms of genre mixing have become much more advanced due to the huge amount of audience research.

End of Days should be called an action film. The main reason for this is the presence of the star of *End of Days*, Arnold Schwarzenegger, who has been called the 'most representative star' of the action film (Arroyo 2000: v). The two other possible generic components of the film, the disaster genre and the apocalyptic genre, need elaboration.

Disaster, Catastrophe, or Apocalypse?

In his book *Disaster Movies: The Cinema of Catastrophe*, Stephen Keane formulates a definition of the genre of disaster films. He looks at the historical development of the genre in the 1970s, 1980s, and 1990s. Keane observes a cyclical movement in the release of disaster films. In his opinion, one should speak of cycles of disaster films, such as the cycle of films released in the 1970s.[5] In this respect, Keane differs from what Maurice Yacowar has argued. Yacowar claimed that, 'disaster films constitute a sufficiently numerous, old and conventionalized group to be considered a genre, rather than a popular cycle that comes and goes' (Yacowar 1976: 90). Yacowar

5. The conception that disaster films appear in cycles is shared by Geoff King (2000). In his book on the Hollywood blockbuster, he compares the cycle of the 1970s to the cycle of the late 1990s and concludes that a good deal of thematic continuity can be identified between the two cycles.

considers the disaster film a solid historical genre, independent from particular periods and trends. In Keane's estimation, however, disaster films adhere to a specific socio-cultural trend.

Keane's chapter on films produced in the late 1990s is particularly useful. He asserts that disaster films address 'issues pertinent to the time they were made' (Keane 2001: 73). The disaster films of the 1970s, such as *Airport* (dir. George Seaton, USA, 1970), *Earthquake* (dir. Mark Robson, USA, 1974) and *The Poseidon Adventure* (dir. Ronald Neame, USA, 1972) are all analyzed with identifiable social and political factors in mind. The disaster films of the 1990s, Keane argues, cannot be read and understood without 'reference to previous disaster cycles or, conversely, the altogether hyperbolic prospect of imminent doom' (Keane 2001: 73). This leads to two important characteristics of the disaster film of the 1990s. Contrary to the disaster cycle of the 1970s, when disaster films spanned the entire decade, the 1990s cycle comprises a wave of films nearly exclusively restricted to the later years of the decade. The release of disaster films reached its peak in 1997; in that year, fourteen disaster films were released. The second characteristic results from the first: since most films were released by the end of the decade, this cycle of disaster films was labeled 'millennial movies' (Keane 2001: 73).

The success of the disaster films of the late 1990s can be explained by several factors, according to Keane. First, these films 'tapped into, and further energised, the 'pop millenarianism' of the time; the tabloid storied, television documentaries and best-selling books which effectively worked in turning 'anxiety' into 'interest'' (Keane 2001: 74). In addition, thanks to the developments in the area of computer-generated special effects of the 1980s and 1990s, scenes of mass destruction could now be shown to audiences in a way never seen before. Viewers had effectively forgotten what disaster films were all about, so 'the time was ripe for bringing disaster movies back round again' (Keane 2001: 74).

In a similar vein, John Shelton Lawrence and Robert Jewett connect the comeback of the disaster film to the revolution in special effects over the past two decades. The possibilities of creating believable images of natural annihilation, Lawrence and Jewett argue, have given the disaster genre a new impetus. In a chapter of their book on the American monomyth, they focus on what they call the catastrophe genre.[6] Comparing the generic cycles of the 1970s and 1990s, characteristics of contemporary disaster films can be pointed out. Two features of recent disaster films are absent in the

---

6. The term 'monomyth' refers to Joseph Campbell's (1949) classic definition of the basic narrative pattern of the hero's journey in his book *The Hero with a Thousand Faces*. Lawrence and Jewett argue that the superhero is the antidemocratic counterpart of this monomyth.

earlier films. Lawrence and Jewett assert that the scale of redemption has increased considerably: 'all human life is at stake in the movies *Armageddon, Deep Impact*, and *Left Behind: The Movie*' (Lawrence and Jewett 2002: 326). Moreover, these films are characterized by the blatant glorification of the United States. As Lawrence and Jewett sarcastically put it, 'A grateful world lifts its eyes to the heavens and expresses relief at being saved by the heroes from the United States' (Lawrence and Jewett 2002: 328).

Apart from these observations, Lawrence and Jewett consider another trait of recent disaster films, which has gone unnoticed by most other theorists of the genre: the 'retribution principle'. There is a relationship between the violation of sexual mores and punishment by the forces of nature: 'The contemporary images of disaster parallel those biblical stories in which the pattern of retribution for sexual infidelity and frivolity is deeply embedded' (Lawrence and Jewett 2002: 314).

The first example of this principle can be found in the flood story in Genesis. Lawrence and Jewett conclude that 'the paradigm was thus established for posterity: sexual improprieties provoke natural disasters, from which only the pure and faithful will escape. The retributive principle is Deuteronomic: sin brings disaster, while virtue brings success and escape from disaster' (Lawrence and Jewett 2002: 315). The retribution principle at work in recent disaster films is paradoxical. On one hand, disaster cinema 'struggles so hard for the modern illusion of visual realism'; on the other, it retains 'archaic biblical conventions of retribution'. This paradox is worth investigating. Lawrence and Jewett conclude that 'while the high-budget special effects provide the believability of the modern disaster film, the archaic biblical fantasy of selective and moralistic destruction remains as the central dramatic convention' (Lawrence and Jewett 2002: 315).

These biblical moral conventions are even more prominent in the genre of the apocalyptic film. Conrad Ostwalt has written extensively on the apocalyptic genre, or what he also calls the cinematic millennial drama, or secular apocalypse. In 'Hollywood and Armageddon: Apocalyptic Themes in Recent Cinematic Presentation', Ostwalt proposes the basic themes of apocalyptic films. In his opinion, these modern, secular, and cinematic representations of apocalyptic themes have an important function: they provide meaning to a chaotic existence. Ostwalt quotes from *The Sense of an Ending* by English literary critic Frank Kermode, suggesting that 'by placing life drama in relation to a beginning, a middle, and an end, the apocalypse provides coherence and consonance—it makes time trustworthy, especially when plot points towards the future, as it does in the apocalypse' (Ostwalt 1995: 61).

Ostwalt's examination of recurring apocalyptic characters, settings, themes, and plots is hampered by his erratic method of analysis. He claims that, in some films, the emphasis is on setting, in others on character development, and in still others, on plot. Ideally, however, a film should be analyzed for the interaction between these aspects. However, Ostwalt is on to something when he looks at the difference between traditional apocalyptic literature and the contemporary Hollywood reworking of that literature:

> Hollywood has captured and fostered the secularization of the apocalyptic tradition. The traditional apocalyptic model presented the end of time and history as an immanent, or at least an imminent, reality from God. The contemporary model of the apocalypse offers the notion that end is avoidable altogether. In other words, the modern apocalyptic imagination removes the end of time from the sacred realm of the gods and places the apocalypse firmly in the grasp and control of humanity (Ostwalt 1995: 63).

Hence, he continues, the modern apocalyptic is characterized by a human, 'messianic figure who prevents the dawning of the new age and the eschatological kingdom' (Ostwalt 1995: 62). This human agent plays a key part in all the films I analyze in this study. In addition, the idea of self-sacrifice is related to this savior figure: to save the world, the redeemer must give up his or her own life.

By focusing so extensively on genre, I have followed Culler's suggestion to limit potential intertextual space. Through this conception of intertextuality, questions of authority and origin are suspended. Yet, *End of Days* and the other films I discuss belong to several genres at the same time, the disaster genre as well as the horror and action genres. Consequently, despite my emphasis on genre, this study does not attempt to define the parameters for an apocalyptic film genre. This is not a genre study in the classic sense of the term. I am not interested in uncovering a possible master narrative for the genre. Though the films I discuss comprise two guiding themes, apocalypse and martyrdom, they do not display fixed generic building blocks such as character type, plot line, or setting. Genre helps me focus on thematic trends in the entanglement of past texts. The notion of genre returns in my selection of biblical, apocalyptic texts.

Apocalypse

The last book of the New Testament, Revelation, tells the tale of the end. Revelation or The Apocalypse of John is a late first century CE text. It is believed to offer the scenario of God's final judgment on humanity. Apocalypse means 'revelation, a revealing' (in Greek, *apokalyptein*, to uncover, take the lid or veil off). Revelation is not the only apocalyptic narrative in the Bible. There are other examples to be found, such as parts of Daniel (7-12), *4 Ezra*, *1 Enoch* and the apocryphal book of *1 Baruch* (the latter three are so-called Pseudepigraphical Books). This has led to the general supposition among biblical scholars that an apocalyptic genre exists.

The definition of the genre is dealt with in two issues of *Semeia* (no.14, 1979 and no.36, 1986). In the introduction to *Semeia* 14, John J. Collins states that the purpose is to 'identify and define a literary genre 'apocalypse'' (Collins 1979: 1). The genre, Collins continues, can be identified by the 'recognizable similarity among a number of texts' (Collins 1979: 1). This similarity is expressed through recurring elements, which function as the 'firm basis for generic classification' (Collins 1979: 2). The elements make up a master paradigm, divided into two sections: the framework and the content of the apocalypse. The paradigm consists of thirteen returning elements, often divided into smaller subsets (Collins 1979: 6-8).

I elaborate on three elements that are identifiable in Hollywood films as well. First, the revelation is visual, in the form of a vision. This element figures prominently in the films I discuss in this study. The second element is salvation. Salvation may take the form of either 'exaltation to the heavens or renewal of the earth' (Collins 1979: 10). Third, exaltation, or rapture, can take the form of a personal afterlife, where 'all the constraints of the human condition, including death, are transcended' (Collins 1979: 10). This feature, Collins explains, is the 'most consistent aspect of the eschatology of the apocalypses' (Collins 1979: 9). Taken together, these features result in a revelatory vision of an afterlife. This, I will argue, is a recurring element in apocalyptic film as well. A final element is the presence of otherworldly beings, often in the guise of Satan. This affirms the transcendent nature of apocalypses, and points to the existence of another world.

On the basis of this paradigm, a comprehensive definition of the apocalyptic genre can be formulated. Collins proposes:

> a genre of revelatory literature with a narrative framework, in which a revelation is mediated by an otherworldly being to a human recipient, disclosing a transcendent reality which is both temporal, insofar as it envisages eschatological salvation, and spatial, insofar as it involves another, supernatural world (Collins 1979: 9).

This definition, which emphasizes the revelatory nature of apocalypses, is far removed from the contemporary popular and predominantly secular conception. In the popular conception, Apocalypse has become a synonym for doomsday, disaster, and the end. Although the academic, biblical definition and the popular notion of apocalypse are divergent, the apocalyptic is, according to Jon Paulien, 'very much alive and well in popular culture today' (Paulien 2003: 158). It is particularly in American society and popular culture.[7]

---

7. For a detailed analysis on apocalypticism in American culture and mentality, see: Harold Bloom (1992), Paul Boyer (1992), and Robert Fuller (1995).

There is a difference, however, between the academic conception of the notion and the popular idea. A three-fold distinction needs to be observed. As David E. Aune argues in *Semeia 36*, there are 'apocalypses' (as literature), 'apocalyptic eschatology' (as a world view), and 'apocalypticism' (as a socio-religious movement) (Aune 1986: 67). The three are closely related; however, their referents do not necessarily coincide. As Collins states in *Semeia 14*: 'if apocalypticism is assumed to be at all related to apocalypses, then the analysis of the literary genre must cast some light on the social phenomenon, even if they cannot be directly correlated' (Collins 1979: 4).

This interconnectedness, direct or indirect, warrants the genre approach. Thus, the biblical pre-text and its generic traits function as a template against which other manifestations of apocalyptic discourse (biblical, social, theological, and cultural) can be read for their similarities as well as their transformations. The other two conceptions, worldview and socio-religious movement, are addressed in the next section.

American Apocalypticism

In *The End of the World as We Know It: Faith, Fatalism, and the Apocalypse in America*, Daniel Wojcik outlines the historical development of apocalyptic belief in the US. Wojcik sketches a historical picture starting with Columbus' landing, an event that the explorer himself interpreted as part of a divine plan, to the present.[8] The US is often historically conceptualized as the 'new Eden', an exceptional terrestrial paradise. This idea, exemplified in the writings of the Puritans, Wojcik demonstrates, entails the religious belief that the foundation of the US was not only part of God's divine plan, but also instrumental in bringing about God's kingdom on earth (Wojcik 1997: 21-24). In short, from its Puritan foundation to the eighteenth and nineteenth century, culminating in the 1960s and 1970s of the last century, American religions are characterized by a fascination with apocalyptic prophecy. One could use the term American apocalypse, since there exists, Wojcik argues, a thorough convergence of general apocalyptic attitudes and a belief in the United States as the culmination of history.

The enduring apocalyptic streak in American culture may be connected to its 'syncretistic' nature. Syncretism is understood as the combination of different forms of religious belief.[9] Wojcik argues that the apocalyptic

---

8. Columbus imbued his role as explorer with divine qualities. In his journal, he writes: 'God made me the messenger of the new heaven and the new earth of which he spoke in the apocalypse of St. John... and he showed me the spot where to find it' (Wojcik 1997: 21). For a thorough study on Columbus's apocalyptic mindset, see Pauline Moffitt Watts (1985).

9. The best example of this apocalyptic syncretism is the belief in UFOs, which is a

beliefs of fundamentalist Christians and those of secular groups, ranging from survivalist groups (such as white supremacist, neo-Nazi groups) and youth subcultures (the Punk and Generation X subcultures of the 1980s and 1990s), offer many points of convergence (Wojcik 1997: 10-11).[10] Wojcik does not develop this notion, but the syncretistic nature of apocalyptic belief and its attendant scenarios can supply one explanation for its enduring appeal in American culture.[11] There is something in it for everyone. Hollywood, eager to tap into elements of the *Zeitgeist*, uses these scenarios to its own benefit. Because apocalyptic stories are syncretistic, they can take on many different shapes. Their potential use by Hollywood, to tell those stories, across different genres, is nearly limitless.

Narrative Theory and a Philosophy of The End

The need to make sense of time and history are not exclusive to religious tradition or American culture. I briefly address two disciplinary traditions, narrative theory and postmodern philosophy, that engage with notions of time, temporality, and the question of the end. Although these traditions are assumed to be secular in character, their imagery and vocabulary have a distinct religious quality.

synthesis of 'Christianity, Theosophy, Spiritualism, Eastern religions, New Age notions, and ideas inspired by science fiction literature and popular films' (Wojcik, 1997: 10).

10. Michael Barkun has written extensively on the apocalyptic tendencies in several American far Right groups, in *Religion and the Racist Right: The Origins of the Christian Identity movement*. See also his article 'Racist Apocalypse: Millennialism on the Far Right' in *The Year 2000: Essays on The End*, Charles B. Strozier and Michael Flynn (editors). New York: New York University Press (Barkun 1997: 190-205). For a discussion on terrorism and religiously motivated acts of war, see Mark Juergensmeyer (2003) *Terror in the Mind of God*.

11. The pervasiveness of apocalyptic thinking can be interpreted as alarming. Feminist theologian Catherine Keller claims that it is impossible to escape apocalyptic thinking: we are '*already* involved in apocalypse' (Keller 1992: 184, emphasis in text). She contends that one should be attentive to the apocalyptic pattern that is dominant in Western history and to the cultural and ideological stretch between biblical and contemporary materializations of the theme. Keller observes the intricate link and, at the same time, considerable distance between biblical and modern and secular forms of apocalypticism. She warns explicitly about the present form of apocalypticism, particularly as expressed by Christian fundamentalists. Their right-wing apocalyptic thinking is pervasive within American society and has gained access to the power of the state. Academics, Keller argues, should rid themselves of their 'ignorance about the conservative Christian movement and to work to expose right-wing apocalypse, with its massive grip on the American populations, as a demonic distortion of the biblical apocalypse' (Keller 1992: 187). Keller takes a political stance against the exploitation of biblical apocalyptic texts to support the agenda of the new religious right, an ideology she characterizes as 'bare-faced sexism and militarism' (Keller 1992: 187).

In his discussion on the importance of narrative, literary theorist Peter Brooks speaks of a 'sacred masterplot that organizes and explains the world' (Brooks 1984: 6). In his influential study on plot and narrative, *Reading for the Plot*, Brooks suggests the human need for 'an explanatory narrative that seeks its authority in a return to origins and the tracing of a coherent story forward from origin to present' (Brooks 1984: 6).

In Brooks' conception, plot is the dynamic logic of narrative, which in turn is a form of understanding and explanation (Brooks 1984: 10). Narratives function as a way of coming to terms with death, since every story presumes an ending. Following Walter Benjamin, Brooks argues, 'only the end can finally determine meaning' (Brooks 1984: 22, 52). The end might take up an even more imperative position if one observes the principle that the end is instrumental in shaping the beginning and the middle of a narrative (Brooks 1984: 22).

This estimation of the end is also crucial for Frank Kermode's classic study on the relationship between fiction and apocalypse, *The Sense of an Ending*. By imagining an end for the world, apocalyptic discourse imposes 'coherent patterns' on history. These patterns 'make possible a satisfying consonance with the origins and the middle' (Kermode 1967: 17). Kermode thus argues for the recognition of apocalyptic patterns in literary fictions; at the same time, he acknowledges that this pattern also functions as one of 'our ways of making sense of the world' (Kermode 1967: 28). The human need for an 'imaginatively predicted future' often results in the calculation of a certain end. As it turns out, these prophesized ends have never come to pass. This, Kermode points out, is an important characteristic of apocalyptic discourse:

> The great majority of interpretations of Apocalypse assume that the End is pretty near. Consequently the historical allegory is always having to be revised; time discredits it. And this is important. Apocalypse can be disconfirmed without being discredited. This is part of its extraordinary resilience (Kermode 1967: 8).

Despite numerous miscalculations in the past, the idea of an impending end remains in place. In relation to this apocalyptic resilience, I would add another narrative mechanism. The historical abundance of failed prophesized endings leads to the assumption that predicted endings never come to pass. This logic is driven by a desire to imagine the end in the certainty that this end will never happen. I return to this below in relation to contemporary Hollywood apocalyptic films.

Whereas Brooks and Kermode support the idea that the grand narratives of history structure the apparent human need for an ending, perhaps the end has already happened or is an illusion altogether.[12] These two assumptions

---

12. Or, it could be argued that the major, or any, narrative of the end has become

are crucial for Jean Baudrillard's postmodern, philosophical conception of time and history. In the aptly titled *The Illusion of the End*, the human need for an end is characterized by Baudrillard as a 'fatal exigency, a false strategy of time which wants to shoot straight ahead to a point beyond the end' (Baudrillard 1994: 8). Understandable as this desire may be, it is futile, according to Baudrillard, since 'hyperreality rules out the very occurrence of the Last Judgement or the Apocalypse or the Revolution' (Baudrillard 1994: 8).[13] There are no longer any events, there is only the endless circulation of consumer goods. Baudrillard's main argument entails the idea that history is already finished: 'All the ends we have envisaged elude our grasp and history has no chance of bringing them about, since it will, in the interim, have come to an end' (Baudrillard 1994: 8).

Baudrillard's notion of an ending is a disappointing one: the end might have taken place but, if so, went unnoticed. Not only have we missed out on the experience of 'the original chaos, the Big Bang', but our hopes for experiencing the final moment, 'the Big Crumb' are similarly useless (Baudrillard 1994: 115). Whether or not one chooses to agree with Baudrillard, his analysis of the 'demonic temptation to falsify ends and the calculation of ends' (Baudrillard 1994: 8) resonates with current narratives in popular culture.

Following Baudrillard, apocalyptic narratives are contradictory in nature. On one hand, they thrive on the imminence of the end, which functions as the catalyst for the story. On the other, the expected ending can never be reached. Or, to be more precise, the ending is cancelled, delayed or postponed. As literary critic Northrop Frye comments, 'We notice that while the book of Revelation seems emphatically the end of the Bible, it is a remarkable open end' (Frye 1982: 137). I call this the paradox of apocalyptic narrative: the anticipation of an end that will eventually be forestalled. This, to me, seems a principal narrative structure in apocalyptic cinema. The films I am discussing here, such as *End of Days*, *Armageddon*, and *Alien3*, all thrive on the narrative of impending apocalypse, only to have that end cancelled at the very last minute.

In my discussion of various interpretations of the end, ranging from

redundant altogether. Naturally, the first example of such an analysis of the end of history that comes to mind is Francis Fukuyama's *The End of History and the Last Man*.

13. According to Baudrillard in *Symbolic Exchange and Death*, postmodern societies, or the postmodern condition at large, are organized around simulation and the play of images and signs. To such an extent that simulation is perceived to be more real than the real itself, hence the name hyperreality. Linked to this is Baudrillard's conception of time. Postmodernity differs from modernity's conception of time as linear and developing in a revolutionary, forward moving manner. Instead, the postmodern is characterized by the discourse of the end: the end of labor, the end of the 'signifier/signified dialectic, which facilitates the accumulation of knowledge and meaning' (Baudrillard 1993: 8).

religious to secular, post-modern perceptions, the similarity between these modes of thought is striking. The distinction between secular forms of narrative and history and religious apocalypticism is not clear-cut. These resemblances, once more, point to the syncretistic nature of Apocalypse as a concept.[14] As Marcos Becquer and José Gatti argue, syncretism 'entails the 'formal' coexistence of components whose precarious identities are mutually modified in their encounter, yet whose distinguishing differences, as such, are not dissolved or elided in these modifications, but strategically reconstituted' (Becquer and Gatti 1991: 447).

In apocalyptic discourse as a syncretistic practice, religious and secular discourse come together; reciprocally alter each other, yet without losing their particular characteristics. This encounter results in something that is more than the sum of its particular parts.

Martyrdom

The Apocalypse demands a subject: the martyr. The figure of the martyr, whether one looks at it from a classical or contemporary standpoint, provokes reactions ranging from admiration to disgust. Because martyrdom is a spectacular performance with the martyr's body as an important medium, martyr stories never fail to fascinate. Martyr figures provoke a wealth of multiple and often conflicting meanings, texts, interpretations, and images. Martyrdom forms one of the founding myths of at least two of the three monotheistic religions. Yet, an exploration of the classical Jewish, Christian, and Muslim sources does not yield an unequivocal understanding of the figure. Instead, it exposes the instability and changeability of the concept. In what follows, I will not attempt to offer an overview of the history and interpretation of martyrdom in Judaism, Christianity, and Islam. Instead, I sketch the open nature of martyrdom.[15]

---

14. For instance, Lee Quinby proposes to understand apocalypticism in all its divergent manifestations in a 'Foucauldian sense as a regime of truth that operates within a field of power relations and prescribes a particular moral behavior' (Quinby 1994: xv). This apocalyptic regime of truth has had a persistent appeal, in ancient as well as modern times. Its discourse—understood as a 'system of dispersion of statements that define, designate, circumscribe, and sometimes eliminate certain objects of its authority'—claims to have access to 'revealed and absolute truth' (Quinby 1994: xv) about the fate of humanity. Quinby stresses that contemporary types of apocalyptic discourse function as a regime of truth.

15. Daniel Boyarin's book *Dying for God: Martyrdom and the Making of Christianity and Judaism* supports my argument. Boyarin analyzes the discourse of martyrdom in both (rabbinic) Judaism and Christianity. His main thesis opposes the traditional emphasis on a dichotomy between Judaic and Christian discourses on martyrdom, and the way this dichotomy functions in 'the process of making Judaism and Christianity as distinct

The starting point for this inquiry is the Book of Revelation, the key text for martyrdom in a Christian context, a text that figures prominently throughout this study.[16] Though it is generally agreed that the Book of Revelation is not a classical martyr story, its persistent influence can hardly be overestimated. Elizabeth Castelli summarizes her view of Revelation's effect on early Christians as follows: 'The gruesome portraits of righteous suffering and vindication in the book of Revelation wrote the story of Christian suffering within the broadest framework imaginable with a driving apocalyptic beat establishing the rhythms for understanding historical experience in cosmic terms' (Castelli 2004: 36).

Revelation is rife with examples of horrible suffering and exoneration. In Revelation 6.9-11, the martyrs appear for the first time in some detail:

> When he opened the fifth seal, I saw under the altar the souls of those who had been slaughtered for the word of God and for the testimony they had given; they cried out with a loud voice, 'Sovereign Lord, holy and true, how long will it be before you judge and avenge our blood on the inhabitants of the earth?' They were given a white robe and told to rest a little longer, until the number would be complete both of their fellow servants and of their brothers and sisters, who were soon to be killed, as they themselves had been killed.

This passage is a good example of the language and imagery that the Book of Revelation employs. The key phrase is 'those who had been slaughtered for the word of God', which denotes the martyrs. The second

entities' (Boyarin 1999: 93). Rather, Boyarin proposes to read Judaism and Christianity not as two separate entities, but as 'complexly related subsystems of one religious polysystem' (Boyarin 1999: 92). Through breaking down the dichotomy and showing its instability, Boyarin argues, the discourse on martyrdom is opened up and demonstrates its development and change. The question of a historic point of origin—which religion invented martyrdom in the first place?—is rendered futile. Instead, Boyarin proposes to be attentive to the circulating and recirculating motifs, themes, and religious ideas in the making of martyrdom, a recirculation between Christians and Jews that allows for no simple litany of origins and influence (Boyarin 1999: 118). Indeed, Boyarin's call to forsake a 'simple litany of origins' reverberates within this study.

16 As Leonard L. Thompson argues in *The Book of Revelation: Apocalypse and Empire*, although commentators on Revelation differ greatly in their interpretations of the exact historical period in which the book was written and, moreover, by whom it was written, it is commonly accepted that Revelation was written by a man who calls himself John in the reigning period of the Roman emperor Domitian, 81-96 CE. In this period the Christian minority in Asia Minor often came into conflict with the Roman authorities and particularly the imperial cult the Romans forced on its people. The imperial cult imposed by Domitian, who is generally regarded by Roman historians as a tyrant and megalomaniac, demanded the emperor to be worshipped as a deity. Christians who did not act in accordance with Roman law in this respect were harassed and persecuted (Thompson 1990: 11-17).

part of this phrase, 'and for the testimony they had given', is important, yet problematic. I return to the aspect of testimony later. The imagery of slaughter and blood is a recurring one. Initially, it refers to the blood of the Lamb (5.9-10), and later it refers to the blood of the martyrs (19.2, where John speaks of 'the blood of his servants'). This shedding of blood invokes the need for judgment and vengeance; the latter is, in part, also carried out by means of blood (16.4-7). Yet, retribution does not come swiftly, and those who expect it are asked to be patient, or to 'rest a little longer'.

With regard to the verses quoted above, Richard Bauckham writes,

> When the fifth seal is opened, the Christian martyrs of the past cry out for their blood to be avenged, but they are told they must wait until the rest of the full complement of Christian martyrs is complete. In other words, the final judgment on the wicked, which will avenge the martyrs, is delayed until the rest of the Lamb's followers also suffer martyrdom (Bauckham 1993b: 79).

He argues that the 'rest of the Lamb's followers', i.e., all Christians, will have to suffer martyrdom. Bauckham argues that Revelation portrays a future that envisages the martyrdom of all Christians: 'The message of the book is that if Christians are faithful to their calling to bear witness to the truth against the claims of the beast, they will provoke a conflict with the beast so critical as to be a struggle to the death' (Bauckham 1993b: 93).

Jesus sets the example of martyrdom through his sacrificial death on the cross. Those who voluntarily chose to mimic the death of Christ giving witness to their faith were called martyrs. Being sentenced to death, which renders the victim passive, becomes invested with an active component. Through the mimesis of Christ, the imposed death sentence becomes a way for the martyr to express his or her desire for a willed death. The martyr gains power over those who have sentenced him to death, actively expressing his joy over his impending death.

The connection between the act of witnessing and martyrdom is a recurring one in the literature. It is based on the supposed etymological connection between the two notions. The assumption is that the Greek noun 'martys' ('witness') and its related verb '*martyrein*' transformed into the early Christian title 'martyr' and into the meaning 'to die a martyr's death'. This hypothesis is, however, no longer valid. As Jan Willem van Henten states, the 'technical terminology referring to martyrdom in the Jewish and Christian contexts appears considerably later than the phenomenon itself' (Van Henten 2004: 164-65). The title of martyr was bestowed upon persons in hindsight.[17]

17. In his discussion on the symbolic motif of witness in Revelation, Richard Bauckham also critiques the incorporation of the act of giving witness within the martyr's act of dying. According to Bauckham, the title of witness 'refers primarily

The relationship between witness and martyr becomes more problematic in the Islamic context. In 'The Revaluation of Martyrdom in Early Islam', Keith Lewinstein shows how a small 'philological observation', namely that the Arabic words for martyr and witness are identical, reveals a crucial unease in the concept of martyrdom. In Islamic martyrdom, the merging of witnessing and suffering into the concept of the martyr is completed, revealing the Christian influence on Islamic martyrdom. However, as Lewinstein argues, the Islamic understanding of martyrdom differs significantly from its Christian counterpart. The major difference lies in the fact that 'for Muslims, one earns the title of martyr (*shahid*; pl. *shuhada'*) without any apparent act of witnessing. The martyr's sacrifice does not generally attest to anything specific, nor does it symbolize much beyond the obvious sense of death in the service of God's plan' (Lewinstein 2002: 78).

Lewinstein argues that *shahid* derives its meaning strictly from the Christian roots of the term martyr, and not from 'any intrinsic connection in Muslim minds between witnessing and martyrdom' (Lewinstein 2002: 78). He considers several 'strained attempts' by Muslim authorities to make sense of the word. What becomes clear is that 'the Muslim tradition had to invent for itself a connection between witnessing and martyrdom, since none was immediately apparent'. Unlike in the Christian tradition, 'the religious value of suffering and death was never the obvious lesson to draw from the career of the Prophet or from the experience of the early Muslim community' (Lewinstein 2002: 79-80).[18]

to the witness Jesus bore to God during his life on earth and to his faithfulness in maintaining his witness even at the cost of his life'. As Bauckham continues, 'the word 'witness' (*Martys*) does not yet, in Revelation, carry the technical Christian meaning of 'martyr' (one who bears witness by dying for the faith). It does not refer to death itself as a witness, but to the verbal witness to the truth of God'. Nevertheless, Bauckham adds, 'it is strongly implied that faithful witness will incur opposition and lead to death' (Bauckham 1993: 72). The two concepts have merged over time and have gained significance in 'technical Christian' discourse. Yet, the relationship as such, Bauckham observes, is not unproblematic or etymologically rooted in the word 'witness', as is often suggested by other authors.

18. To complicate matters further, Islam defines several types of martyrs. The two main types are 'battlefield martyrs' and so-called 'martyrs in the next world only'. The battlefield martyr is comparable to the Christian martyr: this martyr goes into battle in order to spread God's religion. It is considered to be the noblest and bravest way to die. The 'martyrs in the next world only' are divided into three subcategories, namely, persons who die violently or prematurely (murdered, through disease or accident), persons who die a natural death (while engaged in a praiseworthy act, that is to say, prayer, or after a virtuous life), and the 'living martyrs', those who have joined the 'greater jihad', yet are still alive. This final category could be labeled as battlefield martyrs in waiting. The discussion of the several types of Muslim martyrs points to a blurring and expanding conception of the martyr, which has moved out of the confines of the

An unambiguous definition of martyrdom cannot be given. However, keeping the historical pre-texts, particularly Revelation, in mind, it is helpful to regard the martyr as a traveling concept. As Bal remarks, concepts are indispensable, particularly for an interdisciplinary topic such as this, since 'they facilitate discussion on the basis of a common language'. The common language, here, is largely derived from the biblical pre-text. Yet, at the same time, concepts are 'flexible: each is part of a framework, a systematic set of distinctions'. In this sense, Bal argues, one can only use a particular concept if one important characteristic of the concept is kept in mind: its provisional nature (Bal 2002: 22).

Contemporary notions of martyrdom differ from the classical, canonical interpretation. Nevertheless, any definition of the martyr is somehow rooted in a canonical understanding of the concept. Jan Willem van Henten and Friedrich Avemarie propose a functional definition of the concept of the martyr. They contend that the term has become an established expression for persons who die a specific kind of heroic death. They extend the definition as follows: 'A martyr is a person who in an extremely hostile situation prefers a violent death to compliance with a demand of the (usually pagan) authorities. This definition implies that the death of such a person is a structural element in the writing about this martyr' (Van Henten and Avemarie 2002: 2-3). Hence, the execution and death of the martyr should represent the final stage, the narrative climax, in a recurring sequence of events that constitute Jewish, Christian, and Muslim martyr stories.[19]

Christian definition of the term. For a more detailed classification, see E. Kohlberg's entry on 'Shahid' in *The Encyclopaedia of Islam*, C.E. Bosworth *et al.* (editors). Leiden: E.J. Brill, 1995: 203-207.

19. Jan Willem van Henten takes up the general definition suggested above—of the martyr being a person who dies a violent death—and searches the Internet to explore shifting contemporary meanings. Unsurprisingly, the results of Van Henten's search in cyberspace call for an extension of the definition. Particularly the connection between 'violence' and 'martyr', as presupposed in canonical texts, gains new significance. The martyr's voluntary decision to die for his or her faith, taken as an essential part of the martyr's motivational script in the classical sense, is destabilized in contemporary discourses on what constitutes a martyr. The example of the victims of the Holocaust being marked as martyrs, shows that the 'voluntary dimension of martyrdom is not self-evident any longer' (Van Henten 2003b: 199). In other cases, the religious connotation of martyrdom is lost: 'being a victim while fighting for a justified cause seems enough reason to be called a martyr' (Van Henten 2003b: 207). Finally, Van Henten signals another important departure from the classical interpretation of martyrdom, namely the martyr's presumed peacefulness, or the passive and peaceful intentions of the martyr. Van Henten gives the example of the 'Muslim martyrs', a group whose violent, performative acts of retaliation confound the supposedly clear demarcation between victim and perpetrator: martyrs are in many contemporary cases not only victims of

In *A Noble Death*, Arthur J. Droge and James D. Tabor list five characteristics of martyrs, which they distill from biblical as well classical sources. They also attempt to outline a more general notion of martyrs, which might be applicable outside a strictly theological context. Droge and Tabor's five characteristics are:

1. [Martyrs] reflect situations of opposition and persecution;
2. The choice to die, which these individuals make, is viewed by the authors as necessary, noble, and heroic;
3. These individuals are often eager to die; indeed, in several cases they end up directly *killing themselves*;
4. There is often the idea of vicarious benefit resulting from their suffering and death.
5. The expectation of vindication and reward beyond death, more often than not, is a prime motivation for their choice of death. (Droge and Tabor 1992: 75)

This list serves as the template against which the contemporary cinematic texts of martyrdom are read.

In her work on early Christian martyrs, Castelli characterizes the discourse on martyrdom as ambivalent, yet powerful to this day. She argues that there were competing theories of religion, power, and violence at work in the first centuries, the time when the early Christians came into conflict with their surroundings. The numerous conflicts between the Christians and the Romans were recorded in many different sources, Roman as well as Christian. Each side attempted to make its perspective the true and righteous one.[20] Castelli claims that these 'different versions of the past (and its relationship to the present and future) became critical resources for rendering present circumstances meaningful' (Castelli 2004: 34). It is precisely this variety of different versions, Castelli observes, which

---

violence, but also—by the very act of martyrdom—initiators, or perpetrators of violence (Van Henten 2003b: 207).

20. A contemporary example of a conflict of power and identity, fueled by notions of martyrdom can be found in Galit Hasan-Rokem's essay entitled 'Martyr vs. Martyr: The Sacred Language of Violence', which analyzes the semiotics of the term 'martyr'. Hasan-Rokem demonstrates that a historical analysis of the word 'points at its contingent changes in various situations'. Her argument focuses on the 'lethal dialogue' between Israelis and Palestinians, in which the word 'martyr' refers, on one hand, to Palestinian victims or suicide bombers and, on the other, to Israeli victims. Both groups appropriate the word 'martyr' to legitimize violence and to attach powerful collective emotions to it. Following both Boyarin as well as Castelli, Hasan-Rokem argues that the concept of the martyr 'has always served in the generation of mutual relationships of entities contesting their legitimacy over a specific legacy, be it sacred texts of sacred territories' (Hasan-Rokem 2003: 99).

makes past discourses on martyrdom a critical resource for the present. Put differently, there never was one version of martyrdom to begin with. Martyrdom stories have always existed in many, mutually contesting versions. She continues, 'It is precisely because of this tendency to refract the present through recourse to the past that it becomes impossible to generate a stable originary narrative concerning Christian martyrdom' (Castelli 2004: 34).

Central to Castelli's thesis is the connection between the past and the present, and the ways in which memory works to turn martyr stories into a crucial aspect of Christian collective memory and identity. Moreover, Castelli evaluates martyrdom as 'an idea without a precise origin' (Castelli 2004: 35). Since it is impossible as well as unproductive to pinpoint the historical moment at which martyrdom came into existence, Castelli proposes to explore the ongoing manifestations of martyrdom in 'narratives, social formations, practices, and representations' (Castelli 2004: 33). This study follows Castelli's proposition for the sustained investigation of contemporary, popular, and secular representations of martyrdom. Her conception of this history as changing, as it 'oscillates and adapts itself over time' resonates with preposterous history's conception of (historical) time as changeable and simultaneous (Castelli 2004: 137). The discourse of martyrdom is so powerful precisely because of its adaptability and the transformation of the object that it allows. It is not just the concept of martyrdom that is not fixed; it also causes related discourses to change. In particular, acts of martyrdom are interpreted significantly differently when women instead of men perform them. As a consequence, gender is a central theme in this study.

Gender

The two major themes of this study, apocalypse and martyrdom, are analyzed through a gendered lens. In my study, Apocalypse and martyrdom and the stories and representations they construct are problematic from a feminist point of view.[21] According to feminist theologians, a defining

---

21. Catherine Keller stresses the multi-interpretable character of the Apocalypse. Its key text, the Book of Revelation, can be construed and used in different ways and applied to support conservative (Christian right-wing) as well as progressive (ecological, feminist, and socialist) political agendas. The force of this text is undeniable and the numerous uses and abuses of it should not be underestimated. Keller endorses the progressive readings of Revelation. She proposes to read back into scripture, to 'locate the biblical burnmarks in the present' (Keller 1996: 20). Keller's engagement with scripture—despite her assertion that she is unimpressed by the 'patriarchal authority of scripture' (Keller 1996: 25)—is worth exploring. Feminist theology has, according to Keller, an ambivalent and 'fairly abstract relation' to the Bible, in that it tends to 'leave

characteristic of apocalyptic discourse is its malignant representation of women. There are three main female figures in Revelation: Jezebel, the Whore of Babylon, and the Woman clothed with the sun.[22] The first two are sexually impure, since they are no (longer) virgins.[23] Their unchecked sexuality is perceived as dangerous and, hence, needs to be constrained through the use of violence. The Woman clothed with the sun is a stereotypical representation of feminine purity and virginity, despite the fact that she is pregnant. None of the three women, however, escapes physical or mental punishment in Revelation.[24]

biblical interpretation to feminist exegetical and historical scholars' (Keller 1996: 25). Keller, instead, proposes a sustained encounter with the biblical text. Her conception of the biblical apocalyptic text is predominantly intertextual. The apocalyptic narrative is 'intertwined with endless other ones, and therefore intertextually absorbing but also absorbed and absorbable in them, internally contested and externally relativized' (Keller 1996: 27). Keller thus proposes to unravel the threads of this seemingly coherent text. In order to do so, she deploys the tool of a midrashic reading of Revelation. Midrash refers to the ancient tradition of rabbinic commentaries on scripture, in which multiple readings, developing and disputing each other, would literally surround the scriptural text on the printed page (Keller 1996: 31). In such an analysis, interpretations are manifold and are not characterized by a single, coherent theological or other meaning. Furthermore, each reading of the text becomes part of the text, adding yet another layer of meaning to it. Through intertextual reading, meaning becomes multiplied and the closure of the Apocalypse is postponed. A deconstructivist, midrashic reading opens up the text or rather acknowledges its open-endedness.

22. All three figures are symbolic. Jezebel, however, is probably based on an actual historical figure, most likely a false prophet. See, Van Henten 2003a: 745-59.

23. The key word in the judgment of both female figures is 'porneia', meaning 'fornication'. As Van Henten (2008) argues, 'the accusation of fornication […] can be interpreted in a literal as well as a symbolical way', […] 'the basic message of the charge of fornication in Revelation seems to be quite clear, despite its poly-interpretability: it calls for a radical abstention of foreign culture, whether this is exemplified by sexual relationships with foreign women, veneration of foreign deities, corruption through foreign political power or foreign economic transactions, or all of these' (Van Henten 2008: 247). In this interpretation, the nature of the offense is taken out of a strictly sexual context. Bal has commented extensively on the ideological use of metaphors of infidelity, particularly in relation to female sexuality. As she argues, 'first, plurality is correlated with the absence of morality; next, religious plurality with sexual plurality' (Bal 1988: 43).

24. For a close analysis of the basic female archetypes in Revelation, see Pippin 1992. Susan R. Garrett argues similarly in *The Women's Bible Commentary*: 'The stereotyped feminine images in the book do not represent the full spectrum of authentic womanhood, either in John's day or in our own'. And she concludes, 'the dehumanizing way in which he [John] phrased his message will remain deeply troubling' (Garrett 1992). Catherine Keller formulates it as follows: 'Here is the paradox for feminist meditation on 'the end of the world': while innumerable women have found means of private resistance and public voice in the symbols of the Apocalypse, overt or subvert, the *toxic misogyny* of

In the Christian discourse of martyrdom, gender is constructed in conflicting ways. Although one can claim martyrdom to be what one commentator has called an 'equal opportunity employer', martyrdom nevertheless draws on and generates ideals of masculinity (Corrington Streete 1999: 349). In the ancient context, martyr images frequently entail masculine notions of identity, gaining power over one's opponents, self-mastery, and endurance (Penner and Vander Stichele 2003: 177). As Castelli remarks, 'The martyr's death is a masculine death, even when (or perhaps especially when) it is suffered by a woman' (Castelli 2004: 62). However, female martyrs, as I will show, also stretch assumptions of gender. In their acts, they perform a transgression from femininity to masculinity.

From the perspective of film studies, a similar move or transgression in representations of masculinity and femininity can be observed. The heroine of *Alien3*, Ripley, is the prime example of a character who destabilizes conventional imagery of gender. The representation of masculine martyrdom in films as *Armageddon* and *End of Days* is read alongside the transgressive gender of Ripley. Her female masculinity, combined with the act of martyrdom she performs, not only destabilizes male and female representations in film, but also endows classic representations of female martyrdom with new significance. The discourse on male and female martyrdom, as reconfigured in contemporary Hollywood film, I argue, can critique binary oppositions and undercut normative statements that fixate gender representations. A recurring theme is maternity as a required, yet anxiety-raising feminine characteristic. In the final three chapters of this study, the emphatic combination of maternity and a martyr-like death are discussed at length.

In their book on the politics and ideology of contemporary Hollywood cinema, *Camera Politica*, Michael Ryan and Douglas Kellner argue that apocalyptic films address contemporary social tensions. They argue that films do more than mirror these tensions. Films teach viewers how to

much of its imagery cannot [...] be flushed out of the text or its tradition' (Keller 1996: 29, emphasis added). The crucial exception to this feminist interpretation of Revelation is Elizabeth Schüssler-Fiorenza, whose work is characterized by attempts to redeem the text and (re)interpret it positively from a feminist perspective. This takes the form of a socio-historical reading of biblical texts, coupled with an attempt to undermine the patriarchal stance of the Bible. Schüssler-Fiorenza seeks to read biblical texts as useful guides for dealing with present, often political, situations involving inequality and injustice. Interestingly, Pippin's dissertation follows Schüssler-Fiorenza's proposed liberation hermeneutic. Pippin applies a Marxist hermeneutic to reveal the narrative of Revelation to be 'resistance literature'. As she states: 'The Apocalypse was the literary equivalent to a book burning or a food riot or a violent revolutionary takeover' (Pippin 1987: 158). In Pippin's subsequent work she has abandoned the revolutionary and liberating notions of her dissertation altogether.

respond to them: when the social order is stable, the dominant discourses, value-systems, and accompanying symbolic representations are also secure. Men are men and women are women. When the social order is in crisis, a simultaneous crisis occurs in the realm of representation. The films discussed in this study all thrive on an ideology that attempts to resolve a crisis in the gender system. A film such as *Armageddon* (Chapter 2) enacts the re-subordination of a woman. This process is directly connected to the struggle to overcome a threat imposed by contact with space and alien creatures that threaten Earth. To put it bluntly, in contemporary apocalyptic film one can observe the tendency to link feminism with catastrophe.[25] The conclusion is politically repugnant: to avoid the apocalypse, women must be re-subordinated. However, the correctional shift these films display, from transgression back to re-subordination, should not be understood as negative only. Every female film character I discuss in this study seemingly falls victim to this correctional shift, yet, as my analyses will show, their re-subordination only succeeds to a certain extent. The transgressions of these women have a more lasting impression than their eventual re-subordination.

In the first chapter, I lay out my historically preposterous approach as a way to read the film *End of Days*. The central concept of preposterous history, quotation, is applied to the final sequence of the film. The self-sacrificial death of Jericho Cane, played by Arnold Schwarzenegger, is, on one hand, grounded in the Book of Revelation and its concomitant iconographical tradition and, on the other, imported in the new context of Hollywood cinema, the Schwarzenegger/action film. The effect of the finale of *End of Days* originates not only from its employ of the source text, but also from the secular context of Hollywood cinema.

In the film *Armageddon*, the focus of the second chapter, the martyr's act of dying is reconfigured. Harry Stamper, played by Bruce Willis, is invested with novel causes and values to die for, not so much religious but rather masculine, individual, patriotic and, importantly, American. In relation to the construction of the American martyr, I address the specific aesthetics of the film, so-called 'High Concept' characteristics such as music, stars, and high speed cutting. *Armageddon*'s intertextual referencing of religiously inspired discourses of martyrdom is not unproblematic. The use of religion and the preposterous images of martyrdom the film engenders, obscured as these may be by Hollywood aesthetics, result in the abduction of religion for the sake of nationalism.

25. Or, as Joel Martin remarks in an online article on the anti-feminist tendencies in apocalyptic film: 'if space threatens, it has something to do with a professional woman' (Martin 2000).

The first two chapters are explicitly about male and masculine martyrdom. In the third chapter, I turn to a representation of female martyrdom. Female martyrs, exemplified in the heroine of the *Alien* saga, Ellen Ripley, played by Sigourney Weaver, suggest a gendered continuum between masculinity and femininity. I address this gender ambiguity through the concept of 'musculinity'. The crucial marker of the female, the ability to have children, is a recurring element in classical martyr stories. Ripley's maternal qualities, her pregnancy and subsequent delivery of the alien, reconceive classical discourse, which presupposes that mothers cannot become martyrs. My analysis of *Alien3*'s climax is medium-specific: the technology of the DVD provides the analyst with the possibility of endless repeat/rewind and, crucially, offers alternate versions of Ripley's martyrdom.

The theme of female martyrdom is developed in the fourth chapter. I read *The Rapture* for two particular characteristics: the film's depiction of an apocalyptic ending and its misogynistic disposition, which can be traced back to Revelation. The feminist critique of apocalyptic discourse underscores the need to counter its misogynistic tendencies. In my reading, I employ the interdisciplinary concept of the sequel (and the affiliated idea of the Final Girl) to argue against the misogynistic fate of the film's heroine Sharon, played by Mimi Rogers. Finally, I add a preposterous reading of *The Rapture*'s female protagonist. This analysis focuses on the notion of light and lighting as an instance of interdisciplinarity between religion and film studies.

In my fifth and final chapter, I deal with another recurring element in martyrdom discourse: the vision. In the film *The Seventh Sign*, the heroine Abby, played by Demi Moore, receives visions about the possible end of the world. The visions disrupt notions of linear time, and, consequently, the unfolding of the narrative. In the character of Abby, the intimate link between motherhood and martyrdom is further articulated. Finally, through a detailed analysis of the opening sequence, I argue that the ending of the film is already located in the beginning.

Chapter 1

CHRISTIAN WARRIOR:
MUSCULAR MARTYRDOM IN *END OF DAYS*

So here we are, engulfed in a millennial madness utterly unrelated to
anything performed by the earth and moon in all their natural rotations and
revolutions. People really are funny—and fascinating beyond all possible
description.

Stephen Jay Gould (Gould 1997: 22).

Introduction

The end of the world never seemed more imminent to people as on the
last day of the twentieth century, December 31, 1999. In his book on the
significance of the millennium, Stephen Jay Gould addresses the question of
why this date is so central to apocalyptic thinking or, better, why it should
not be since, he persistently argues, millennial thinking is not rationally or
scientifically grounded in any way. The 'millennial madness' Gould ridicules,
as far back as 1997 when his book was published, took on many different
shapes, not the least of which was in popular culture. This pre-millennium
tension also pervades the film *End of Days* (USA: Peter Hyams, 1999), set
on the potentially ominous eve of the new millennium. In the film, Satan
(Gabriel Byrne) escapes from hell to earth in the guise of a human body. If he
is capable of impregnating his bride-elect, called Christine, before the turn
of the millennium on January 1, 2000, she will give birth to the antichrist, a
birth that will signal the inauguration of Satan's earthly kingdom. It is the
suicidal, washed-out ex-cop Jericho Cane (Arnold Schwarzenegger) who,
reluctantly at first, has to protect Christine. Ultimately, he saves the world
by sacrificing himself to defeat Satan.

In this first chapter, I lay out the preposterous history approach as one
way to read *End of Days*. The central concept of preposterous history,
quotation, is specifically applied to the final sequence of the film. This
approach, I argue, differs significantly from readings that position the Bible
as the precursor to cinema. To demonstrate this, I take as my point of
departure the analysis of the film offered by biblical scholar Richard Walsh.
His reading is a good example of the allegedly 'interdisciplinary' work done

in the field of religion and film. Walsh's approach shows the strengths—a strong commitment to the biblical text—as well as the weaknesses—a disregard for visual analysis—of this kind of reading between Bible and film. My analysis, on the other hand, is influenced by the work of French film theorist Raymond Bellour. Throughout this study, his method, characterized by Bellour as 'a methodical kind of work' of close visual analysis is deployed (Bellour 2000: 15).

End of Days offers a case of martyrdom within the context of Hollywood film and is therefore a good place to start the analysis of cinematic representations of martyrdom. The sacrificial death of Jericho Cane, played by Arnold Schwarzenegger is, on one hand, grounded in the Book of Revelation and its concomitant iconographical tradition and, on the other, imported in the new context of Hollywood cinema, specifically of the Schwarzenegger/action film. I argue that the effect of the finale of the film stems not only from its references to the source text in Revelation, but also from the secular context of Hollywood cinema in which it is played out. In this respect, the film is crucial to my study of preposterous relationships between Hollywood cinema and the Bible: it adds new characteristics to the action film *as well as* to the Bible. The film, as a whole, is an example of how Hollywood cinema engages with, and 're-writes' biblical images and biblical narrative structures.[1]

One-Way Reading: Scripture as Precursor

Richard Walsh analyzes *End of Days* as a contemporary manifestation of the Book of Revelation in American culture. He argues that Revelation has acquired a popular American reading in which three themes dominate: first, the calculable end; second, sectarianism; and third, fantasies of innocent revenge. Walsh then asks the question 'whether one can read Revelation in another, less American way' (Walsh 2002: 6). Nevertheless, Walsh proceeds to read the film exactly for these three dominant themes, which appear to be inescapable to him. In the end, he offers one possible alternative interpretation of the film. Put differently, he provides the viewer with the opportunity to turn away from Revelation's warrior figure and focuses instead on the figure of the lamb.

As Walsh argues, in the final sequence of the film, Jericho abandons his anger, 'eschews his guns for prayer', and finds sacrificial faith. Walsh rightfully concludes, 'So, while Revelation moves from suffering to (redemptive)

---

1. *End of Days* is, however, not the sole example of a film in which Schwarzenegger chooses to sacrifice his life in order to save mankind. In *Terminator 2: Judgment Day* (USA: James Cameron, 1991), Schwarzenegger's cyborg character asks to be destructed or better yet 'terminated'.

violence, the movie moves from violence (guns) to faith' (Walsh 2002: 12). This reversal is surprising: the action film presents faith as superior to guns. As Walsh is offering a close analysis situated between scripture and film, particularly examining how the former influences the latter, one can hardly disagree with his reading. However, Walsh does not take the reversal of this process of influence into account. This is most telling in the title of the introduction to the book in which Walsh's article was published, *Screening Scripture: Intertextual Connections Between Scripture and Film*, called 'Introduction: Scripture as Precursor'. I consider Walsh's method of reading the film to be one-sided. Of course, Scripture 'came first', but rather than being a second and secondary scripture, *End of Days* is an active re-working of its precursor. Such rereadings may reveal neglected aspects of even the most canonical of pre-texts, so that they can be claimed to 'influence' their so-called sources.[2] This reversed perspective is called preposterous history. I propose to set up a dialogue between the biblical and secular aspects of the film. This implies not only taking the earlier, biblical contents of the film into consideration, but also analyzing the secular elements of the film.

Exchanging Looks: Shot List of the Final Sequence

As a starting point for my investigation into the concept of preposterous history, I analyze the final sequence of *End of Days* in detail. The film is a prime example of action cinema, the kind of blockbuster cinema of which I will discuss other examples throughout this study. The film is dominated by the presence of the action genre's most notable star, Arnold Schwarzenegger. What is interesting about the film is its finale. Uncharacteristically, it denies the viewer the usually violent and triumphant *denouement* of action cinema. Even though Schwarzenegger's character Jericho conquers the ultimate evil, Satan, he does so by sacrificing his life. Hence, the film is also a fine example of martyrdom in Hollywood cinema.

The final sequence of the film starts with a shot of the crowd gathered at Times Square, waiting for the countdown to the New Year. At the same time, Christine and Jericho are chased by an angry mob of Satan worshippers. They run into a church and bolt the doors. Jericho orders the congregation in the church, which is in heavy prayer, to leave. When there is no response, he fires his machine gun. The congregation flees, turning the church into a silent place. Jericho tells Christine to hide somewhere in the church. He moves to the front of the illuminated massive altar. The centerpiece of the altar shows a triptych depicting the crucifixion of Christ.

---

2. I define a predecessor as a pre-text. It is a 'text', which can be verbal as well as visual, from the preceding artistic tradition. The Book of Revelation functions as a verbal pre-text for the film.

From this point, I will break down this sequence into a shot list, that is, divide the sequence into its major building blocks, the distinct shots of which it consists. This shot list will help me to focus on what Raymond Bellour has called the 'textual volume' of a film, its separate shots and the relation they have to a larger group of shots. Since I will be using the heuristic tool of the shot list as the primary way to analyze the filmic image, this approach merits some explanation. As Bellour argues, the written analysis of film is 'the product of a double transgression', since the analyst has to resort to the use of words to describe a moving image. The literary analyst, in contrast, does not encounter this problem, 'thanks to the signifying osmosis of writing in relation to itself' (Bellour 2000: 17). As Bellour's own work demonstrates, the written analysis of film can be excruciatingly detailed; however, 'the written text can never capture anything but a kind of elementary skeleton' (Bellour 2000: 16). Despite the inadequacy of the word to describe the image, let alone a *moving* image, it is the only tool available.[3] I combine the written analysis, in this case the shot list, with a picture of the shot that is described. This combination of descriptive words and image is the closest one can get to a rendering of the moving image within a written medium.

The shot list can give insight into instances of repetition. These are significant because, as Bellour states, 'meaning emerges in the succession of a story in pictures by the double constraint of repetition and variation' (Bellour 2000: 28). Even though it often goes unnoticed by viewers, repetition is an important tool for making sense of a film and for assigning meaning to acts, objects, and even mental states of mind. The Hollywood style of filmmaking, represented by continuity editing, is highly efficient: every shot has its function within a scene or sequence. Furthermore, the editing style is subservient to the narrative. The aim of the film is to tell the story, as if it were unfolding in front of the viewer's eyes. This means that film style, represented in its editing, should be unobtrusive, that is, the viewer should not notice it at all. The editing presents a smooth flow from shot to shot. By repeating a particular shot so that the viewer becomes aware of that repetition, attention is temporarily directed at the film itself. As an effect, the narrative spell is temporarily suspended, and the viewer will try to incorporate the eye-catching element back into the narrative by treating it as a clue. The repetition of shots can occur both within a given sequence, as well as within the larger frame of several sequences and finally the film as a whole.

---

3.   The inevitable paradox of film analysis is that one has to momentarily halt the flow of the moving image in order to grasp the image, an image that derives its meaning from its forward motion in time. In this sense, the filmic text is, in Bellour's words, 'unattainable'. I return to this paradox in the following two chapters.

The scene lasts approximately one minute and 23 seconds, and contains a total of 25 shots. The average shot length in this scene is 3.3 seconds. This may imply rapid cutting but, because of the pacing of the scene, the short shots are not very numerous: I have counted only four instances of above average speed. The average shot length indicates the genre of the film, the Hollywood action film. Combined with the fact that this sequence is positioned at the very end of the film (the climax), certain assumptions about its dynamics will arise. As I will show, however, the sequence contradicts these viewer assumptions.

Let me briefly elaborate on the characteristics of cinematography and the frame. In film, the frame (the border of an image) is never simply a neutral border. The frame projects a certain vantage point onto the material within the image. The frame is important because it actively defines the image for us. Framing can supply a sense of being far away from or close to the mise-en-scene of the shot. This aspect of framing is usually called camera distance. The standard measure for perceiving distance from the camera is the human body. In the *extreme long shot*, the human figure is barely visible. This is the framing for landscapes, for example. In the *long shot*, figures are more prominent, but the background still dominates. The *plan Américain* ('American shot') is very common in Hollywood cinema. Here, the human figure is framed from about the knees up. This type of shot permits a nice balance between figure and surroundings. The *medium shot* frames the human body from the waist up. The *medium close-up* frames the body from the chest up. The *close-up* traditionally shows just the head, hands, feet, or a small object. The *extreme close-up* isolates a detail and magnifies small objects. In film it is possible for the frame to move with respect to the framed material. This is called mobile framing, or more commonly, camera movement. In the *crane shot*, the camera moves above ground level. Typically, it rises or descends, often thanks to a mechanical arm, which lifts and lowers it. In the *tracking shot*, the camera, as a whole, changes position, traveling in any direction along the ground.[4]

1. Long shot of Jericho (with his back to the camera) facing the altar
2. Circular tracking shot, encircling a cautious Jericho. He clings to his gun and scans the church for possible intruders. He reloads his gun, or is about to, when he faces the altar directly. Jericho hesitates

---

4. For a complete list of the key terms in cinematography, see David Bordwell and Kristin Thompson 1997: 210-69.

3.   Plan Américain of Jericho holding the gun

4.   Plan Américain of the statue of Michael holding his sword. This shot is a mirroring of the previous shot, visually forging a link between the two warriors Michael and Jericho

5.   Medium close-up of Jericho, who starts to lower his gun

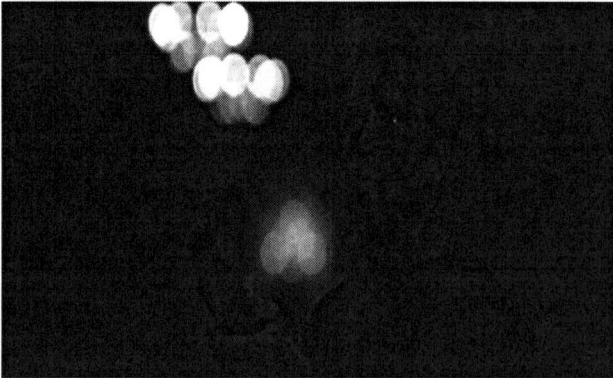

6. Close-up of Michael's face

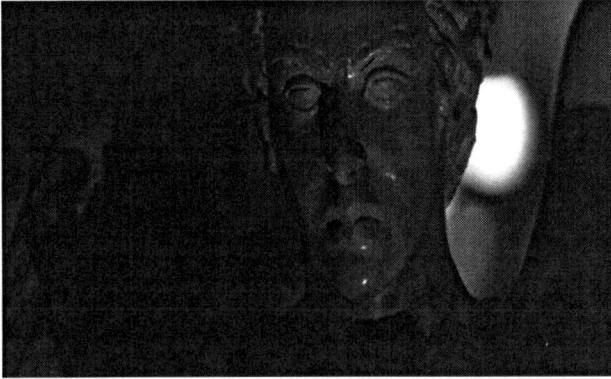

7. Medium close-up of Jericho, who turns his head at –
8. Insert of a tableau depicting the four apostles and Jesus, followed by a quick cut to –
9. Another part of the altar
10. Jericho in medium close-up. He is still cautious and cocks the hammer of his gun
11. Insert of a tableau depicting a group of saints, rapid cut to—
12. Another insert, in more detail, of saints
13. Medium close-up of Jericho looking at –
14. The centerpiece of the altar, the triptych of the crucifixion of Christ

15. Medium close-up of Jericho looking at the gun in his hand
16. Long shot of Jericho facing the altar (exactly the same shot 1)
17. Close-up of Jericho looking up to the altar and nodding his head in some kind of recognition, rapid cut to –
18. Medium close-up of Jericho with the gun, he lowers his gun. Through a rapid cut (match on action) to—

19. Crane shot from above, moving down and forward toward Jericho who drops his gun, resulting in a close-up of Jericho's face. The downward movement seems to suggest an encroaching of the altar upon Jericho

20. Close-up of the face of Christ. (This shot could also represent Jericho's point of view.)

21. Close-up of Jericho imploring, 'please God, help me' –

22. Plan Américain of Jericho (with his back to the camera), 'give me strength'
23. Close-up of Jericho closing his eyes
24. Close-up of the triptych (according to the rules of the continuity system, this shot cannot be a point-of-view shot)
25. Close-up of the face of Christ, same as in shot 19

Mere seconds after this shot, Satan makes his entrance into the church.

If one looks at this shot sequence, it is possible to divide it into two parts: the first part consists of shots 1 to 16. This is the first part of Jericho's quest for faith, or the initial step in the process of finding God (Christ) and letting go of his anger and violent behavior. This first part of Jericho's transformation is framed and closed off by shot 16, an exact repetition of shot 1. In my view, shots 1 and 16 bracket the first part; the symmetry of the shots gives it a rounded-off status. The second half of the sequence commences with shot 17 and ends with shot 25. In this part of the sequence, Jericho finds and accepts Christ as his leader. I will return to the second part of the sequence below.

In the first part of the sequence, there is a particular aspect that immediately stands out: the exchange of close-ups in shots 3 to 7. Through these close-ups, the warrior connection between the archangel Michael and Jericho is established. In the entire sequence, two religious icons and symbols are juxtaposed: the armed warrior-hero Michael and the crucified lamb Jesus. Yet, as becomes obvious in the rest of the sequence, though he seems torn between choosing either Michael or Christ, Jericho eventually chooses the lamb, Christ, over the warrior. In the next section, I will address Jericho's alignment with Christ.

Warrior Becomes Christ

Following Panofsky's model of iconological analysis, it is necessary to analyze the figure of Michael on an iconographic level. This means one has to search the literary source that features Michael. Michael is explicitly mentioned in Revelation 12.7: 'And war broke out in heaven; Michael and his angels fought against the dragon. The dragon and his angels fought back'.[5] Despite being mentioned by name only once in the Book of Revelation, Judith Kovacs and Christopher Rowland argue that the scene of Michael battling with the dragon is one of the most prominent motifs in artistic representations of the Apocalypse (Kovacs and Rowland 2004: 32).[6]

Michael is the protagonist of the war in heaven, a war between him and the dragon, Satan. According to Kovacs and Rowland, this war is a familiar theme in both Jewish and Christian sources, yet it has presented interpretative problems for Christian theologians. Kovacs and Rowland point to the fact that Michael, who eventually defeats Satan, is an angel, 'which seems to threaten the unique rule of Christ' (Kovacs and Rowland 2004: 136). Several commentators have attempted to identify Michael with the figure of Christ or the Holy Spirit. Another interpretation of Michael is that his defeat of Satan in heaven is the counterpart to Christ's earthly

5. All biblical citations in this study are taken from the digital New Revised Standard Version of the Bible, http://bible.oremus.org.
6. There are two other instances in which Revelation speaks of John's angel, an allusion to Michael, namely in Rev.1.1 and 22.6.

death on the cross.[7] Kovacs and Rowland remark that Revelation 12 was long seen as a source giving 'insight into the larger cosmic struggle between God and the forces of darkness' (Kovacs and Rowland 2004: 136, 138-39). The image of Michael is a conventional one, and the theme of the battle between good and evil he represents is too.[8]

One can conclude from this that the figure of Michael clearly belongs to Panofsky's history of types. By reading the figure of Michael from an iconographical perspective, the spectator of *End of Days*, who may not be familiar with the Book of Revelation, may interpret the scene on another level. The iconographical method has, however, a major disadvantage. It is a method that aims at what Bal calls a 'naturalization of symbolic meaning' and to fixate that meaning (Bal 1999: 223). Indeed, by assuming the biblical source as crucial to the only correct understanding of Michael, the process of signification is closed off. Moreover, the specific framework in which the character of Michael occurs, Hollywood cinema, is rendered irrelevant. I believe the opposite to be the case. The manifestation of Michael in *End of Days* opens up a range of possible intertextual meanings, which go beyond the iconographical reading of Michael.[9]

Crucial for Hollywood cinema is that the viewer can dispense with the specific iconographical reading of Michael and still make sense of the scene. The two elements that guide the viewer are the mise-en-scene and the editing of the scene. With regard to editing, the shot list clearly demonstrates the exchange of looks in shots 3 to 7 between Jericho and Michael. This constitutes a speechless dialogue between the two. This is repeated when Jericho turns to Christ and again, through editing, a rapport between the two is constructed. The mise-en-scene operates in tandem

7. See Resseguie 1998: 155.

8. Timothy Beal considers the story of Michael defeating the dragon an inspiration for many other legends of saints slaying dragons. His examples range from *Beowulf* to the character of Draco Malfoy in the *Harry Potter* novel series (Beal 2002: 83-84).

9. Bal defines iconography as, 'interpreting visual representation by placing its elements in a tradition that gives them a meaning other than their 'immediate' visual appearance suggests' (Bal 1991: 177). Instead of 'seeing' the image, iconography uncovers the symbol and then 'reads' the image. Therefore, it 'subordinates the visually represented element to something else'. An iconographical reading is potentially limiting, yet it can also be productive. Iconography can be deployed to 'ward off threatening interpretations, to fit the works into a reassuring tradition, but which can also be taken beyond its most obvious use to yield a powerful critical reading' (Bal 1991: 178). By reading the figure of Michael iconographically, the verbal element takes over the reading, since the prime pre-text to Michael is biblical, and as such 'colonizes the image'. The recognition of Michael as a biblical figure is an important and primary reading strategy, but it should not be the only reading strategy.

with the editing; they support each other. The mise-en-scene shows a strong visual resemblance between Michael and Jericho. In the juxtaposition of shots 3 to 7 in my breakdown of the scene, a strong visual alliance is forged between Jericho and Michael, as both are warriors. The key element that brings the two characters together is Jericho's gun, which is juxtaposed with Michael's sword. The mirroring of Jericho and Michael in both their stature and their weapons, which occurs in shots 3 and 4, constitutes a clear moment of recognition. This recognition happens on a diegetic level. The contemporary warrior Jericho armed with his automatic gun encounters his ancient, biblical counterpart, Michael. Likewise, the viewer connects Jericho with Michael. However, the scene continues. Almost instantly, the established alliance between Jericho and Michael is torn down in favor of another one: the association of Jericho with Christ.

Before I turn to Jericho's transformation into a Christ-like figure, I want to explore the warrior aspects of Jericho and, more importantly, of the Schwarzenegger embodiment of the warrior. The conversion from warrior to Christ is the most important element in this sequence precisely because, in this conversion, a whole field of intertextual significance, regarding images of warriors and specifically images of the film star Arnold Schwarzenegger, is opened up. The concept of quotation functions as the key to unlocking these divergent visual connotations.

Intertextuality: Star Text

So far, I have looked at the warrior image from an iconographical stance. Now I will deploy the concept of intertextuality, the second concept that, together with iconography makes up quotation, to make the image both more dynamic as the medium of film requires, and more 'preposterous' as historical analysis demands.

The star text of Arnold Schwarzenegger enables me to analyze the dominant conception of Schwarzenegger as film star. As I suggested at the beginning, *End of Days* is an exceptional entry in the Schwarzenegger filmography. In this film, Schwarzenegger acts against the type of character that has made him an international star. Richard Dyer's theory of stars serves as a good starting point to analyze the star image of Schwarzenegger. To begin, the relationship between a star and a particular film has to be taken into account. As Dyer states, stars are made for profit: they are an integral part of the marketing of a film. Dyer argues that the presence of a star is 'a promise of a certain kind of thing that you would see if you went to see the film' (Dyer 2004: 5). Stars play an important role in selling a film to a particular audience.

Furthermore, stars and their images are constructed. According to Dyer and other theorists such as John Ellis and Paul McDonald, a star text consists of everything that is publicly available about stars. A star text is based on the films of a particular star, and also on the promotion of those films, pin-ups, public appearances, interviews, and biographies. The latter types of text can, according to Ellis, be characterized as 'subsidiary forms of circulation', which serve to maintain the hype surrounding the activities of the film stars (Ellis 1982: 91). Star texts, according to Dyer, have two main characteristics. First, a star text is by definition always extensive, multimedia, and intertextual. Second, star texts are subject to historical change; they are by no means stable and they take on different dimensions in certain stages of a star's career. Moreover, as Dyer remarks, the star text can outlive the star's own lifetime (Dyer 2004: 2-3).[10]

The films of a star shape a particular star text to a large extent. Hence, the filmography of Arnold Schwarzenegger should be the starting point for coming to terms with his star text. Schwarzenegger's films predominantly belong to the genre of the action film and, more specifically, the action film of the 1980s and 1990s. As Yvonne Tasker points out in her book on action cinema, *Spectacular Bodies*, the white male bodybuilder has dominated the American action cinema since the 1980s. In her analysis of the genre, Tasker claims that the centrality of muscular heroes is by no means an entirely new phenomenon; rather, it harkens back to earlier cinematic traditions, such as the Tarzan films and the mythological epic. However, the scale of the budgets, production output, and box-office success of these muscular action films makes the genre incomparable with its predecessors. One possible explanation for the huge success of these films is that they serve as a kind of backlash against the feminism of the 1970s. In the wake of that social change, these films signal, as Tasker puts it, the 'extent to which masculinity itself has been called into question' (Tasker 1993: 1-5).

It comes as no surprise, then, that in the explosive genre of the action film the display of the white male body is most welcome. The bodybuilder Schwarzenegger serves as the embodiment of this muscular, white action hero. The fact that Schwarzenegger was a world famous bodybuilder (seven times Mr. Olympia) before he switched to acting explains why his star text hinges on his body. Moreover, one can easily argue that, had it not been for his spectacular physique, Schwarzenegger would never have been capable of breaking into the movies. He is generally regarded as a limited actor at best, hampered by his heavy Austrian accent. Turning this weakness into

10. The two characteristics of the star text are not exclusively applicable to film stars within the context of popular culture. In a similar vein, the epitome of 'high art', Rembrandt, can also be defined as a cultural text, and star text. By treating Rembrandt as a cultural text, the imaginary boundaries between 'high' culture, that is, the work as a thing, and popular culture, meaning the reception as an event, can be transgressed (Bal 1991b: 11).

strength, Schwarzenegger's trademark one-liners make excellent and effective use of his pronunciation. By limiting the dialogue to the bare essentials, Schwarzenegger's comical one-liners are highlighted and provide a comical counterpoint both to his threatening physique and the menacing characters he often portrays. His best asset, the one thing that sets him apart from most other actors (except perhaps Sylvester Stallone), remains his physique. One could claim that Schwarzenegger's films not only make excellent use of this body, but also *originate from* Schwarzenegger's body. That is to say, the extraordinary body is the starting point for particular films. Without that body, many of Schwarzenegger's films would never have been made. Schwarzenegger's limited acting qualities and, even more so, his typical pronunciation play an equally important role in his oeuvre, restricting the range of characters he plays to non-American or non-human characters (cyborgs).[11]

The film in which these two defining characteristics of the Schwarzenegger star, the body and the accent, are put to maximum effect is the 1982 film *Conan The Barbarian* (USA: John Milius), a film adaptation of Robert E. Howard's sword and sorcery adventures of the 1930s. The film is an important one in the star text of Arnold Schwarzenegger. The film was crucial in shaping the image of Schwarzenegger as a Teutonic superman; it brought the unique qualities of Schwarzenegger to the attention of a large audience; his previous films had only been minor successes. This film marked Schwarzenegger's breakthrough in Hollywood. The success of *Conan the Barbarian* and the effect it had on Schwarzenegger's career demonstrates that the film was tailor made for Schwarzenegger: he had the body to be Conan. The story is basically a study in primitive living and fighting, set in the 8th century B.C. and is inspired by old myths, legends, and the Bible, ranging from the biblical strongman Samson and the wheel of pain to the crucifixion of Christ. Conan itself is also a hybrid of other action heroes such as Tarzan and Superman. He is skilled in the art of sword fighting, looting, and plundering.[12]

---

11. Schwarzenegger has proven to be a skilful master in reinventing his star persona. Even though he became famous as a muscular action hero in films such as *Commando* (USA: Mark l. Lester, 1985) and *Predator* (USA: John McTiernan, 1987), he made a conscious decision to accept roles that went against his usual character. Films such as *Twins* (USA: Ivan Reitman, 1988) and *Kindergarten Cop* (USA: Ivan Reitman, 1990) foreground Schwarzenegger's comic timing and delivery instead of his physique. I will return to stars acting against their established persona in the next chapter. With *End of Days* (and one can argue, *The 6th Day* (USA/Canada: Roger Spottiswoode, 2000), Schwarzenegger invented himself once more. In these two films, he wished to deal with more serious themes, expressed in Jericho Cane's fallibility and mortality. Perhaps this was prompted by Schwarzenegger's brush with mortality. In 1997, he underwent emergency open heart surgery to have an aortic valve replaced (Andrews 2003: 233).

12. The book of Judges (Judges 16.21) tells the story of Samson and his love for

The barbarian aspect of the Conan character needs some elaboration. In a chapter on the representation of white masculinity in *White*, Richard Dyer makes an important connection between bodybuilding and the ways in which it shapes the body drawing on a number of white representational traditions. Bodybuilding makes reference to classical Greek and Roman art. This is expressed in both the body shape and the posing of bodybuilders. Bodybuilding is also an American lifestyle or, to be more specific, a Californian lifestyle characterized by health, energy, naturalness, and also pain. The aspect of pain is closely related to Christian imagery, another recurring representational tradition in bodybuilding. As Dyer claims, bodybuilding is a painful activity, which involves 'bodily suffering, and with it the idea of the value of pain' (Dyer 1997: 150). Finally, bodybuilding draws on the primitivist image of the barbarian. *Conan the Barbarian* is indeed the prime example of the relationship between primitivism and bodybuilding, and Dyer even speaks of a 'host of largely straight-to-video movies' based on the barbarian theme (Dyer 1997: 149).

Paradoxically, the pairing of white bodybuilding with the primitive, exotic barbarian might, at first, seems to result in the construction of a *non-white* image. This, Dyer asserts, is not the case. On the contrary, these films will always cast an unambiguously white hero, which 'mobilises a sub-Nietschian rhetoric of the *Übermensch* that, however inaccurately, is strongly associated with Hitlerism and crypto-fascism' (Dyer 1997: 150). Schwarzenegger, with his massive body and his persona of Teutonic confidence is, to many, the personification of the *Übermensch*. The meaning of the word Barbarian, literally a person who does not speak Greek and whose utterances sound to Greek speakers like '*bar bar bar*', is nicely illustrated in the film. Schwarzenegger speaks very little and, if he speaks, it is barely comprehensible. The production company Universal Pictures feared that Schwarzenegger's accent would have a negative influence on the box office result and cut much of the dialogue out of the film.[13]

Conan the Barbarian is the key film in Schwarzenegger's subsequent career and star text. All the roles he has played since this film not only capitalize on the image of the barbarian, but also return to and expand on this image. The sequence in *End of Days* where the Schwarzenegger character encounters Michael cannot be read without taking into account this aspect of the star text of Schwarzenegger. It is almost inescapable, if

his philistine wife Delilah. After she betrayed him, he was set to grind at the mill in the prison. In *Conan the Barbarian*, this device, used only for torturing the strongest of men, is called the wheel of pain. See also, Bal 1987, for a critical deconstruction of the Samson and Delilah story.

13. For a discussion on the designation of the Other as barbarian, see Papastergiadis 1997: 257-81.

not impossible, to read this scene without remembering the template of visual representations of Schwarzenegger.[14]

As Bal contends, cultural images such as films 'come to the subject from the outside but arrive in an environment of memories' (Bal 1999: 198). Moreover, 'fragments from other discourses, visual scraps are loaded with memory. The image does not forget where it has been' (Bal 1999: 100). The moment Schwarzenegger's character Jericho encounters Michael, one is instantaneously reminded not only of Michael (in the iconographical tradition of Christian imagery), but also of earlier images of Schwarzenegger as a sword-wielding barbarian. For an instant, the images of Conan and Michael collide. The clash and blend of these images recasts the image of Michael as a barbarian, instead of a Christian warrior. Michael takes on Conan-like and, as collateral effect, also Schwarzenegger-like qualities: a physical giant with a taste for death and destruction. Conversely, Jericho-Schwarzenegger is imbued with Michael's Christian qualities: he becomes a warrior of God.

Let me stress that the viewer need not know the specific iconographical context of Michael nor, for that matter, that of Schwarzenegger. The fact that this character is positioned in the mise-en-scene as a statue in a church provides enough clues with regard to the Christian standing of Michael. Likewise, the fact that Jericho recalls familiar images of the white, super male physique provides enough clues to operate the blend. The striking facet of this scene in *End of Days* is that the new image of Jericho as the Christian warrior is cast aside immediately after it is established.

Jericho Cane as Christ

In the second part of the sequence, a transformation takes place in the character of Jericho Cane: he moves away from his warrior-like characteristics, his use of guns and excessive physical force, and takes on the characteristics of a Christ-like persona. Before I analyze this conversion in detail, it is necessary to consider whether Jericho should be regarded as a personification of Christ. The Christ-figure, like the warrior, has a long history of representation in film. Depictions of Christ range from the reverential portrayals of a solemn savior in films from the 1960s, such as *King of Kings* (USA: Nicholas Ray, 1961) to the 1970s musical *Jesus*

---

14. Stephen Moore makes a provocative argument regarding representations of Christ/God in the Book of Revelation. In his study of God as bodybuilder, Moore notes that the Son of Man in Revelation has feet of bronze (1.15). He links this image with the vision on the bronzed bodybuilder who is like a bronze statue. For Moore, the God of Revelation is a posing bodybuilder, an Arnold Schwarzenegger with throne in *Conan the Barbarian* (Moore 2001). I owe this reference to Pippin 1999: 123.

Christ Superstar (USA: Norman Jewison, 1973).[15] Generally speaking, the depiction of Christ reached its peak of popularity in the 1950s and 1960s, but the genre of the biblical epic can effectively be presumed dead these days. One of the last films that attempted to represent the life of Christ is *The Last Temptation of Christ* (USA: Martin Scorsese, 1989). This film has been held responsible for the extinction of the genre of Christ films.[16]

It can be argued, however, that Christ made way for an alternative manifestation: the messianic figure in film. This is a character that shares many features with the Christ figure of the biblical epic, but has moved beyond the generic boundaries of the biblical spectacular (McEver 1998). The genre that has incorporated the Christ/Messiah character is the contemporary action film. Films such as *Armageddon* (USA: Michael Bay, 1998), *End of Days*, and *The Matrix* trilogy (USA: Andy and Lana Wachowski, 1999, 2003) all feature the messianic superhero character, a selfless male who is called upon to carry out a redemptive task, usually for the greater good of a society in distress. This character and script can be found in thousands of popular culture artifacts and is often considered to be the American monomyth. In their book on the divergent manifestations of this American monomyth, John Shelton Lawrence and Robert Jewett claim that the archetypal hero functions as a replacement for the Christ figure, 'explicitly designed to offer contemporary moviegoers this new Christ' (Lawrence and Jewett 2002: 6-7).

In an analysis of the heroic Christ character, one often looks for a number of divine signature signs that relate to both the appearance and behavior of the hero. In *End of Days*, the obvious clue is the initials of the protagonist: J.C. (Jericho Cane). Furthermore, Jericho has blue eyes. This may seem a trivial detail; however, the blue eyes are an established trait of celluloid saviors and belong to the cinema conventions regarding the depiction of Christ. The gentilising and whitening of Christ is the object of critical study in Dyer's *White*. The historical fact that Christ was a Jew plays an important part in his representation. As Dyer contends, Jews have historically constituted the 'limit case of whiteness' (Dyer 1997: 53). On one hand, their racial visibility was undisputed. In the representation of Jews, certain physical differences such as skin, eyes, and hair color, were recurring. On the other, there was uncertainty. The characteristics attributed to Jews were undermined by a theory that attempted to fix

15. For a good overview of films about Christ, see Walsh 2003, Barnes Tatum 1997 and Reinhartz 2007.

16. Mel Gibson's *The Passion of the Christ* (USA, 2004) proved to be responsible for a minor yet controversial revival of the genre. However, it remains to be seen if Gibson's film turns out to be an incentive for the production of other biblical epics. For an overview of responses to the film, see Brent Plate 2004.

Jewish color geographically and in its ability to adapt to surroundings. This 'adaptability', as Dyer explains, 'could easily be viewed as the capacity to infiltrate, passing for gentile as a kind of corruption of whiteness' (Dyer 1997: 57). In the depiction of Christ and the Virgin Mary as well, skin color is a mark of otherness. Even though both Christ and the Virgin Mary are Jews, 'they are rendered as paler, whiter, than everyone else'. In this instance, the color of the skin is a sign of their enlightenment: 'Christ and Mary are actually saved Jews, that is, Christians' (Dyer 1997: 66-67).

In this respect, it is worth mentioning *The Passion of the Christ* (USA: Mel Gibson, 2004), in which, according to some people, a more truthful representation of Christ is attempted. Hence, Christ has brown eyes and a more Semitic appearance.[17] This film breaks with the Hollywood rule in order to heighten its realism and assumed truthfulness, ignoring the fact that, even though blue-eyed Messiahs may not constitute a realistic depiction of Christ, the rules of Hollywood, a system in itself, equate the color blue with divinity, truth and, fidelity. Another common sign of divinity is the evil temptation the hero has to resist, which harkens back to the biblical Satan's lure of Christ in the desert. In *End of Days*, Jericho rejects Satan's temptation, a scene to which I will return in more detail below. By resisting this temptation, he sets himself up to be the recipient of Satan's wrath.

Satan's particular method of punishment, crucifixion, resulting in divine (near) death points to Jericho's possible rebirth as a Christ figure or, at least, to his celestial status. Moreover, in the punishment, discourses on martyrdom and masculinity merge. In a memorable scene that takes place halfway though the film, Satan crucifies Jericho, who is left to die. However, like Jesus, Jericho is resurrected: he is found by a priest and survives. The cross as a symbol of punishment, epitomized by Jesus' slow and agonizing death on the cross, is effectively used in *End of Days*. Jericho is punished as well as saved by the cross. The punishment, the physical torture, ties in with what Tasker understands to be a recurring scene in action cinema: the revelation of the body of the hero. This revelation is often characterized by 'suffering, and torture in particular, [it] operates as both a set of narrative hurdles to be overcome (tests that the hero must survive) and as a set of aestheticised images to be lovingly dwelt on' (Tasker 1993: 125).

The scene echoes martyr stories, in that it draws on the Christian imagery that depicts bodily suffering as benevolent to the human spirit. Consequently, pain ennobles those who are able to endure that torment. This results in what Dyer calls the establishment of 'the moral superiority of not specifically Christian characters' (Dyer 1997: 150). This is the case in *End of Days*: Jericho Cane is marked by human weaknesses: he is an

17. For an overview of scholarly reconstructions of the physical appearance of the historical Jesus, see Moore 2001: 90-130.

egoistic and violent alcoholic. Moreover, the crucifixion connects two different discourses, action film and martyrdom, and shows them to be remarkably similar. The two discourses converge in their conception of masculinity as the control over one's body, specifically when the body is in tremendous pain. Jericho's capacity to withstand this brutal form of torture echoes action film narratives in which the hero 'struggles for physical self-control and for control over one's body' (Tasker 1993: 126). Ultimately, it signals Jericho's nascent talent for becoming a fully-fledged martyr in that it demonstrates his uncontested masculinity.[18]

What is striking is that Jericho's conversion does not take place immediately after he has been saved from being crucified. The crucifixion is an important test and foreshadows Jericho's connection to Christ. However, Jericho is not a personification of Christ. Rather, as his ability to endure torture demonstrates, he finds faith in order to become a martyr. In that sense, Jericho emulates Christ, in that he follows his example and dies a sacrificial death from which all humankind benefits. The completion of Jericho's transformation occurs in the second part of the sequence, when he faces his biblical mirror image Michael. Only then does the conversion from warrior to martyr take place.

The Materialization of the Christian Warrior

The conversion of Jericho is depicted in the second half of the sequence, starting with shot 17 in the shot list. As I mentioned above, the first part of the sequence runs from shot 1 to 16. In its exact mirroring of shot 1, shot 16 functions as a way of bracketing that part of the sequence. However, it could also be argued that the second part of the sequence *begins* with shot 16 instead of shot 17. The main motivation for this is that shot 16 could function as a re-establishing shot: it returns to a view of an entire space after a series of closer shots. As Bellour points out, the demarcation of a sequence is always arbitrary: 'neither the beginning nor the end can properly be said to constitute this segment of film as a closed and strictly definable unit' (Bellour 2000: 29).

I want to focus on what I consider to be the key shot of the second part of the sequence, shot 19. This shot is important because it consists of an unusual, elaborate camera movement. All previous shots were static (except for shot 2) and showed little variation in height of framing; hence, the sequence is dominated by medium close-ups and plan Américain shots. Shot 19, however, is a descending crane shot, segueing neatly into a

---

18. For a discussion of ancient hegemonic constructions of masculinity connected to martyrdom and, in particular, the classical martyr text of 4 *Maccabees*, see Moore and Anderson 1998.

tracking shot, which results in framing Jericho in a medium close-up. With this shot, the symmetry and balance of the sequence is disrupted. According to Bellour, disruption serves an essential goal. Variation in the symmetry of shots has as its objective the continuity of the narrative. Bellour writes, 'the regulated opposition between the closing off of symmetries and the opening up of dissymmetry gives rise to the narrative, to the very fact that there is a narrative' (Bellour 2000: 75).

The difference of shot 19 has a crucial consequence for the point of view of the narrative. Whereas previous shots, for instance shots 8,9, and 14, can be aligned to Jericho's point of view (or could at least be considered to be Jericho's eyeline matches), shot 19 has the reverse effect: it is as though the altar, the figure of Christ and his saints, is 'looking down' at Jericho. The position of point of view is reversed from Jericho to the altar. The altar appears to come to life, and perhaps does so literally, since this is the moment that Jericho becomes a believer. Christ, of whom the altar is a personification, has come to life for Jericho. The dialogue of the sequence underscores Jericho's conversion. For the first time in the entire film, Jericho pleads with God for help. Moreover, for the first time, Jericho realizes that his weapon is of no use in his battle against Satan. Instead he begs God to give him spiritual strength. By casting away the gun and addressing God directly, Jericho's conversion from warrior to lamb is completed. The redemption of the character, which began with his crucifixion by Satan, has now been achieved: Jericho is a believer and ready to sacrifice himself for God. As a warrior of a different kind, a warrior of God, Jericho is empowered by divine influence, faces Satan, and saves mankind.

The *denouement* of *End of Days* offers a reworking of its source text, Revelation: the film and its depiction of the warrior and the lamb, makes an interesting volte-face. In order to demonstrate in what respect *End of Days* diverges from its iconographical source text, and thus constitutes a case of preposterous history, it is necessary to return to the source text. According to James Resseguie, there are three major visions of Christ in Revelation: the first is the Son of Man (1.12-20; 14.14), the second is the Lamb (5.6-14), and the third is the rider called Faithful and True (19.11-21) (Resseguie 1998: 111). The differences between these visions are striking. The Son of Man vision presents Christ with 'sublime features of divinity'. The second depicts him as the slaughtered and resurrected lamb, which accentuates his humanity. In the first two versions, Christ appears in heaven. In the final vision, however, 'Christ descends from heaven with his entourage to conquer the powers of deception on earth. Heaven and earth meet in the final and dramatic scene in which Truth dispels falsehood and casts it into the lake of fire' (Resseguie 1998: 113-14). This final vision has strong militaristic connotations: the rider called Faithful and True is riding a white horse together with the armies of heaven, who are also on white horses

(Revelation 19.14). The rider wears a robe that is dipped in blood, unlike his armies who are dressed in white linen. The striking feature of the rider, though, is the two-edged sword that protrudes from his mouth. [19]

The images of the robe dipped in blood and the sword have yielded diverse interpretations. Resseguie contends that the blood-soaked robe, 'likely comes from the shedding of Christ's own blood on the cross' (Resseguie 1998: 116). Other commentators claim that the blood belongs to those slain in battle. As these readings suggest, the image brings about opposing views. This is even more the case with the imagery of the sword. Again, Resseguie downplays the violent connotations of the two-edged sword by stating that it 'symbolizes truth's double-edged testimony. On one hand, it slays falsehood and releases those bound by the lies and deceits of the beast. On the other, it condemns those who reject Jesus' testimony to the true God and cling to the beast's delusions' (Resseguie 1998: 114-15). He concludes his analysis by claiming that the Christian warrior in Revelation has no need of a real sword since 'The only weapon this warrior needs is the proclamation of the gospel, his confident testimony, the word of God' (Resseguie 1998: 115).

In their reading of Revelation 19, Kovacs and Rowland draw up a list of biblical passages in which God is portrayed as the divine warrior. Kovacs and Rowland reach the same conclusion as Resseguie. They conclude that 'most of these passages suggest that judgment in the context of an eschatological battle comes by the power of the Word of God rather than through force of arms' (Kovacs and Rowland 2004: 94-195).

What both Resseguie and Kovacs and Rowland endorse is that the violent language and its corresponding metaphors in Revelation are a means of conveying the message of divinely sanctioned violence. Richard Bauckham makes a similar argument in his exhaustive study of Revelation. He states that 'Revelation makes lavish use of holy war *language* while transferring its *meaning* to non-military means of triumph over evil' (Bauckham 1993a: 233, emphasis in text). The conclusion he eventually reaches is somewhat confusing: 'the distinctive feature of Revelation seems to be [...] its lavish use of militaristic *language* in a non-militaristic *sense*'. Nevertheless, Bauckham adds, 'there is ample space of the imagery of armed violence' (Bauckham 1993a: 233). So, though Revelation does not denounce militarism *per se*, and its language and imagery are predominantly militaristic, Revelation should be understood as *not* sanctioning militant violence. The discrepancy between language and intended or preferred significance maneuvers its interpreters into a position to make inconsistent claims.

---

19. As Kovacs and Rowland suggest, the rider called Faithful and True is, in a sense, echoed and foreshadowed by the first of the four horsemen of the Apocalypse (Kovacs and Rowland 2004: 194).

David L. Barr, who, unlike Bauckham, seems aware of his awkward position, attempts to read Revelation from an ethical point of view, stressing what he calls 'the ethical problem of John's language' (Barr 2003: 102). He states that, 'while it is possible to appreciate the meaning of John's violent language, the language itself remains a problem. There is too much violence' (Barr 2003: 102).

Though the violent nature of Revelation is partly subverted by the act of sacrifice of the lamb, its dominating rhetoric remains violent. According to Barr, the moral dilemma is that, though one may rejoice at Revelation's 'vision of the overthrow of evil [...], the images and actions that are used to portray this overthrow' are indeed very hard to stomach (Barr 2003: 105).

To come to terms with this surplus of violence, Barr divides the acts of violence into four categories: cosmic upheavals, war, harvest scenes, and judgment scenes. The fourth category of judgment is ethically the most problematic. The primary scene of judgment is the one in Revelation 19.20-21, in which the rider called Faithful and True makes his appearance. The rider exercises a judgment after the battle has been fought:

> And the beast was captured, and with it the false prophet who had performed in its presence the signs by which he deceived those who had received the mark of the beast and those who worshipped its image. These two were thrown alive into the lake of fire that burns with sulphur. And the rest were killed by the sword of the rider on the horse, the sword that came from his mouth; and all the birds were gorged with their flesh.

The most brutal aspect of this scene is the useless killing of 'the rest', the followers of the two leaders, the beast and the false prophet. As Barr argues, 'one might justify the punishments of the leaders as stemming from their crimes of war, but what of the rest? Is it right to kill combatants after the war is over?' (Barr 2003: 103). Indeed, scenes such as these highlight the brutal nature of Revelation.

As a reader, I find it hard to get past these depictions of destruction. At the end of his article, Barr gives validation for the violent language. He points out the intended purpose: 'What must always be kept in mind, however, is that these images of the conquest of evil, however immoral they may appear to be, always correspond to the innocent suffering of Jesus and of those who hold the testimony of Jesus' (Barr 2003: 107).

In a sense, Barr justifies the violent nature of Revelation by suggesting that it is a means to an end. The language John uses is a way of uncovering 'the violence of this world, offering a glimpse of the cosmic war between good and evil, a war only won through suffering' (Barr 2003: 107). Although Barr attempts to criticize Revelation's violence, in the end he cannot help but rationalize and excuse that violence nonetheless. By relating violence to suffering to the point where the two converge, Revelation's violence is morally neutralized.

An interesting parallel between biblical and cinematic violence can be observed. Namely, a similar rhetoric to the one outlined in relation to Revelation pervades discussions on extremely violent film as well. The issue of excessive violence in action cinema, and particularly the moral response to graphic violence—condone it as an element of the text, or condemn it—mirrors the exegesis of Revelation. The analogy between Revelation and *End of Days* as controversial texts also affects the interpretation of the Michael, the rider called Faithful and True, and Jericho as protagonists. These are not unreservedly 'good', morally just heroes. Their use of violence is problematic because it obscures the wished-for meaning, 'the good will prevail, with violence if necessary', of both biblical and cinematic text. By placing the biblical warriors next to the cinematic one, the analogy of violence between both texts is further accentuated. By reading backward from the contemporary warrior to its biblical predecessors, the earlier text is altered: the rider called Faithful and True and Michael are infused with the muscular qualities of Schwarzenegger's Jericho.

The End: Death Shall Be No More

The war between good and evil, violence, suffering, and eventual redemption through suffering, are all visualized in the finale of *End of Days*. The devil, now no longer represented in its earlier human incarnation but in its true form of a gigantic dragon, enters Jericho's body. Although Jericho physically tries to fight this intrusion, after some struggle Satan takes over. Satan, now in the guise of Jericho, lures Christine out of her place of hiding, grabs her and lays her down at the altar where the final act, impregnating her and inaugurating Satan's reign, will take place. Christine implores Jericho to fight Satan. Jericho has not given up yet: there is an 'internal' struggle taking place between Jericho and Satan. Similar to the sequence I have analyzed in detail, Jericho turns again to both Michael and Jesus, and again, seems torn between them. This time, though, Jericho first looks at the triptych of the crucified Jesus. In an instant, Jericho is inspired by the image of the lamb Jesus. It becomes clear to him that the only way to fight Satan is by committing the non-violent act of self-sacrifice, giving one's life for the greater good of mankind.

Immediately after looking at the triptych of Christ, Jericho turns to the statue of Michael, which now lays broken on the church floor. His sword is the one thing that is not broken. This is emphasized in one particular shot, which is a close-up of the shiny tip of the sword, rendered through the device of pulling focus. This is done by adjusting perspective by refocusing the lens on an object in the background and racking it to the foreground, making it 'jump' into focus. Jericho does not hesitate and falls into Michael's sword, killing, or at least casting out, Satan from his body. His release is represented by an overwhelming wave of fire erupting from Jericho's belly, which temporarily sets fire to the church. The image of Satan appears briefly in the flames before he vanishes into a hole in the church floor.

After this act, Jericho, who is dying, sees the image of his deceased wife and daughter. They look at him smiling and appear to be waiting for him. This short scene underlines Jericho's status as a martyr. In it, two recurring elements, or themes, of martyr stories are present, namely the vision and the reward. The martyr's susceptibility to visions is outlined in the next four chapters of this study. Since Jericho's vision is not a prominent feature of the film, I will not deal with it here in more detail. The apparition of Jericho's wife and daughter recalls the temptation scene earlier in the film. In that scene, Satan conjured up the past, in which Jericho's wife and child were still alive. The image was intended to coax Jericho into choosing Satan's side. Jericho saw through the deceitfulness of the image, a mirage, and denied Satan. This denial led to Jericho's crucifixion, which, I argued, was a crucial step in his transformation into a martyr. In the final scene of the film, Jericho's deceased loved ones appear once more, only this time the image is not conjured up by satanic forces but by Jericho's newfound belief in Christ. Consequently, the image should not be understood as tempting but as rewarding. Jericho's act of sacrifice is rewarded by the victory over death, the reunion with loved ones, and an afterlife.

This compensation echoes Revelation 21.4: 'He will wipe every tear from their eyes. Death will be no more; mourning and crying and pain will be no more, for the first things have passed away'. The theme is also persistent in non-biblical or theological sources, as Arthur J. Droge and James D. Tabor point out, 'the expectation of vindication and reward beyond death, more often than not, is a prime motivation for their [the martyrs] choice of death' (Droge and Tabor 1992: 75). The secular *End of Days* adheres to this convention and, moreover, uses it to its own benefit. Since the film denies its viewers the usual *denouement* of action films, typified by the hero's triumphant victory over his adversaries, Jericho's triumph in the afterlife comes to function as a substitute. The reunion of Jericho with his family is a makeshift happy ending.

As I stated at the beginning of this chapter, *End of Days* is a popular representation of millennial anxieties. This is illustrated by the film's main narratological premise: the unleashing of Satan in order to thwart the turn of the millennium. This caused the disturbance of the present day situation. The return to the status quo, brought about by Jericho's death, is confirmed by the New Year's celebration at the very end of the film.[20] In the film's

---

20. The imminence of the New Year, represented throughout *End of Days* as a countdown to 00.00 hours, also serves another function in apocalyptically themed action

ending, which is neither cataclysmic nor apocalyptic since the world is saved by the sacrifice of one human being, the dreaded end, the Apocalypse, does not take place. As such, *End of Days* adheres to Baudrillard's conception of the Apocalypse, which I outlined in the introduction, as inherently disappointing. Particularly, what Baudrillard calls the temptation to calculate the end dominates the film. Its narrative structure is grounded on the anticipation of the end, signaled by the constant reminders of the remaining time before midnight, December 31, 1999. Yet, this seemingly inescapable end is cancelled at the very last minute. The turn of the century takes place. The Apocalypse does not.

Conclusion: Scripture as Precursor and Successor

At this point, I return to the article of Richard Walsh, with which I started my analysis of *End of Days*. I argued that Walsh's reading is one-sided, in that it posits the Book of Revelation as the inescapable precursor of the film. Walsh argues that *End of Days* presents an inverted reading of Revelation: 'while Revelation moves from suffering to (redemptive) violence, the movie moves from violence (guns) to faith' (Walsh 2002: 12). Walsh draws this conclusion, which I believe is right, by taking Revelation as the precursor of the cinematic rendering of Revelation. He concludes that '*End of Days* improves Revelation because it refuses to externalize evil to the extent that Revelation does'. Walsh continues, 'placing *End of Days* alongside Revelation, then, exposes the anger and resentment at the heart of Revelation' (Walsh 2002: 13). Walsh uses the film to point out the violent nature of Revelation. By use of a contemporary film, his reading highlights a familiar and problematic trait of Revelation. Walsh credits the film for improving on its source text. However, the preposterous notion that the film might also influence our estimation of the source text is not accounted for.

In my reading of *End of Days*, I have attempted not just to regard Revelation as the historical source for the film, but also to read in the opposite direction as well. The film is not merely a cinematic adaptation of Revelation, as Walsh argues; the film in turn affects Revelation as well. The focal point for my analysis is the presences of Arnold Schwarzenegger as film star, whose images, packed together in his star text, constitute a source of iconographical and intertextual meanings. By juxtaposing Schwarzenegger with archangel/warrior Michael and with Revelation's manifestation of Christ as the rider called Faithful and True, new images emerge. The comparison between Schwarzenegger and Michael results in an augmentation of the latter, as the

cinema: that of the deadline. The notion of the countdown to a deadline returns in the next chapter.

image of the biblical warrior becomes infused with Schwarzenegger's physical and barbarian aspects.

However, in the final part of the film, there is an ultimate reversal occurring in imagery. In Schwarzenegger's act of sacrifice, the film transcends both its pre-text Revelation, as Walsh argues, and the popular genre of the Hollywood action film. Whereas the final part of Revelation manifests Jesus personified as an uncompromising judge who will rule the nations with a rod of iron (Revelation 19.15), *End of Days* emphasizes the sacrificial act performed by Schwarzenegger. In both contexts, the singularity of Schwarzenegger's martyrdom stands out. As I will argue, this act is congruent with the sacrificial acts in other films I discuss in subsequent chapters. One can claim that the motif of self-sacrifice has a strong biblical, iconographical grounding, since the motif refers back to the textual source of the martyrs in Revelation. However, the motif has been imported within a new context, that of Hollywood cinema. Interpretation should then focus on the interpretation of the borrowed motif of self-sacrifice or martyrdom in its new context. The effect of the finale of *End of Days* originates not merely from its renunciation of violence, as it seeks to *improve*, to paraphrase Walsh, on its source text Revelation, but also from the context in which this is played out. In the juxtaposition of Schwarzenegger and the act that he commits, the new-fangled meaning of self-sacrifice can be found.

Chapter 2

AMERICAN MARTYR:
HIGH CONCEPT VISIONS IN ARMAGEDDON

The pursuit of making money is the only reason to make movies. We have
no obligation to make history. We have no obligation to make art. [...] Our
obligation is to make money, and to make money it may be necessary to
make history, [...] art or [...] some significant statement
(Fleming 1998: 192).

Introduction

The epigraph of this chapter is the opening statement taken from the
'Paramount Corporate Philosophy' memo, written by top Hollywood
producer Don Simpson in 1980.[1] The memo encapsulates a conception of
film as primarily an economical device, a product, not an artistic expression,
that should generate as much money as possible. This idea, embodied in so-
called 'high concept' films, of which Simpson together with Jerry Bruckheimer
produced many, ruled the film business in the 1980s and 1990s. The films
echo the machismo of Simpson's bold mission statement in his corporate
memo. High concept films are fast, loud, and, most of all, masculine. They
present the spectator with a male, emphatically macho hero, who eventually
prevails, but not before he has gone through the standard three-act plot
structure summarized as incident, crisis, and triumph. The film I analyze in
this chapter, *Armageddon* (USA: Michael Bay, 1998), is an example of high
concept film. What interests me about this film is its representation of the
hero's masculinity in combination with the martyrlike act of dying. In this
sense, the present chapter follows up on the previous one, as both explore
the representation of male, masculine martyrdom.

The story of *Armageddon* is uncomplicated. After New York City is
damaged by hundreds of small meteorites, NASA discovers that an asteroid

1. An elaborate account of this memo, and its subsequent implications for
Hollywood film in the 1980s and 1990s, can be found in Fleming 1998: 191-193.

the size of Texas is on a collision course with Earth. NASA recruits the best deep core driller in the world, Harry Stamper (Bruce Willis), to train astronauts who will travel to the asteroid, drill into its center, and detonate a nuclear warhead. With only eighteen days left to destroy the asteroid, a race against time begins to save creation and prevent Armageddon.

Armageddon became the most profitable film of 1998. With an estimated budget of over $140 million, it took over $200 million at the American box office and another $300 million outside the US. Additional profits were garnered from DVD rentals and sales. With figures such as these, *Armageddon* epitomizes the mixture of economics and aesthetics of which post-classical Hollywood cinema is generally accused by its critics and, consequently, dismissed. To accept the first point and reject the second, and develop a constructive way of looking at this film, a way that takes it seriously as an aesthetic object, though with important economic ramifications, departs precisely from taking into account its commercial context.

Armageddon gives new meaning to the concept of martyrdom. On one hand, it does so by means of the evocation of the earlier, canonical discourse on martyrdom. A reading of the film will reveal such instances of a historical echoing. On the other, *Armageddon* invests this precursory discourse with new and additional significance. To be more precise, I will argue that *Armageddon* articulates the martyr's act of dying as performative, which echoes earlier discourses on martyrdom. In addition, the film invests the figure of the martyr with novel causes and values for self-sacrifice, which are not so much religious as they are individual, patriotic, masculine and, most notably, American. In my analysis, I look at three separate moments, before, during, and after death that, taken together, amount to the martyrdom of Harry Stamper. Even though martyrdom is effectively achieved after death, I argue that the moments before and during the martyr's death are equally important for the contemporary making of a martyr.

To address the ways in which *Armageddon* is a representation of a new type of male martyrdom, I focus on the film's mode of production, the so-called 'high concept' film. Defining *Armageddon* as a case of high concept cinema enables me to take into account the economic as well as the aesthetic context of this film. It is of crucial importance to address both high concept style and the influence that style exerts on the substance of the film. High concept style, I argue, is an intricate blend of economic and aesthetic powers that must be addressed. I begin with a short historical sketch of the factors responsible for the advent of high concept cinema, followed by its essential characteristics in narrative and characters. High concept cinema depicts in its style and substance a particular kind of masculinity, which has several implications for the type of martyrdom that is constructed in *Armageddon*. Subsequently, I highlight one particular aspect of high concept style, the visceral combination of sound and image through rapid montage. This type of editing, known as the 'MTV aesthetic', governs the key sequence in relation to *Armageddon*'s thematic of martyrdom. My argument will be built on the close analysis of this sequence and supported by the critical evaluation of divergent readings of the film. Finally, the type of close analysis I perform exposes a problematical issue in film analysis, namely, the pause of the moving image in order to be able to read that image. Raymond Bellour has addressed this issue at length; therefore I refer to his work to tackle this paradox.

Characteristics of High Concept in Armageddon

The simplest definition of high concept is a film of which the narrative can be described in a single sentence, making it obvious and highly marketable. High concept is often regarded as the dominant style of Hollywood film production in the 1980s and 1990s. As Justin Wyatt suggests in his study *High Concept: Movies and Marketing in Hollywood*, this style of filmmaking can be considered the central development within post-classical cinema (Wyatt 1994: 8). Wyatt's argument points to the fact that modes of film production, the industrial aspect, and styles of filmmaking, together resulting in the cultural product of film, are all subject to historical change. As film historians Robert Allen and Douglas Gomery contend, 'each mode of production produces its own set of production practices: normative conceptions of how a particular film "should" look and sound' (Allen and Gomery 1985: 86). So, mode of production and film style are both intricately linked to a particular period of time. In this respect, high concept cinema is a mirror of its time: the outcome of far-reaching economic and institutional changes in Hollywood after the 1960s. Wyatt outlines some notable factors in the creation of high concept: the conglomeration of the film industry, the rise of television, and new marketing methods (Wyatt 1994: 16).

As I have indicated, the defining characteristic of high concept is the fact that its content can be captured in a single sentence. This is a key factor in the two distinct valuations high concept cinema evokes. From a film industry point of view, the single-sentence description, known as the pitch, spells out a movie's marketability: its specific narrative can be conveyed and sold easily.[2] Its content is straightforward, easily communicated and

---

2. The act of pitching a movie is effectively parodied in Robert Altman's 1992 film *The Player*. The film shows some hilarious examples of how screenwriters attempt to sell their stories to producers. In order to gain the producer's interest and time, the story needs to be pitched in less than 25 words. Moreover, writers often refer to their proposed projects in shorthand. The story is thus often pitched as a combination of several previous successful films, for instance, the incredible amalgamate of *Ghost* and *The Manchurian Candidate*.

readily comprehensible. Film critics stress the other side of the equation. To them, high concept represents the zero point of creativity, and signals the creative bankruptcy of Hollywood in the 1980s and 1990s. Specifically, they condemn the collapse of classical narrative cinema and Hollywood storytelling in favor of superficial spectacle and style. Moreover, these critics evaluate high concept as sensationalist, tasteless, and aesthetically suspect (Wyatt 1994: 13-14). I do not intend to take sides with either of these two positions in my analysis.

According to Wyatt, high concept is based on two main components. First, narrative and characters are predictable and uncomplicated. The story consists of stock situations and is 'firmly set within the bounds of genre and viewer expectation' (Wyatt 1994: 16). Secondly, the style of high concept film is instrumental to the functioning of its characters and the development of the narrative. Another attribute of high concept style is the strong match between powerful, stylized images and a dominant musical soundtrack (Wyatt 1994: 16-17). This match is commonly expressed through montage sequences that summarize a topic or compress a passage of time in symbolic or stereotypical images. The driving force behind the montage sequence is music, specifically rock music. These sequences are aesthetically similar to music videos shown on MTV and other music stations. The abundance of such sequences entails a further reduction of both narrative and character development which, in the latter case, results in character typing.

One important consequence of character typing is that high concept relies strongly on star persona. The film star, as my analysis of Arnold Schwarzenegger in the preceding chapter elaborates, comes with a particular star text that consists of a constellation of images and knowledge. Ideally, the high concept movie creates a strong connection between the star text and the new project; Wyatt gives the example of Clint Eastwood in a crime thriller (Wyatt 1994: 10-11). However, high concept may also create the exact opposite: the familiar element of the star can be placed in a different context. In this case, stars are consciously working against their well-established and commercially viable image. Illustrative of the latter approach is Arnold Schwarzenegger's comic turn as the first man capable of having a baby in the film *Junior* (USA: Ivan Reitman, 1994). Here the effect is based on the uneasy fit between Schwarzenegger's Mr. Universe physique and preconceived notions of pregnancy, femininity, and vulnerability. This indicates an important aspect of the star: his or her physical characteristics. As Wyatt argues: 'Stars are […] a particular set of physical characteristics, demeanor, and attitude. This emphasis often overwhelms the character being portrayed so that the character is identified more strongly with the star than as an integral part of a unique story' (Wyatt 1994: 53, 55). In this sense, stars and their particular qualities might even hinder the viewer in constructing a particular diegetic character. Moreover, stars encourage the viewer's recognition of character types.[3]

In *Armageddon*, Bruce Willis is the star. The rest of the cast supports and accommodates his character and presence. By casting Willis, the producers secured one of the biggest action stars of the 1980s and 1990s. Particularly his *Die Hard* series (1988, 1990, 1995, and 2007), which is considered as paradigmatic of the new Hollywood action-adventure movie, also known as the male-rampage film, cemented Willis' status as one of Hollywood's popular male heroes, among the ranks of Sylvester Stallone and Arnold Schwarzenegger. The casting of the all American hunk Ben Affleck (playing AJ) and of his love interest played by Liv Tyler (playing Grace, Stamper's daughter) appealed to the female demographic of spectators. In this respect, the film works to secure what Geoff King in his study on blockbuster film calls 'the potential to achieve the useful economic status of a 'date movie', offering something at least to meet dominant expectations associated with male and female viewers' (King 2000: 173).

The significance of the formation of the diegetic couple, AJ and Grace, lies not merely in its means to draw a larger viewer demographic. It also has consequences for *Armageddon*'s narrative, as I will elaborate below. Interestingly, the supporting cast of *Armageddon* consists of 'serious' actors, that is to say, actors who often work outside Hollywood's blockbuster system, such as Billy Bob Thornton, Peter Stormare, and indie favorite Steve Buscemi. The film has a remarkable combination of *bona fide* stars and actors.[4] However, the characters they play are restricted to and reminiscent of characters they have portrayed in some of their previous films. Therefore, the Southern-type tough guy plays tough (Thornton), the heartthrob (Affleck) is just that, and the freaky guy (Buscemi) is still freaky, albeit in a blockbuster production.

The reduced narrative and characters of high concept film imply its dependency on generic conventions and iconography. As Wyatt states, 'generic iconography has been utilized increasingly as an 'economical' means of transmitting information' (Wyatt 1994: 55). High concept film assumes a genre-aware audience and refers to genre conventions and

3. David Bordwell contends that film stars do *not* play a crucial role in high concept film. He claims, based on what one screenplay manual prescribes, that high concept 'denotes a movie sold on the strength of an unusual plot idea that will work without stars' (Bordwell 2006: 6-7). This claim seems incorrect. Bordwell almost immediately retracts it, stating that stars have embraced high concept projects and that a report showed that high concept films without stars had trouble gaining publicity or even release. On the basis of this, I think it is safe to claim that stars are an indispensable feature of high concept film.

4. For an exploration of the differences and overlap between stars and actors in relation to the diegetic characters they can play, see Dyer 1979.

iconography to address it. *Armageddon* is a mixture of action-adventure, science fiction, and thriller genres, and is also firmly located in the series of disaster films released in the second part of the 1990s. With respect to iconography, *Armageddon* is predominantly situated in the science-fiction genre. Apart from allusions to well-known classics of that genre, such as *Fantastic Voyage* (USA: Richard Fleischer, 1966), *Star Wars* (USA: George Lucas, 1977) and *Apollo 13* (USA: Ron Howard, 1995), *Armageddon*'s sleek technological look, particularly its blue, metallic color schemes, is clearly based on a lesser-known film in the genre, *The Right Stuff* (USA: Philip Kaufman, 1983).

Such referencing is not only limited to other genres, or to mixtures of genres, as is often the case in post-classical cinema, but also extends to television shows and other forms of mass media. This pervasive practice of referencing is what Noël Carroll calls allusion, which covers 'practices of quotations, the memorialization of past genres, […] *homages*, and the recreation of 'classic' scenes, shots, plot motifs, lines of dialogue, themes, gestures, and so forth' (Carroll 1998: 241).

The intertextual field of meaning evoked in high concept film functions as a way to convey information by establishing an already familiar context. The practice of allusion presupposes a group of informed viewers, who are able to recall past films. At the same time, these viewers do not take allusion as a form of plagiarism. Allusion, ideally, results in the reciprocal recognition between film and audience of an 'iconographical code': a code which, through its evocation of the past, comments on and influences the present. The knowledgeable audience is able to 'fill in the blanks' or 'connect the dots' easily.

In the case of *Armageddon*, another and unusual type of intertextuality, which stems from its authorial source, is brought into play. Usually, the *oeuvre* of a particular director provides an intertext. This approach is exemplified by the auteurism approach in cinema studies, which postulates the director as the source of a film's intentionality, value, and meaning. However, in the case of high concept films such as *Armageddon*, the director is not the auteur. Rather, the producer has a decisive role in the narrative, aesthetic, and economic choices that are being made. Even though it is contested who actually invented the term high concept, there is no disagreement about naming the two producers responsible for bringing it to life, resulting in a string of trademark high concept films over the last two decades.[5] Don Simpson and Jerry Bruckheimer were the creative team behind many blockbusters of the 1980s and 1990s. In a sense, their films, such as *Top Gun* (USA: Tony Scott, 1986), *Beverly Hills Cop* (USA: Martin Brest, 1984), *Flashdance* (USA: Adrian Lyne, 1983), and later films such as

5. See Wyatt 1994: 8 for a short history of the genesis of the term.

Bad Boys (USA: Michael Bay, 1995) and *Crimson Tide* (USA: Tony Scott, 1995) have had a decisive influence on contemporary pop culture. The Simpson and Bruckheimer films are instantly recognizable though their use of popular music, montage sequences and male stars. *Armageddon* is another example of a Simpson and Bruckheimer production, even though Bruckheimer produced the film without Simpson, who died of heart failure in 1996.

To sum up: the reduction of narrative and character in high concept results in three particular aesthetic strategies: the use of stars, the referencing of many different genres, and the broad intertextual allusions. As a consequence of these aesthetic strategies, high concept is often charged with being a cinema of visual excess, a cinema that chooses style over substance.[6] Even Wyatt, whose book is one of the few studies available giving a thorough analysis of the genre, proposes a critical evaluation of high concept that is reminiscent of the viewpoint of cultural critics alluded to above: 'The modularity of the films' units, added to the one-dimensional quality of the characters, distances the viewer from the traditional task of reading the films' narrative. In place of this identification with narrative, the viewer becomes sewn into the 'surface' of the film, contemplating the style of the narrative and the production' (Wyatt 1994: 60).

Wyatt argues that high concept aesthetics disengage the viewer from the narrative to such an extent that it becomes subservient to the surface qualities—stars, music, and production design—of the film.[7] One may argue that the viewer of high concept cinema is not fully engaged on a narrative level, although what constitutes total narrative engagement to begin with is difficult to assess. High concept's intertextual strategies of referencing, allusion, and iconography certainly result in a diminished importance of the narrative. Instead, high concept tells the story in shorthand by means of generic characters, images, and situations.

However, what I consider to be high concept's most important solution to, or means to overcome, its recognizable narrative is its emphasis on the visual. High concept movies create excess, or visceral impact, with their overall look and sound. Or, to put it more constructively, the viewer is engaged, or 'sewn into the film', as Wyatt phrases it, by the effective combination of sound and image (Wyatt 1994: 60). I will elaborate on this specific stylistic trait of high concept in detail. My analysis of one scene in

6. For a convincing refutation of this still dominant assumption, see Bordwell's study on contemporary Hollywood narration (2006).

7. In this sense, high concept is akin to early cinema or what film historian Tom Gunning has labeled 'cinema of attractions'. The concept relates the development of cinema to forces other than storytelling. For an exhaustive overview of the concept, see Strauven 2006.

Armageddon will attempt to demonstrate how style and substance coalesce to make meaning.

The High-speed Climax of Armageddon

In the sequence I analyze first, I focus on the stylistic peculiarity of *Armageddon*: its high speed editing. This rapid editing, which is maintained through the entire film, produces a kind of kinetic energy. This is a central characteristic of high concept movies. Sound and image are combined to create maximum effect which, as I mentioned above, is known as the MTV aesthetic. The MTV aesthetic is defined by the visual motifs that originated in music video and now also appear in motion pictures. Its most important characteristic, Kay Dickinson argues is, 'the submission of editing to the customary tempi of popular music' (Dickinson 2003: 143). Moreover, and this particular trait can be observed in *Armageddon*, the MTV aesthetic presents, according to Dickinson, 'shots which defy the standard broadcast rhythm of around three seconds minimum each' (Dickinson 2003: 143). I return to *Armageddon*'s average shot length below. The effect of this type of editing on the viewer may be unsettling. As Michel Chion has pointed out, there is a temporal difference between the human senses:

> The ear analyzes, processes and synthesizes faster than the eye. Take a rapid visual movement—a hand gesture—and compare it to an abrupt sound trajectory of the same duration. That fast visual movement will not form a distinct figure; its trajectory will not enter the memory in a precise picture. In the same length of time the sound trajectory will succeed in out-lining a clear and definite form, individuated, recognizable, distinguishable from others ... the eye is more spatially adept and the ear is more temporally adept. (Chion 1994: 10-11)

Thus, according to Chion, the viewer, when viewing a sequence for the first time or when viewing it just one time, fails to grasp it. The rapid visual movement will not enter memory as a precise picture. The combination of visual and musical motifs combined with a breakneck speed of editing will leave the viewer numb.

The sequence I focus on is where the narrative climax of the film occurs: Harry Stamper is about to push the button that will detonate the explosives and destroy the asteroid and, importantly, will kill Stamper himself. Prior to the act of pushing the button, Stamper has a vision of his daughter. This sequence is significant for two reasons.

First, it combines the eventual event of dying with a simultaneously formed mystical rapport between Stamper and his daughter Grace. The mystical rapport or, as I would call it, the vision of Stamper, is a recurring aspect of martyr stories. Therefore, I will treat it as an instance of preposterous history. The vision can be motivated through the troubled father-daughter relationship that *Armageddon* addresses. This father-daughter relationship and, more generally, the male-female dichotomy represented in *Armageddon* and similar films in the catastrophe genre, is subject to criticism. As I will argue on the basis of my analysis of this sequence, the supposedly anti-feminist content of *Armageddon* can be deflected to a certain extent. Nevertheless, a certain anti-feminist streak can be observed in most of the films I analyze in this study. This apocalyptic misogyny will feature prominently in the three subsequent chapters of this study, in which I focus on female martyrdom.

Second, Stamper's death is shown as a performative act: he actively and knowingly decides to sacrifice his life. Rather than accepting the danger of the job and coming to terms with a possible fortuitous death, Stamper actively seeks his death. The flaunting performance of choosing to die is an important aspect of claiming the role of a martyr and of eventually becoming a martyr in the eyes of other people. This constitutes Stamper as an American hero and martyr. Moreover, the performance of Stamper suggests a connection to an earlier discourse on martyrdom, namely the case of Ignatius. Both Ignatius and Stamper are good examples of the active dimension of martyrdom. The full extent of Stamper's actively willed martyrdom becomes clear in the climax of *Armageddon*.

The Quotable Climax: Shot List of Armageddon

As the shot list indicates, the editing of this scene alternates shots of Stamper's vision with shots of the countdown mechanism of the NASA clock, which displays the estimated time before the impact of the asteroid. The climax sequence takes only 19 seconds to unfold. In these 19 seconds, I have counted 36 shots. Hence, the average shot length (ASL) in this sequence comes to precisely 0.5 seconds (half a second per shot). The average shot length in the cinema of the 1940s is around nine to ten seconds.[8] The average shot length of contemporary Hollywood cinema is around three seconds. In *Armageddon*, the average shot length in the entire film is, according to Bordwell (Way Hollywood Tells It), 2.3 seconds, substantially shorter than most other Hollywood films.[9] A below-average shot length, an indication of high-speed cutting, characterizes *Armageddon*.

8. See Bordwell 2006: 121-23 for a short historical sketch of the accelerated speed of editing. In his book *Film Style and Technology: History and Analysis*, Barry Salt has done extensive research on what is now called statistical style analysis. Calculating average shot length is a key component of Salt's method of analysis (Salt 1992). For an introduction and overview of statistical style analysis, see: Elsaesser and Buckland 2002.

9. Several critics, such as *Variety*'s Todd McCarthy, mention the editing of *Armageddon* as a reason for its lack of character development. McCarthy states that the editing 'resembles a machine gun stuck in the firing position for two and a half hours', and that 'perhaps someone will someday reveal how many separate shots make up

The modern technology of the DVD player enables me to dissect the sequence into its constituting shots. Moreover, through DVD technology, one can establish the exact number of frames and the duration of each single shot. In this sense, I am able to overlook the fundamental and most confusing, or blinding, element of this particular sequence: its speed. Once the images have been drained of their speed, I can open my eyes and begin to see. By compiling a shot list, I make the frozen image the condition of my discussion, ignoring or violating the law of continuity that is cinema's primary principle.

The French film analyst Raymond Bellour struggled with this problem. In his essay 'The Unattainable Text', Bellour engages the key paradox in which film analysis is trapped. If one agrees, following Roland Barthes, that the film is a text, Bellour argues, the film text should receive the same kind of attention that the literary text receives. However, the problem of equating a filmic text with a literary text arises when the analyst attempts, like the literary analyst, to quote (a part of) the text. Here, film discloses its 'fatal flaw': the text of the film is beyond the film analyst's reach because it is an unquotable text. It is extremely difficult to translate verbally even one stopped image. According to Bellour, following the work of Christian Metz, the filmic text consists of a mixture of materials: phonetic sound, written titles, musical sound, noises, and the moving photographic image. The first four elements are quotable to a certain extent. The image, Bellour posits, cannot be quoted. The moving image, Bellour argues, has a twofold effect: 'on the one hand it spreads in space like a picture; on the other it plunges into time' (Bellour 2000: 25). The attempt to quote a moving image results in the loss of its defining characteristic, its movement: 'the written text cannot restore to it what only the projector can produce: a movement, the illusion of which guarantees the reality' (Bellour 2000: 25). Bellour concludes, 'the written text is the only one that can be quoted unimpededly and unreservedly' (Bellour 2000: 22).

Although Bellour has no solution for the impossibility of quoting the image, the use of film stills, preferably as many as possible, is one possible yet inadequate tool. As he states, 'stills are essential, they represent an equivalent, arranged each time according to the needs of the reading' (Bellour 2000: 26).[10] His work of the 1960s and 1970s reflects his preference

---

Armageddon, but the count has to be one of the highest in Hollywood history'. *Variety* 371:8, June 29-July 12, 1998. http://www.variety.com/index.asp?layout=review&review id=VE1117477644&categoryid=31&cs=1.

10. Bellour's use of the word 'still' is somewhat problematic and confusing, since the word 'still' is often used to denote so-called 'production stills'. These are photographs taken during filming by a 'still photographer'. Usually, these stills are not taken from the position of the motion picture camera and, as a result they do not correspond to any image in the finished film. Naturally, any analysis on the basis of production stills would

for freezing the image on the editing table: 'I have seen what happens to film writing when one writes from memory or with the help of a few notes taken in the theater—when one wants to avoid the very costly, perhaps too costly penalty for freezing the image' (Bellour 2000: 5).

For a remotely accurate analysis of film, the image has to be frozen, though this disrupts the fundamental element of the image, its movement. Simply trying to write from one's memory of a film, as Bellour endeavored before the advent of the VCR and the DVD, does not suffice. Bellour resolves the paradox by accepting the fact that analysis originates from the interruption of the moving image. As he argues with reference to Thierry Kuntzel, 'we' [as film analysts] 'must situate ourselves neither on the side of the motion nor on the side of the stillness, but *between* them, in the generation of the projected film by the film-strip, in the negation of this film-strip by the projected film' (Bellour 2000: 16 n. 55).

Kuntzel signals the double bind in which every film analyst is involuntarily caught. Analysis of film is always determined by the distinctiveness of the medium, particularly with its dual characteristics of movement and stillness. The proposed way out is to be attentive to both of these features.

In my shot list, I have attempted to demonstrate the separateness of each individual shot while, at the same time, looking at the relationship between the shots and at the sum of the shots that constitute this sequence.[11] The shot list is as follows:

1. Extreme long shot representing the point of view from the asteroid toward planet Earth. The movement of the asteroid toward Earth enhances this shot
2. Insert of a computer screen, located at Kennedy Space Centre, indicating the 'zero barrier'. This is the critical point in space and time before which the asteroid must be destroyed. Once the asteroid passes the zero barrier, it cannot be destroyed without also destroying Earth
3. In profile close-up of Grace, positioned on the right side of the

prove to be fruitless, since there is no indexical relation with the actual moving image. Bellour continues his analysis and uses the word freeze frame, a more apt term since it exactly describes the nature of the image: that of the frame that is temporarily frozen in its movement. However, he needlessly complicates the matter again by referring to the 'frozen frame and the still that reproduces it' (Bellour 2000: 26). For matters of clarity, I call what Bellour calls the frozen frame a screen shot, since I take the shot and the transition between the shots as the key element for my analysis. My definition of the shot is derived from Bordwell and Thompson. They describe the shot as follows: 'in the finished film, one uninterrupted image with a single static or mobile framing' (Bordwell and Thompson 1997: 481).

11. For technical definitions of framing distances, see the previous chapter.

frame. She turns her head to the right, looking at the clock ticking down the seconds to the zero barrier. The clock is brought into focus through the device of pulling focus, again constituting a movement within an otherwise static shot

4. Close-up of Stamper, screaming, 'We win Gracie'
5. Extreme close-up of Stamper's hand on the verge of setting off the detonation device that will destroy the asteroid
6. Insert of digital clock in extreme close-up, counting down
7. In profile close-up of NASA's executive director, positioned to the left side of the frame
8. Frontal close-up of Stamper, positioned to the right side of the frame. This is also not a static shot; there is a short zoom toward his face
9. Extreme frontal close-up of Grace, particularly on her eyes. Again, the camera zooms in as Grace closes her eyes
10. Extreme close-up of Stamper's hand as he flips the switch on the detonating device

Shots 1 to 10 are the introductory shots, leading up to the central event of the film: the exploding of the asteroid and the sacrificial death of Harry Stamper.

11. Frontal close-up of Stamper's face, blinded by the blast of the explosion[12]

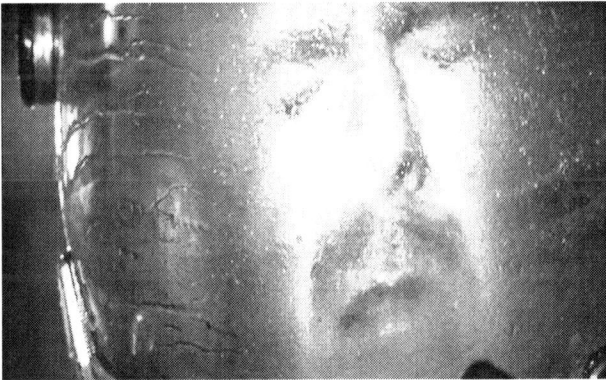

12. Insert of an empty, white frame[13]

Shots 11 and 12 represent the actual explosion. These two shots have a

---

12. The transition between shots 10 and 11 is extremely quick. The freeze-frame function of the DVD player occasionally could not capture shot 11. The extreme editing pace creates a strobing effect.

13. The inserts of white frames are a stylistic trademark of director Michael Bay.

bracketing function within the sequence. This will become clear when I continue to break down the sequence into separate shots.

13.   Extreme close-up of Grace's still closed left eye (see shot 9), again the camera zooms in toward the eye. Grace opens her eyes. The camera continues its movement, entering through the now open eye. In this transitional moment, there is a graphic match between the dark pupil of Grace's eye and the darkness of outer space, surrounding the Earth, the image of which emerges on the left side of the frame

This is the key shot of the sequence. It represents the literal disappearing of the spectator into the eye of a character, Grace. It is reasonable to assume, at least for the moment, that the following sequence can be attributed to Grace's point of view.

14.   Medium shot of a little girl sitting on a swing

The coloring of this shot differs dramatically from the rest of the sequence (as well as the rest of the film). The shot has an overexposed look, with bleached-out colors. According to Hollywood conventions, this particular coloring signifies that the image is a dream, vision, or memory. Furthermore, the viewer will assume that the little girl in the image is Grace. Although, at this moment, it is not certain whose dream or memory is represented, the spectator will, following the logic of the preceding shot, assume it to be Grace's memory. Another possibility is that this shot represents the beginning of a vision that can be attributed to Stamper.

15.   Insert of an 'empty' frame, that is to say, an entirely white image
16.   Plan américain of the girl sitting on the swing. A very slight tilting of the camera again creates movement in the shot
17.   Close-up of the girl, looking directly into the camera or turning her gaze toward a diegetic character over her right shoulder

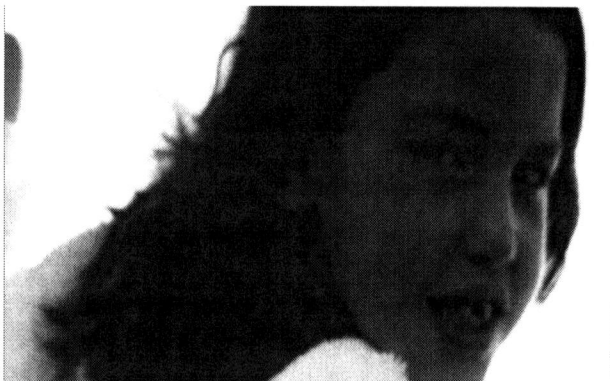

18. Insert of another white frame
19. Extreme long shot of a hill with a tree. Attached to the tree is a swing with the girl sitting on it. The blue sky above her head is rapidly filling with dark, menacing clouds. This shot functions as a belated and purposely withheld establishing shot
20. Long shot of the girl, running toward the camera or another diegetic character
21. Extreme long shot of the girl running toward the camera. A pair of hands belonging to a diegetic character emerge on the left side of the frame

Now, the uncertainty of shots 17 and 20 is resolved. She is running toward a diegetic character, probably Stamper. This shot gains the status of belonging to Stamper's point of view, as do shots 17 and 20 in retrospect. Since point of view is now assigned to Stamper, it is essential to analyze what the diegetic status of shots 14 to 21 signifies.

22. Frontal medium close-up of Grace (not the little girl Grace) combined with a zoom toward her face
23. Insert of an empty, white frame
24. Close-up of Grace, dressed as a bride, looking over her right shoulder

Here one should notice the parallel with shot 17, which points to the possibility that this is another instance of a point of view shot belonging to Stamper. Furthermore, note the mirroring in shots 17 and 24. In this instance, years have passed in the blink of an eye.

This shot, 24, is the key shot in answering my question about the status of the sequence. A casual observer may call the sequence, and particularly shot 24, an example of a flash-forward. This hypothesis can be strengthened by the simple fact that the final sequence of *Armageddon* shows the marriage of Grace to AJ. Shot 24 is subject to further scrutiny in the following section. For now, I want to conclude by emphasizing that, by using Bellour's mode of analysis, which focuses on the distinction between a series of shots recorded in a numbered shot list, one can achieve a restricted quotability of the image. The image can be quoted, provided that two restrictive conditions are taken into account. First, despite the inherent limitations of freezing the moving image, the stilled image is necessarily the source for the quotation. Second, the visual quotation needs to be augmented by a written description. On these conditions, the moving image yields to analysis.

Final Vision

I propose to read the sequence, culminating in the crucial shot 24, as an instance of a vision, as 'something seen in a state of trance or ecstasy' and an 'unusual discernment or even foresight', rather than a dream, memory, or flashforward emanating from Stamper's mind.[14] The main reason for this lies in shot 24. Shots 14 up to 23 can be defined as a dream, since a vision can also be experienced in a dream or memory, or in a combination of the two. My reading of shot 14 points to both possibilities. However, shot 24 is of a different nature than the preceding ones. Here, the spectator shares Stamper's vision of the future, which he will not experience. This also dispenses with the possibility of the shot being a flashforward, as it is tied to Stamper's perspective.

As David Bordwell and Kristin Thompson point out in *Film Art*, film is capable of manipulating the temporal relations through the basic distinction between story and plot. A flashforward is an instance where plot shuffles story order. As Bordwell and Thompson remark, flashforwards are used to 'tease the viewer with glimpses of the eventual outcome of the story action' (Bordwell and Thompson 1997: 283). In the case of the flashforward, the authority that orders the organization of the relation story and plot resides with a non-diegetic agent, say the director or editor of a film. Unlike flashbacks, flashforwards cannot be easily attributed to a character. As I have already emphasized the dominance of Stamper's point of view in this

---

14. These definitions are taken from the Merriam-Webster Online Dictionary.

sequence, the shot cannot be defined as a flashforward. All this, I believe, points to the fact that shot 24 represents the vision of Stamper.

David Bordwell gives one plausible motivation for the attribution of subjectivity to a flashforward: 'One might argue that a film could plausibly motivate a flashforward as subjectivity by making the character *prophetic*, as in *Don't Look Now*. But this is still not parallel to the psychological flashback, since we can never be sure of a character's premonitions as we can be of a character's powers of memory' (Bordwell 1985: 79, emphasis added).

Bordwell's distinction between, on one hand, premonition as subjectively uncertain and unreliable and, on the other, memory tied to the psychological flashback as subjectively clear-cut and trustworthy, strikes me as rather naïve. Numerous films capitalize on the viewer's expectation, the convention of the reliable flashback from a character.[15] Even though Bordwell may have a point when he claims that classical narrative cinema has hardly used the subjective flashforward (contrary to art cinema), *Armageddon* is the exception. Stamper's vision should be regarded as highly prophetic.

The prophetic, visionary dimension of the sequence ties this moment to a preposterous approach. A recurring element in martyr stories is the martyr's vision shortly before his or her death. The vision arrives at the moment he or she is on the brink of leaving the painful reality of this world and about to enter the next one, envisioned as the afterlife. In the martyr's transcendent state of being, caught between two parallel realities, a vision of immense clarity and truth is revealed. An example of this can be found in Acts. Stephen has a vision of God and Jesus in heaven; he gazes into heaven shortly before he is stoned to death.[16] Another well known example can be found in the story of Perpetua, who has no less than four visions before she is martyred in the arena (Castelli 2004: 85-92). The case of Perpetua takes center stage in the next chapter.

This motif of the martyr scenario is unambiguously quoted but also altered in Hollywood cinema. In the previous chapter, I discussed the scene in *End of Days* in which Jericho Cane sacrifices his life. In the final moment of his life, he experiences a vision of his murdered wife and daughter. They appear to be waiting for him in the afterlife. A similar scene can be found in *Gladiator* (USA: Ridley Scott, 2000). Again, the dying protagonist Maximus, caught

15. A film like *The Usual Suspects* (USA: Bryan Singer, 1995) thoroughly tricks the viewer into believing the elaborate confession, presented in voice-over and flashback, by its main character.

16. Acts 7.54-58, 'When they heard these things, they became enraged and ground their teeth at Stephen. But filled with the Holy Spirit, he gazed into heaven and saw the glory of God and Jesus standing at the right hand of God. 'Look', he said, 'I see the heavens opened and the Son of Man standing at the right hand of God!' But they covered their ears, and with a loud shout all rushed together against him. Then they dragged him out of the city and began to stone him'.

between two realities, the physical here and now in which he is dying and the afterlife, will be reconciled with his murdered wife and son, similar to *End of Days*. The transition between the two realities is expressed in a medium close-up shot of Maximus' body, lying in the arena, being lifted off the ground and moved. The shot suggests that Maximus' body, as well as his mind, journey in the direction of the afterlife. The reward of the afterlife is foreshadowed earlier in the film, when one of the characters consoles Maximus by saying, 'Your family will meet you in the afterlife'.

An obvious interpretation of these two examples would be that the prospect of a happy reunion in the afterlife provides a postponed happy ending to the non-Hollywood ending. The protagonist is redeemed and will receive his reward, despite the fact that he is no longer alive. Hollywood thus quotes an aspect of canonical martyrdom, but invests it with a different meaning. In both cases, *End of Days* and *Gladiator*, the vision discloses the truth about the afterlife, similar to classic examples but, crucially, Hollywood's representation of it is dominated by family. The classic depiction would stress an afterlife in the presence of God in heaven. The idea of what constitutes a reward for martyrdom has significantly changed. Bellour has remarked that American cinema is 'powerfully obsessed by the ideology of the family and of marriage, which constitutes its imaginary and symbolic base' (Bellour 2000: 14). This American obsession with family relations is further developed below, when I discuss several recurring thematic traits of the contemporary disaster film.

Hence, the vision of Stamper in *Armageddon* can be considered another instance of the 'dying-hero-who-will-be-rewarded-in-the-afterlife' scenario. However, Stamper's vision is dissimilar to the visions of Jericho Cane and Maximus, as well as to the visions of the 'classic' martyrs, such as Stephen and Perpetua. The visions of Jericho Cane and Maximus adhere to the classic paradigm that postulates a reward for the martyr in the hereafter. Importantly, the vision itself refers to, and is positioned in, the next world, a different reality than the present one. Stamper's vision, however, is linked to present reality, the present world, of which he will no longer be part. The vision functions not so much as a reward for Stamper, although the vision may well give him feelings of joy or pride. It transforms his sacrificial act into a less egoistical, more benevolent act. His reward is the gift of the future he bestows upon Grace and AJ. As such, *Armageddon* offers an elaboration of the classic paradigm. It invests the older form of the martyr story with new, additional meaning. This new meaning, reflecting back on the older cases, makes Stamper's vision in *Armageddon* 'preposterous'. My reading uncovers the visionary quality of Stamper and connects this trait to an earlier discourse on martyrdom. I argued that Stamper's act might be labeled as benevolent with regard to Grace and AJ's future. However, several readings of *Armageddon* exactly critique this act of Stamper as paternalistic.

Containment and Catastrophe

An example of this reading of *Armageddon*, closely connected to the sequence, criticizes the ideological content of recent apocalyptic cinema. Joel W. Martin contends that films such as *Independence Day* (USA: Roland Emmerich, 1996), *Deep Impact* (USA: Mimi Leder, 1998), *Contact* (USA: Robert Zemeckis, 1997) and particularly *Armageddon* thrive on narratives that 'enact the re-subordination of a woman and that these films connect this process of subordination directly to the struggle to overcome a threat that contact with space, space rocks, and space beings supposedly represent' (Martin 2000). Implicitly, these films display 'the tendency to link feminism with catastrophe', Martin claims 'it is a crisis in the gender system that has produced the genre of 1990s apocalyptic films. If space threatens, it has something to do with a professional woman' (Martin 2000).[17] In *Armageddon*, Martin argues: 'It is the sexuality of the daughter that needs to be contained. Only after the father has transferred his authority over her to her male lover can the father perform the sacrifice that will save the earth' (Martin 2000).

Though Martin does not perform a close analysis of the film, his assertion about the misogynistic tendencies of these films appears convincing. His claim that the sexuality of women, in this case of the daughter, needs to be contained is in agreement with Stephen Heath's critique of the representation of women in Hollywood film. His reading of *Touch of Evil* (USA: Orson Welles, 1958) centers on the role of the woman as both a good, yet missing or otherwise lacking object, and as a bad object that needs to be restored to its proper function. Woman is the impetus for male action, yet she herself is absent or at least a passive factor: 'the woman [is] set aside: expelled from the main action until she can be brought back into place' (Heath 1981: 139).

Armageddon is a textbook example of this containment thesis.[18] The film needs woman-as-trouble to function, yet male-female relations remain marginal. The strained relationship between Stamper and AJ is fueled by AJ's attempt to gain Stamper's permission to have a relationship with Grace. Furthermore, Stamper acts as a surrogate or even stepfather to AJ. After AJ's

17. For a similar argument, see Lawrence and Jewett 2002: 327-28.

18. In his renowned article 'Symbolic Blockage' on Alfred Hitchcock's 1959 film *North by Northwest*, Bellour argues that the heroine Eve has a double function, symbolically tied to two different bodies. On one hand she represents the threatening body of the forbidden mother. On the other, in the climax of the film, that body, represented as a statue, is literally broken and Eve is reborn as a non-threatening body for the hero to claim and possess. She then comes to function as the reward for the hero's journey throughout the film (Bellour 2000: 191).

father died in an accident on Stamper's oilrig, he made Stamper promise him to raise AJ. Like the son Stamper never had, one might add. When Stamper finally approves, the film arrives at an ideologically acceptable form of closure: the marriage of Grace and AJ. In his evaluation of the disaster film genre, Keane summarizes *Armageddon* as follows: 'go to work, save the world, get married, populate the species' (Keane 2001: 95). King phrases it differently; he observes a tendency to 'square its foregrounding of action-adventure with ideologically potent domestic concerns' (King 2000: 170).

A potent domestic concern in *Armageddon* is the absence of the mother of Grace, the wife of Stamper. In the beginning of the film, Grace alludes to the fact that her mother 'split' at a particular moment. From that moment on, Stamper was forced to raise his daughter by himself. The troubled, fractured family is a recurring motif in the action films of the 1990s. In an article entitled 'With Violence If Necessary', Karen Schneider argues that the action-thriller film consists of three related components: 'family fracture, confrontation with various perceived threats to the family, and family recovery' (Schneider 1999: 4). Her analysis is based on three distinctive subgenres of the action film, of which the category of the apocalypse film is most relevant here.

As Schneider argues, in the apocalypse film an imminent danger threatens the family as well as mankind in its totality. These threats are intricately related, and are to be solved by the same agent, namely a father. Schneider considers the films *Volcano* (USA: Mick Jackson, 1997) and *Jurassic Park: The Lost World* (USA: Steven Spielberg, 1997) as prime examples of the apocalyptic action film, in which 'fathers alienated from their adolescent daughters salvage their relationships through decisive heroic action that simultaneously quells a catastrophic threat to the community' (Schneider 1999: 5).

This synopsis is also perfectly applicable to *Armageddon*. Following both Keane and Schneider, one can argue that disaster films are also emphatically 'family values' films. I would, however, propose a further specification of both these readings on the basis of my close analysis of the remainder of the sequence. For this purpose, I continue my analysis with shot 25 of the sequence.

25.   Dynamic medium close-up of the girl: the zoom changes the shot from a medium close-up to a close-up
26.   Repetition of shot 22 (frontal medium close up of Grace)
27.   Frontal medium close-up of Stamper. The change in background lighting, from dark to light, provides the dynamic in this otherwise static shot
28.   Close-up of Grace, zoom to extreme close-up
29.   Medium close-up of Grace, a repetition of shots 22 and 26

30. Close-up of Stamper, with a slight zoom
31. Close-up of Grace
32. Close-up of Stamper, with a slight zoom
33. Close-up of Grace

34. Close-up of Stamper

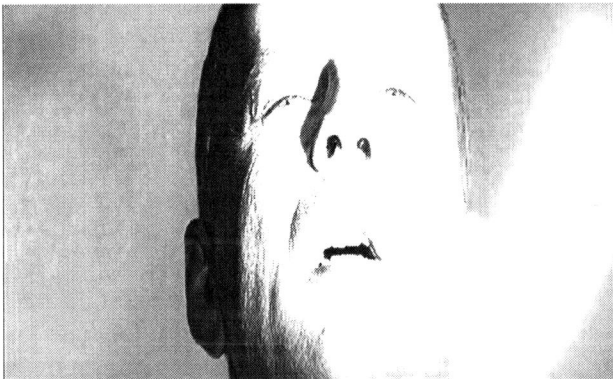

35. Close-up of Grace
36. Long shot of the explosion of the asteroid

The final shot of the sequence functions as the return to the diegetic world. The blast that was initiated in shots 11 and 12 is continued. This shot functions as the closure, by means of bracketing, of the sequence.

The connection that is created between Grace and Stamper through the climactic exchanges of close-ups is expressed in shots 29 to 35. Joel Martin speaks of the plot as revolving on the transfer of authority over a woman between two men. Stamper can only make his sacrifice and save the world after he has made sure that his daughter will be married to the man he considers to be the right one for her. However, Martin's contention that

Grace is simply an object of exchange between the two men leads to an
incomplete reading of *Armageddon*.

As the entire sequence, and particularly this final part consisting of shots
25 to 36, demonstrates, Grace and her father share an intense relationship.
At the moment of the explosion and Stamper's death, the two characters'
thoughts, memories, and feelings are 'in sync'. The exchange of close-
ups between Stamper and Grace profoundly visualizes the union of the
two characters. The most convincing aspect of their rapport rests in the
uncertainty in assigning point of view. The crucial part of the sequence
is launched by the elaborate shot of Grace's eye, shot 13, constituting her
point of view. However, this initial assumption proves to be wrong: it turns
out to be Stamper's vision of the future, which he is about to safeguard by
dying, that is expressed in the sequence.

Grace is not just an object that needs to be handed over to another male;
instead the father-daughter dynamic itself is expressed. At the moment of
his death, they find they are in each other's minds, as equals, and they find
peace in this union. Crucially, by ending the sequence with a close-up of
Grace, authority and approval are transferred from Stamper onto Grace.
Stamper grants Grace permission to marry the man she loves, AJ. Stamper's
death is his ultimate act of approval of the marriage bond. Through his
death, Stamper will safeguard the future, in which the marriage can take
place.

What is striking in this sequence, and at odds with the containment
thesis, is that the father grants permission to the daughter. In a standard
containment scenario, the woman would be a passive object of exchange
between two men. In this case, however, the woman is an active receiver
of the paternal gift of permission, while the third party, AJ, is noticeably
missing during this transfer of approval.[19] Nevertheless, in line with the
containment thesis, one can still argue that Grace functions as a reward
for the hero's successful journey. This is made very clear in the final scene
on the runway of Kennedy Space Center, where Grace eagerly awaits AJ's
return. In *Armageddon*, the motif of the successful journey has a double
meaning. First, AJ has survived the mission, only with the help of Stamper,
of course. Moreover, Stamper's death inaugurates the exchange of power
from Stamper to AJ. The film constantly plays with the notion that AJ
is the natural successor to Stamper; being his adopted son is one aspect
of this. Stamper and AJ share a unique characteristic: they are 'naturals'
at the art of drilling oil, meaning that rather than relying exclusively on
technology, they drill on instinct. This unique, individual quality, common

19. The transfer of authority takes place in the final conversation between Stamper
and Grace, with Grace in the control seat of Mission Control in Houston. In this
conversation, Stamper tells Grace to take care of AJ.

to all high concept protagonists, sets them apart from all other oil drillers. Stamper's death promotes AJ to the position of heir, together with Grace, of the Stamper Oil kingdom. But he bestows this legacy through Grace, with whom he mystically bonds as he dies.

Though Stamper's act may have the undertone of paternalism and female containment, rightfully observed by Martin, Keane, and Schneider, I contend that Stamper is transcending mere paternalism. The effect of his voluntary death extends beyond the realms of an approved marriage to the survival of the whole of humankind, exemplified by the love and marriage of Grace and AJ.

Overtures to Martyrdom

The mystical aspect of the dying seconds of Stamper's life, underscored by a host of short, fleeting images that are presented through high-speed cutting, divert attention from two vital events of the film: the destruction of the asteroid and the death of Harry Stamper. I would suggest that Stamper's death itself is of minor relevance to both the spectator and the diegesis. Saliently, the sequence does not strive to create audience apprehension about his death. The sequence is, on one hand, dominated by the spiritual bond between father and daughter and, on the other, by the combination of fast cutting with a classic action film deadline structure: the NASA clock steadily counting down to zero. Unlike canonical martyr stories, which often focus in detail on the actual death of a martyr, in *Armageddon* the significance of dying is relegated to the sideline. The act itself seems of minor importance.

I contend that the kind of contemporary martyrdom constructed in *Armageddon* does not merely originate through death, but rather through the acts of the protagonist that are performed before his death and by the way he secures his commemoration as a martyr after his death. Both these aspects need to be addressed through the mode of high concept cinema. I want to focus on the sequence in which Stamper actively takes on the role of martyr, which precedes the sequence analyzed above. The pivotal scene shows the drawing of straws to decide who has to stay behind to detonate the bomb. Before the straws are drawn, Stamper volunteers to take responsibility and stay behind. His crewmates appear to talk him out of this idea, and the straws are drawn. AJ is the unlucky one. Stamper volunteers to escort AJ outside to the surface of the asteroid. Once outside, Stamper quickly sabotages the air supply of AJ's astronaut suit, leaving him temporarily paralyzed. He rips the NASA badge of his own uniform and stuffs it in AJ's pocket, saying, 'Make sure Truman gets that'. Now Stamper, no longer under the badge, that is to say, under orders of NASA, is able to do things his way, without anyone being able to stop him. At this moment, Stamper's defiance of the system, partly responsible for bringing him into this situation, is complete. Since the system obviously failed (the technology of NASA turns out to be defective, leaving the team no option than manual detonation), Stamper has no one to rely on. Tearing off his badge, he chooses an actively willed death to prove his point to the system, NASA as personified by Truman. Stamper reverses his passive dependency on technology, and invests it with the active component of individual will power, even in sacrifice.

This act echoes the path that was chosen by one of the classic martyrs, Ignatius. In *A Noble Death: Suicide and Martyrdom among Christians and Jews in Antiquity*, Droge and Tabor discuss the example of the second century bishop of Antioch, who was sentenced to death by the Roman authorities. In a letter to the Christians of Rome, Ignatius stresses the fact that he actively desires his imminent death and implores his fellow Christians not to take any action to prevent the death sentence from being executed. Ignatius' letter expresses in explicit and visual language his desire to die for God: 'Let there come on me fire, and cross, and struggle with wild beasts, cutting, and tearing asunder, rackings of bones, mangling of limbs, crushing of my whole body, cruel tortures of the devil, may I but attain to Jesus Christ!' As Droge and Tabor conclude, Ignatius was inspired by the crucifixion of Christ, which resulted in an *imitatio mortis Christi* (Droge and Tabor 1992: 130).

Like Ignatius, Stamper reverses the situation and takes active control over his own life and subsequent death. This control may render his dying as suicide. However, this is not the case with Ignatius and Stamper. Droge and Tabor remark that there is a fine line between what is considered to be suicide, a pejorative term, and what constitutes martyrdom, a positive term. The perspective depends on the position one takes within a given situation.[20] To overcome the distinction, they propose the morally neutral term 'voluntary death', indicating 'the act resulting from an individual's intentional decision to die, either by his own agency, by another's, or by *contriving* the circumstances in which death is the known, ineluctable result' (Droge and Tabor 1992: 4, emphasis added).

The use of the verb 'to contrive' is of interest in this definition. It means 'to trick a particular situation' and, in a more negative vein, implies 'to do something stupid'. Stamper can be said to contrive the circumstances in *Armageddon*. His character possesses a lethal combination of bravery and stupidity. Stupidity is characterized in his decision to replace AJ; bravery is exemplified in his decision to renounce Mission Control in Houston. Equal parts of bravery and stupidity constitute the contours of the American male martyr.

---

20. The example of the violence in the Middle East and the evaluation of these acts immediately comes to mind: 'the western press speaks of Islamic "suicide squads"; the Arab side speaks of "holy martyrs"' (Droge and Tabor 1992: 4).

The creation of the Harry Stamper character through the mold of high concept production is of crucial significance here. I return once more to a crucial feature of high concept, the lack of character development. This is what Wyatt calls a form of 'one-dimensional stylish characterization'. To which he adds 'major characters exist in a void, with little motivation or background' (Wyatt 1994: 57). One-dimensional characterization leads to greater emphasis on physicality, and on the appearance and demeanor of a character. The introduction of Stamper is a case in point.

In his introductory scene, he is caught in the act of teeing off golf balls from the platform of his own oilrig, located somewhere in the South China Sea. The significance of this seemingly innocent activity becomes clear: a Greenpeace ship, protesting against the Stamper Oil drilling activities, is Stamper's target. He is instantly typed as self-made man who does not play by the rules. Moreover, his remark that 'I give you [Greenpeace] 50.000 a year in donations', emphasizes his individualistic and egoistic worldview. Since he donates money to Greenpeace, apparently to buy off his guilty conscience, Stamper assumes he should have free reign of the seas he is polluting. Stamper's redeeming quality is his exceptional skill for oil drilling, a skill called upon to save the world. The main character of *Armageddon* is a good example of the values a typical protagonist in high concept cinema incarnates: individualistic, abrasive, defiant, yet special.

The specific character of Stamper's ardent martyrdom lies precisely in the individualistic approach to the task he is chosen to perform. Being the only person capable of saving the world does not have a paralyzing effect on him. Quite to the contrary, if he is called to do it, he will do it, and do it the way he wants. The technological surface appearance of *Armageddon*, its generic science fiction and action film characteristics, cannot disguise that the film deals with the theme of the stubborn individual, Stamper, who defies the system of the majority, the rocket scientists as personified in the figure of the executive director of NASA, Dan Truman. In many disaster films, the failure or arrogant misuse of technology results in catastrophe. As King argues, the inadequacy of technology presents 'the opening through which can be asserted the importance of frontier-style heroics at the individual level' (King 2000: 155).

In this sense, *Armageddon*'s narrative resembles the Western, typified by the appearance of the outsider, Stamper, chosen to save a community (in this case, the entire world). The outsider is able to save the community because he is not a member of the system that was supposed to protect the community in the first place. NASA is supposed to protect mankind but, since it proves unable to do this, the intervention of an outsider is necessary. At first, Stamper is reluctant to take on the job. What is more, the NASA experts make the mistake of not taking him seriously, as they are unaware of Stamper's unique qualities. The outcome of the taunting of the outsider—

the stubborn, individualist, 'won't–take-no-for-an-answer' man Stamper personifies—is his willingness to die in order to prove his point and beat the established system of experts. In this sense, Stamper's act echoes the core definition of a martyr, namely, a person who sacrifices life for the sake of principle.

What makes Stamper a contemporary, American martyr is the combination of his individualism with the cause for which he chooses to die. As Jan Willem van Henten argues, contemporary martyrs do not exclusively die for religious causes, or a particular religious identity (Van Henten 2003a: 195). Instead, Stamper sacrifices his life for a kind of collective ideology, which could be called liberalism or Americanism. Stamper's act preserves the continuation not only of his own oil drilling business, but also of the American way of life, exemplified by the future marriage between Grace and AJ. This aspect is linked to another characteristic of the modern martyr, his or her status as representative of a group identity that is religious, political, ethnic or other (Van Henten 2003a: 201). Stamper is the personification of American values: liberalism, individualism, capitalism, free enterprise, belief in yourself, the American Dream, and family.

Armageddon indicates its Americanism not just in its protagonist. Although the whole world is in danger, it is America's job to save the world. The technological dominance of the US is underscored by the fact that the other space traveling nation, Russia, can only offer its MIR space station as a refuel station for the American shuttles on their way to the asteroid. *Armageddon* reduces Russian space technology to an outer space gas station. Apart from technological leadership, overall American leadership is repeatedly stressed in the film. A telling sequence is the crisis speech delivered by the American president—the natural leader of the world *Armageddon* seems to suggest—intercut with shots from a worldwide audience.[21] Somewhat subtler is the appearance of the Stars and Stripes in the mise en scène, with Stamper strategically positioned in front of it. *Armageddon* never fails to emphasize the fact that an American makes the ultimate sacrifice.

Patch of Commemoration

A final aspect of classical martyrdom that is echoed in *Armageddon* needs to be addressed. After the hero's sacrifice, those who were saved must maintain its significance. It would lose its value if it were forgotten. Commemoration is of crucial importance in the narrative of martyrdom. As Castelli puts it,

---

21. As Todd McCarthy of *Variety* puts it: 'In a lame attempt to globalize the drama, insert shots show thousands of natives praying in front of the Blue Mosque in Istanbul and the Taj Mahal (not a religious site) in India, which somehow increases the jingoistic, thank-you-America-for-saving-the-world message' (McCarthy 1998).

'martyrdom is not simply an action but rather the product of interpretation and retelling'. It is, she continues, 'rhetorically constituted and discursively sustained' (Castelli 2004: 173). The constitution of a martyr's story can be done verbally, by telling and retelling, and writing and rewriting. The story can also be augmented by material or visual components. Stamper's NASA mission patch functions as the material remnant of his martyrdom and takes on special significance. After the safe return home of the remaining crew, AJ hands Truman the patch, which reads: 'freedom—for all mankind'. The message commemorates the spectacular dimension of Stamper's martyrdom. Its meaning is clear: Stamper's martyrdom has liberated mankind. Though Truman and Stamper were each other's adversaries throughout the film, now Truman admits his defeat. Stamper's moral victory is underscored. The patch gives Stamper the last word. AJ's responsibility is increased: not only is he Stamper's son-in-law and business heir, but also the sole witness to Stamper's martyrdom. His task is to give witness and sustain Stamper's martyrdom.

Earlier in the film, the importance of remembrance is accentuated. Shortly before the launch of the two space shuttles, the viewer is presented with a shot of the plaque at NASA headquarters that reads: 'In memory of those who made the ultimate sacrifice so others could reach for the stars, ad astra per aspera (a rough road leads to the stars) God speed to the crew of Apollo 1'.

The plaque makes martyrs of the deceased astronauts of NASA. This signals what Castelli describes as the martyr's function as a 'placeholder for a touted virtue or ideal'. The astronauts become the objects of 'shared memory in the service of a contemporary institutional or ideological interest' (Castelli 2004: 136). The institutional interest the astronauts serve is NASA, and the larger ideological concern is the status of the US as a space traveling nation. The commemorative inscription opens up a field of intertextual meaning. The Latin proverb is more commonly translated as, 'To the stars through thorns'. 'Thorns' evokes the connotation of suffering, as in the crown of thorns Jesus wore during his crucifixion. The 'stars' are not merely astral bodies; they are part of heaven. They signify not just a higher point literally, but also a higher state of being, detachment from earth. The connection can be observed in one of the key apocalyptic texts of the Old Testament. Daniel 12.1-3 speaks of 'Those who are wise shall shine like the brightness of the sky, and those who lead many to righteousness, like the stars forever and ever'. The phrase could be read as follows: Those who make a sacrifice will gain transcendence through their suffering.

Unlike the crew of the Apollo 1 space ship, who died collectively in their quest for the stars, however, *Armageddon* emphasizes the individuality of Stamper, who can and will make a difference. The scene where the crew draws straws is the first indication that the individual will perform the task at hand. Initially, the draw emphasizes the arbitrary, individual nature of the sacrificial act. The possibility of a collective detonation is never seriously considered. Instead, each of the crew members expresses the wish for the others to be able to return home. An awkward discussion ensues about which crew member has the least valid reason for living, which is quickly resolved by drawing straws. However, by sabotaging the draw, Stamper invests the sacrifice with individual motivation. He emphatically claims the right to save the world.

The straw-drawing scene stands in contrast to the rest of the film, where Stamper's team of oil drillers is repeatedly presented as a team. As Keane suggests, Stamper's 'leadership principle is tempered with the value of teamwork: "I'm only the best because I work with the best"' (Keane 2001: 93). In this light, the film can also be read through the metaphor of sport. The two shuttles are the two opposing teams, the military, represented by NASA, the Pentagon and the American President versus the workers, Stamper and his crew. There is a red and a blue team, with different types of players and different tactics. Both, however, have the same objective, the destruction of the asteroid. When one of the teams scores, the rest of world, depicted as a global crowd of sports fans, cheers. The sports metaphor uncovers another principal subject of disaster movies, which is, according to Keane, class (difference) (Keane 2001: 93-94). *Armageddon* represents the clash between Stamper's blue-collar workers, who value physical labor above technology, and the scientists of NASA and the military, who value technology above everything else.

NASA director Truman functions as the link between the two opposing groups. Even though his background is in the military, a war injury has prevented him from becoming an astronaut. He decided to become an engineer for NASA. Keane claims that Truman is 'the decent worker made group leader' (Keane 2001: 94). Though I agree with Keane's assertion of class being of major importance for the genre, his reading of Truman is limited. I propose to read Truman as a man torn apart between the two groups. His loyalty remains firmly with the military for most of the film. Only at the last minute does Truman have a change of heart. Giving Stamper the chance to perform his sacrifice, he ignores a military order. Truman is a non-believer; he prefers to believe in protocol and systems, not in the power of the individual, Stamper. When the magnitude and single-mindedness of Stamper's sacrifice finally dawns on him, he is, at least temporarily, converted and moves against the system.

The interaction between Truman and Stamper is based on a clash of perspective and class. Truman is well aware of the fact that the system sometimes needs individual sacrifice in order to survive.[22] With no other

22. As is often the case, the name of a character can be telling: in the end, Truman

options left, Truman realizes that the sacrifice of Stamper is the only chance of preserving the system. Truman's initial reluctance can be explained through the fate of the astronauts of Apollo 1. Unlike them, Stamper does not bow before a collective institutional or ideological interest. His rogue methods go directly against NASA policy. Truman, though, is a pragmatist, who adheres to the credo that it is better to 'have one man die for the people than to have the whole nation destroyed'. Truman's decision to allow Stamper to blow up the asteroid resonates with the pivotal discussion between Caiaphas and the council about what measures to take against the agitator Jesus. Caiaphas exclaims: 'You know nothing at all! You do not understand that it is better for you to have one man die for the people than to have the whole nation destroyed' (John 11.47-50). Stamper's death not only saves an entire nation; it also resolves class conflict. His individual sacrifice transcends class and ideology.

Individually Defined Martyrdom

As I have argued in this chapter, *Armageddon*'s representation of male martyrdom functions as an instance of preposterous history. The film's recasting of past images affects the original source of images which, in their turn, shape the historically preceding images. We have seen that a recurring element in martyr stories is the fact that the martyr has a vision shortly before his or her death. This trait of the martyr scenario is quoted, but also altered, in Hollywood cinema. The prophetic, visionary dimension of the sequence thus ties into a preposterous approach: Hollywood quotes an aspect of canonical martyrdom, but invests it with a different meaning. Similar to classic examples, Stamper's vision in *Armageddon* discloses a truth about the future, namely the marriage between his daughter Grace and AJ. However, classic martyrs, such as Stephen and Perpetua, envisioned the afterlife as a reconciliation with God. Family and loved ones, their relations and futures, dominate Hollywood's representation of the afterlife. Hollywood's preposterous turn resides in the substitution of a religious context for a familial and secular one. Moreover, in classic visions, the vision refers to, and is positioned in, the next world, a reality different from the present one. Stamper's vision in *Armageddon*, however, is linked to present and future reality, of which he will no longer be part. The vision

finally lives up to his name and acts like a 'true man'. That is to say, a 'true man' would not merely rely on technology or put his faith in the abstract instance of a system. A 'true man' would value both physicality and individuality. An even more obvious association of the name is the reference to former US President Harry S. Truman which, in its turn, points to the leadership qualities associated with this president.

conveys to a dying Stamper that his paternal wish will be carried out in the future through the marriage of Grace and AJ.

A second recurring element in martyrdom discourse is the emphasis on the act of dying as performative. *Armageddon* represents Stamper's death as a deliberate performance. The actively willed death of Stamper suggests a connection to an earlier discourse on martyrdom, namely the case of Ignatius. However, unlike canonical martyr stories, which focus in prolonged detail on the actual death of a martyr, in *Armageddon* the representation of Stamper's moment of death is short. The moment, expressed through high speed editing, is of minor importance.

The contemporary martyrdom constructed in *Armageddon* does not merely originate through death itself but, on one hand, through the acts of the protagonist *before* his death and, on the other, through the way he secures his commemoration as a martyr *after* his death. The construction and commemoration of the contemporary martyr are both addressed through the mode of high concept cinema. The particular character of Stamper's martyrdom lies in his individualistic approach to the task he is chosen to perform. What makes Stamper a contemporary, American martyr is the combination of his individualism with the cause he dies for. First, he dies for the continuation of the family. Second, he dies for the safeguarding of freedom for all mankind which, throughout the film, is typified as an American value. Finally, his death readjusts the relationship between individual and collective, favoring the former over the latter.

In conclusion, *Armageddon*'s intertextual referencing of religious discourses of martyrdom is by no means unproblematic. Obscured as it may be by Hollywood aesthetics, the martyrdom of Stamper is motivated by the will to preserve a severe Americanism. *Armageddon* grants Stamper a martyr's death, commemorating him as a true man, a true American, and an American martyr. Stamper may die, so that the spirit of American beliefs and values can live on.

Chapter 3

MUSCULAR, MONSTROUS, MATERNAL:
FEMALE MARTYRDOM IN *ALIEN3*

Observe how complex is a mother's love for her children, which draws
everything toward an emotion felt in her inmost parts…

4 *Maccabees* 14.13

Introduction

The Book of Maccabees, from which the epigraph of this chapter is taken,
is one of the earliest examples of female martyrdom in the Judeo-Christian
tradition. 4 Maccabees recounts the martyrdom of a Jewish mother and her
seven sons, who refused to break Jewish law and eat forbidden food. One
by one, the seven brothers are gruesomely martyred, while the mother is
forced to watch them die. As David A. DeSilva argues, the apocryphal Book
of Maccabees is an influential martyrological text.[1] It is a philosophical
demonstration, influenced by Platonism and Stoicism, on the 'mastery
of devout reason over the passions'. In 4 *Maccabees*, DeSilva notes, 'the
principal emotion that the mother has to master is maternal love' (DeSilva
1998: 71). She urges her sons to die for their faith, rather than renounce that
faith and remain alive. Renouncing their faith would mean only temporary
security, whereas a courageous death guarantees eternal life. Therefore,
DeSilva argues, 'by urging her sons on to die for God's Torah, she is not
losing them but rather "giving rebirth for immortality to the whole number
of her sons (16.13)"' (DeSilva 1998: 73-74). Thus, the mother displays
an extreme form of maternal love, which is expressed in her wish to see
her sons die, knowing that in death she and her sons will be reunited for
eternity. The complexity of maternal love, exemplified in the epigraph with
its paradoxical and lethal qualities, is the focus of this chapter.

---

1. In the view of DeSilva, the text influenced the thinking of Ignatius (whom I
mentioned in the previous chapter). Furthermore, the ideology of the text resembles
Revelation. Both 4 Maccabees and Revelation are concerned with bearing witness,
conquering the enemy occurs by dying, and the death of the martyr is 'not a degradation,
but rather the path to eternal honour' (DeSilva 1998: 148).

In this chapter, I explore a number of representations of female martyrdom, cases where women take up the role of the martyr. My aim is not to
contrast these representations with the representations of male martyrdom
to point out the difference between male and female martyrdom. Rather,
female martyrdom, in my view, should be regarded as a separate entity. Its
significance lies in the fact that women who chose the role of the martyr,
determined by masculine values as this concept may be, in their act of
martyrdom, at least temporarily, transgress the prevailing binary. Although
some discursive elements of male martyrdom are relevant for female
martyrdom as well, such as the defiance of authority and the manifestation of
visions, a simple comparison between the two would reduce the significance
of the female martyr.

I present the cases of three classical female martyrs, Thecla, Perpetua, and
Blandina, whose martyrologies show the diversity among female martyrs. I
develop my position in contradistinction to Elizabeth Castelli, whose final
assessment of female martyrdom deems it no more than a 'Pyrrhic victory'
(Castelli 2004: 67), suggesting that the women who could endure the
most gruesome acts of physical torture in the end still remained, and were
valued by society as, women. Instead, I argue that these martyrs lay bare
a gendered continuum between masculinity and femininity. The crucial
marker of the female, the ability to bear children, is a recurring element in
classical martyr stories. This repetition of the maternal in martyr discourse
is of particular interest to me.

Subsequently, these texts will be read against a secular and contemporary
manifestation of female martyrdom: Ellen Ripley (played by Sigourney
Weaver) of the science fiction film series *Alien*.[2] The character of Ripley,
who is smart, competent, moral, and courageous, has had a profound
influence on the genre of the action film. She serves as the prototype for
a new female lead, which differs from the typical action, science fiction,
and fantasy film heroine.[3] Apart from these masculine qualities, Ripley also
embodies a feminine quality: a mothering instinct. This instinct was latent
in *Alien*, although it almost got her killed as she searched for her lost cat.[4]

---

2.   The series now consists of four films: *Alien* (USA: Ridley Scott, 1979), followed
by *Aliens* (USA: James Cameron, 1986), and *Alien3* (USA: David Fincher, 1992), the
supposedly final installment of the series. However, Ripley was brought to life one more
time in *Alien: Resurrection* (USA: Jean-Pierre Jeunet, 1997).

3.   More than any other film genre, science fiction has served to reinforce stereotypical notions of masculinity and femininity. The genre is even more dominated by
males than the western (Bell-Metereau 1985: 209). An exception to the rule is the
science fiction television series *Star Trek*, which features many female characters.

4.   In one of the first articles on *Alien*, Judith Newton reads Ripley's search for
Jonesey the cat as 'as impulsive, humanitarian, and therefore traditionally feminine

In the sequel, *Aliens*, Ripley discovers a little girl named Newt and begins to transform from the accidental heroine of the first film into the Good Mother of the second.[5] The character of Newt functions as a surrogate daughter. Ripley actively sets up a new nuclear family, consisting of her, Newt, and corporal Dwayne Hicks. At the end of the film, Ripley manages to rescue her new 'family' from the impending nuclear detonation of the planet.

Unfortunately, Ripley's newly forged family is wiped out at the beginning of *Alien3* (USA: David Fincher, 1992). After the narrow escape at the end of *Aliens*, Ripley ends up on a planet populated by monkish men. In this setting, her femininity, read as transgression, becomes a pronounced aspect of her character. In *Alien3*, Ripley's perennial battle with the alien(s) reaches its climax. The film ends with the gruesome event of Ripley giving birth to the alien.[6] In the final scene of the film, she chooses a martyr's death by deliberately plunging into a cauldron of molten lead. Her death, I argue, is governed by intertextual and iconographical elements from classical martyrdom discourse. I address two readings of the *Alien* film series. The films of the *Alien* series have been subject to extensive analysis in film studies, particularly with regard to the representation of their female hero. Analogous to the classical martyrs, the character of Ripley, the self-sacrificial heroine of *Alien3*, is endowed with feminine as well as masculine traits. The two readings upon which I focus appear to be different: while the first, by Yvonne Tasker, proposes a 'positive' evaluation of the female heroine, the second interpretation, by Barbara Creed, uncovers a 'fundamental problem' within the general representation of women in film, and hence cannot but be negative in conclusion. Yet, the two readings share a common denominator: both highlight the conflation of the female with the maternal. The question then is, when Ripley's martyrdom is read against classical martyrdom, to what extent does this contemporary representation reconfigure its historical predecessors?

action'. This, Newton suggests, robs Ripley of her feminist qualities and 'subtly reinvests [her] with traditionally feminine qualities' (Newton 1990: 86).

5. The sequel also reveals an important aspect of Ripley's character background: the fact that she has a daughter. Due to Ripley's 'hypersleep', which lasted over 57 years, her daughter has died of old age by the time Ripley is rescued and awakens again in *Aliens*.

6. The traumatic event of an alien birth is by no means novel within the *Alien* series; in the two preceding films, several characters fell victim to this gruesome death. Ripley's destiny is cleverly foreshadowed in *Aliens*, when she, just awakened after 57 years of sleep, is troubled by the nightmare of her giving birth to an alien. As Lynda K. Bundtzen remarks with respect to this scene, the spectator's confusion about the actual status of a scene (is it a dream or is it real?) is a common 'cinematic trick'. She argues, 'we believe the dream to be reality, and the film thereby enacts an unthinkable horror, the potential birth of Alien otherness in Ripley's body' (Bundtzen 2000: 106). Ripley's dream can also be read as a sign of premonition.

Dynamics of Repetition

Before I turn to the cases of the classic female martyrs, I want to point out the *a priori* preposterous nature of the two components in my constellation of cultural texts. As Castelli argues in relation to the martyr Thecla, her martyr story exemplifies the 'culture making' dimensions of martyrdom that 'depend upon repetition and dynamics of recognition' (Castelli 2004: 136). The continual retelling and rereading of this story in literature as well as in the visual arts raise the question of historical accuracy and the relevancy of the past today. Castelli inquires into the status of the historical predecessor as well as into its 'function as a meaningful resource for the present' (Castelli 2004: 136). Castelli's argument has strong affinities with my own. Factual historicity recedes (Castelli 2004: 136). The question of whether Thecla, or any of the other classical martyrs, are actual historical figures cannot be unequivocally answered. That question is irrelevant, Castelli argues, since the 'commemorative narratives and representations take on lives of their own in rereadings, retellings, reinscriptions' (Castelli 2004: 136). Crucial in this quote is the 'lives of their own' these martyrs take on. These 'lives' should be understood as a-historical, in the sense that they exceed their historical context, although they trace an alternative historicity of their own.

The crux of her argument regarding martyrdom and history resonates with my approach of history as preposterous in Bal's sense. If there is a history, Castelli claims, it 'oscillates and adapts itself over time, sacrificing none of its authority in its changing focus, its amplification of details, and its *transformation* of its object' (Castelli 2004: 137, emphasis added).

This formulation exemplifies the analytical usage of the concept of preposterous history. Although my prime object, the contemporary manifestation of female martyrdom in Hollywood cinema, may be centuries away from Castelli's object, her method of reading the object, through quotation, citation, allusion, and iconography, is as relevant for my project as for hers. The discourse of martyrdom is powerful because of its adaptability and, critically, the transformation of the object that it allows. The object is not only appropriated and translated, but changed inherently.

The second element in my preposterous constellation, the film *Alien3*, displays a similar form of historical transformation. The adaptability of the film rests on a particular technological quality, namely, the DVD player. I want to emphasize an important, but often overlooked connection between the matter of film, celluloid, and the analysis of film. In her book entitled *Death 24x a Second: Stillness and the Moving Image*, Laura Mulvey addresses the effect of the digital revolution on cinema. New technologies such as video, but more importantly DVD, have transformed the way we experience film. The experience of watching a film on DVD is far removed from that of the traditional cinema audience bound to watch a film in its given order at 24 frames per second, Mulvey claims. A new kind of interactive spectatorship is introduced, as the viewer is capable of skipping, repeating, slowing down, speeding up, and reversing the traditional flow of cinema.

This type of spectatorship has implications, Mulvey argues, 'for the cohesion of narrative, which comes under pressure from external discourses, that is, production context, anecdote, history' (Mulvey 2006: 27). This argument has far-reaching consequences for the traditional methods of film theory and film analysis. The release of old films in a special edition format, which often includes restored and previously unseen material, Mulvey argues, 'transforms the ways in which old films are consumed' (Mulvey 2006: 21). A restored and extended version of a film can, and perhaps should, be the incentive for a new analysis. Due to technological development, the original object is transformed, no longer what it was before. Here one can observe the link between Castelli and Mulvey. In their work, they emphasize the transformative powers of history and technology respectively. For that reason, their work constitutes the theoretical frame that carries this chapter. I call the DVD an instance of preposterous technology. In the case of *Alien3*, one should reconsider earlier interpretations since, thanks to the DVD, a crucial augmentation has been incorporated into the film text: an alternative ending that has not been seen before in the film version. Before discussing the preposterousness of the film, located in both its main character and its several endings, I will elaborate on the paradoxical gender status of classical female martyrs.

The Paradox of the Classical Female Martyr

In the Christian discourse of martyrdom, gender and power often work in conflicting ways. Although one can claim martyrdom to be what one commentator called an 'equal opportunity employer' for women and men, martyrdom largely draws on and generates ideals of 'masculinity' (Corrington Streete 1999: 349). The previous two chapters showed the connection between martyrdom and masculinity, and how the two mutually reinforce one another. In the historical context, martyr images frequently entail masculine notions of identity such as gaining power over one's opponents, self-mastery, and endurance (Penner and Vander Stichele 2003: 177). As Elizabeth Castelli remarks, 'the martyr's death is a masculine death, even when (or perhaps especially when) it is suffered by a woman' (Castelli 2004: 62). This paradox points to the subversive influence that stories of female martyrdom can exert over discourses of gender.

Castelli continues to argue that notions of masculine and feminine characteristics within the discourse of martyrdom are, at the same time, ambivalent and unstable. Gender is flexible to a certain extent, in that women can take on male characteristics. One explanation for this ambivalence resides in the status of gender as 'a dimension of worldliness that can be left behind with enthusiasm and without regret', Castelli states (Castelli 2004: 62). The spiritual act of martyrdom transcends the earthly sufferings of the flesh, and renders that flesh, whether male or female, obsolete. However, Castelli adds, this dynamic at the same time preserves the intrinsic dichotomy between male and female: 'the gender binary need not always be binding though its intrinsic value system ... [yet] remains relentlessly intact' (Castelli 2004: 63). Women can be martyrs on the condition that they abandon their femininity and adopt the masculine values of strength, endurance, and steadfastness. Hence, gender difference is at once transgressed and reaffirmed by the female martyr who dies like a man. Castelli's evaluation of martyrdom as a paradoxical domain where gender rules may be transgressed, though ultimately reaffirmed, opens up a range of possible readings of female martyrs.

Three Christian martyrs serve as the basis for my discussion on female martyrdom. Two of them are well known, Thecla and Perpetua. The third, Blandina, is more obscure; yet, her story has close intertextual connections with the story of Perpetua as well as with the already mentioned Jewish account of female martyrdom in *4 Maccabees*. Blandina's text functions as a possible connection between earlier, Jewish, martyrdom and later, Christian, martyrdom. The similarities between these three stories point out the intimate relationship of influence between accounts of Jewish and Christian martyrdom.

Daniel Boyarin proposes to read the Jewish and Christian discourses on martyrdom not as two opposing entities, but as two complexly related parts of one larger religious system. Rather than focusing on the prevailing dichotomy, it should be broken down through a close analysis of recurring motifs, themes, and images. Analogous to Boyarin's claim on the futility of pinpointing the origin of martyrdom—pointless in view of the fact that martyrdom came into being as a perennial recirculation the starting point of which cannot be traced back—are the striking similarities and variations on themes and images these texts display.

My starting point for dissecting this network is the account of Thecla's martyrdom. The text is collected in the *Apocryphal Acts of the Apostles*, a series of post-biblical writings that transmit deeds and experiences of apostles and other persons of the apostolic generation. Thecla's story, which has the characteristics of a romance novel, can be found in the 'Acts of Paul and Thecla'. Thecla meets the apostle Paul when she overhears him preaching, and becomes mesmerized by his message. She is converted to Christianity, and breaks off her engagement to another man in order to follow Paul. When Paul is banished from the city of Iconium for his teaching, Thecla is condemned to death by burning. When she voluntarily climbs the pyre, God quenches the fire with a great thunderstorm. Thecla and Paul escape together to the city of Antioch. There, Thecla is courted by an imperial priest named Alexander. When she scornfully rejects him, she is condemned to death for a second time. This time, she will have to fight with wild animals. Again, Thecla is saved, as the animals refuse to attack her; the lioness sent out against Thecla sits down at her feet.

Thecla escapes death and martyrdom proper for the second time in a row. This leads to the paradox that Thecla is commemorated as a martyr, while not having actually suffered a martyr's death. Instead, she is released by the prosecuting authorities and rejoins Paul, who instructs her to teach the word of God. Thecla now cuts her hair and puts on men's clothing in order to be able to travel and evangelize. She rids herself of the external markings of her gender in order to take up the role of teacher and evangelist, a role that was not readily available to women.[7] This aspect of Thecla's story suggests an important element of female martyrdom: the renunciation of femininity in favor of masculinity. Thecla's masculinity resides in the taking on of the external trappings of masculinity. Femininity cannot only be discarded in favor of an exterior display of masculinity, as Thecla did, but the female martyr can also adopt a masculine mental state. This asset of the female martyr will be dealt with in more detail in the story of Perpetua.

The third century Christian and partly autobiographical text, *Martyrdom of Perpetua and Felicitas*, recounts the imprisonment, dreams, visions, and ultimate death in the arena of the young Roman lady Perpetua and the slave woman Felicitas. It is no exaggeration to claim that Perpetua is the most famous female martyr in Western culture, perhaps only exceeded by the illustrious Joan of Arc. The key point I want to highlight is the gender transformation that Perpetua experiences in her vision the night before she is to be martyred. Perpetua's gender transformation differs significantly from Thecla's. Thecla takes on the visible markers of masculinity, whereas Perpetua undergoes a transformation in her way of thinking about herself as a woman and, crucially, as a mother. In Perpetua's account, the reader can trace her decision to become a martyr and to break away from traditional female and family patterns. In comparison to Thecla, this implies a more subversive transformation: Perpetua may be feminine on the outside, but she is masculine on the inside. The case of Perpetua is thus useful in two ways: it serves as a classic instance of female martyrdom as well as an example of the complex association and connection between the feminine

---

7. One could argue that Thecla is an example of what is called 'passing'. What typifies the act of passing are the appropriation of physical gender cues, in this case the cutting of hair, as well as certain behavioral attributes.

maternal and the masculine martyr. This connection is absent in Thecla's story, but plays a crucial part in Perpetua's narrative.

The martyrdom of Perpetua has been the subject of much scholarly attention because it consists of an autobiographical section, the prison diary of Perpetua, and a pro- and epilogue written by an anonymous editor. The authenticity of the diary is generally undisputed and, as such, it presents the earliest extant writing by a Christian woman. Perpetua belonged to a group of Christians who were arrested and subsequently executed. In her diary, Perpetua recounts the sufferings of prison life, her strained relationship with her father who desperately tries to convince Perpetua to abandon her Christian faith and, above all, the visions she experiences. Her fourth vision especially has attracted the attention of feminist scholars.

In this fourth and final vision, Perpetua finds herself in the arena facing an Egyptian opponent.[8] She is stripped of her clothes and, at that moment, discovers that she has become a man: 'And I was stripped naked, and I became a man'. In this dream, the physical markers of the male sex have replaced the markers of Perpetua's female sex. The implication of this change is that Perpetua's womanly weakness, a weakness that is taken to be physical as well as mental, is replaced by masculine strength, in the physical and mental way. Her mental strength and fervor, already immense as the story points out time and again, is matched by an equally powerful physical strength. Perpetua's masculine mind, ready to face martyrdom, fits her male body, which will serve as the vehicle of that martyrdom. In the remainder of her vision, Perpetua defeats her Egyptian adversary by stepping on his head and she leaves the arena victoriously through the Gate of Life. This divine vision provides Perpetua with the mental strength and conviction that she will be victorious in the case of the real execution that will take place the next day.

According to the editor, who introduces the account of Perpetua's death, she acted exceptionally bravely. He writes that the gladiator who was supposed to kill Perpetua was unable to do so. Perpetua guides and steadies his sword to her neck, which the editor views as a truly courageous act: 'Perchance so great a woman could not else have been slain [...] had she not herself so willed it'. Perpetua's shift from femininity to masculinity is different from Thecla's shift, in that Perpetua undergoes a symbolic physical change. Her body takes on male characteristics in her vision, in contrast to Thecla who hides the female characteristics of her

---

8. Perpetua interprets her own vision, and particularly her Egyptian adversary, as a metaphor of the battle she, as a Christian, will have to wage against the Devil (personified by the Egyptian). She writes in her diary: 'And I awoke; and I understood that I should fight, not with beasts but against the devil; but I knew that mine was the victory'. *The Passion of Perpetua and Felicity*, translated by W.H. Shewring (1931).

body. Perpetua's masculine transformation also entails her repudiation of maternity, ultimately of her own child. Perpetua's body, from the onset of the story marked as a maternal body capable of bearing children and feeding them, is adjusted to her mind. As a result, after her vision, Perpetua's mind and body are aligned: they both have, in a symbolical manner, become masculine.

Margaret Miles provides an explanation for Perpetua's miraculous gender transformation. The metaphor of 'becoming male' was frequently used for women 'who undertook to live an uncompromising Christian faith' and by women who 'sought to union with Christ in martyrdom' (Miles 1989: 55). Perpetua's vision seems directly related to this metaphor. The vision's physically powerful image provided her with the strength to prevail in the arena. In accordance with Miles' interpretation, Castelli argues that Perpetua's martyrdom problematizes conventional thought on the constrictions of gender: 'Perpetua's spiritual progress is marked by the social moving away from conventional female roles' (Castelli 1991: 35).

The text recounts how Perpetua, the daughter, moves away from her father, who begs her to give up her faith to survive persecution by the Roman authorities. In the final move, which completes Perpetua's detachment from femininity, she gives up her baby, refusing the maternal function.[9] Perpetua gradually strips off what Castelli describes as 'the cultural attributions of the female body' (Castelli 1991: 35). This process is completed when even the physical marks of femaleness have been removed. Only then is Perpetua ready to enact her martyr's death. The potential conflict between the roles of mother and martyr become apparent. Perpetua's story points to the incompatibility between these roles: mothers cannot be martyrs and vice versa. The two roles are mutually exclusive.

In her book *Perpetua's Passion: The Death and Memory of a Young Roman Woman*, Joyce Salisbury addresses the question whether Christian women had to renounce their motherhood to attain 'Christian spiritual perfection' (Salisbury 1997: 87). A relevant document in this respect is *4 Maccabees*. The influence of *4 Maccabees* on early Christians is evident.[10] Salisbury notes

9. Mary R. Lefkowitz states with regard to the stories of Christian women martyrs that many of them display a 'surprising eagerness to abandon young infants'. Felicitas gives away her newborn daughter. Similarly, Lefkowitz mentions the case of Eutychia and the Greek myth of the women of Theban, who abandoned and, in some cases, murdered their sons (Lefkowitz 1976: 419).

10. Galit Hasan-Rokem points out the close similarities between *4 Maccabees* and the story of Perpetua. She states, 'the further development of the female martyrological legend in early Christian and rabbinic Jewish cultures occurs not only simultaneously but also in mutual communication, constituting a dialogue of narratives' (Hasan-Rokem 2000: 123). See also DeSilva on the influence of *4 Maccabees* on the martyrs of Lyons, one of the martyrs there was Blandina (DeSilva 1998: 151).

that the story functions primarily as an indication of what had changed in the conception of martyrdom from the Jews to the Christians. In the context of Judaism, the text is read as an account of the preservation of a brave, separate community within a dominant culture. The mother plays a vital part in the continuation of religion, law, and family. Christianity, however, created new communities, urging individuals to break away from existing family or societal structures. Therefore, Salisbury concludes, 'Christian witness was more individual than Jewish community solidarity' (Salisbury 1997: 89). Perpetua's becoming masculine and her renunciation of the values of maternity can be read as signs of this Christian individuation in martyrdom in contrast to the Jewish conception of martyrdom, which stresses the centrality of family identity.

Perpetua may have been in doubt as to whether she should, or could, combine the roles of Roman mother and Christian martyr. As Salisbury puts it, 'motherhood represented a physiological state that seems to have been inconsistent with martyrdom' (Salisbury 1997: 142). Initially, she had allowed her family to take care of her infant son but, after her sentencing, she wanted to have her son with her in prison. Her father refused. From that moment, Perpetua is no longer a mother. She is strengthened in this decision by the appearance of a sign of divine approval: her baby has no more need for her breast. Unlike the mother of 4 Maccabees, she gives up her son and dies alone. So, Perpetua's story adds another characteristic to the female martyr: next to the renunciation of femininity, these women deal with the impossibility of being a mother and a martyr at the same time. Perpetua's vision of becoming male is a literal representation of this impossibility, whereas the vision simultaneously provides her a momentary way out of this impossibility, or suspends the impossibility temporary. However, once Perpetua fulfills her actual martyrdom, both her femininity and her maternity come back with a vengeance.

Female Martyrdom as Ambiguous Spectacle

In my discussion on gender and martyrdom so far, it may appear that the physicality of the martyr is insignificant. The stories of Thecla and Perpetua point to the gender bending and transformation of the female body, and thereby render that particular body obsolete. The attainment of martyrdom comes at the cost of female appearance and physique, which are traded for a masculine body and mental state. However, as these stories unfold and reach their climax in the arena, the spectacular return of the female body is inevitable.

The stories of both Thecla and Perpetua are often considered rare examples of models for the behavior of female Christians or, more generally, women. However, as Gail Paterson Corrington argues, these seemingly positive images should not be taken for granted. The valuation of Perpetua as what Bal has called a 'proto-feminist heroine', alluring as this description may be, ignores the underlying gender model upon which the figure of Perpetua is based (Corrington 1992: 241). This model, Corrington argues, is distinctively masculine. Perpetua's act of making herself masculine signals not only her denial of the female body and sexuality, but also indicates a clear valuation of masculinity over femininity. Corrington's line of argumentation reiterates Castelli's evaluation of female martyrdom: the female martyr remains caught in a gender binary that privileges the masculine over the feminine. Put differently, masculinity, separated from a strictly anatomical fact, is taken to be the measure of virtue. As Corrington explains, women such as Perpetua 'pattern themselves after models of power and autonomy available in their world and in its literature: the male apostles, who in turn are patterned on the model of Christ' (Corrington 1992: 23).

Since representations of women in the early Christian world were absent, male models were the only ones available to women who wished to gain spiritual empowerment. Miles is even more pronounced in her assessment of the development of a religious self in women: 'for women, then, courage, conscious choice, and self-possession constituted gender transgression' (Miles 1989: 55). However, Perpetua's masculinity also works the other way around. Castelli observes that a woman taking on masculine virtues delivers a strong message to male readers, effectively 'shaming [them] into more forthright displays of piety' (Castelli 1998: 15).

Even though 'becoming male' was applauded by male Christians and regarded as a crucial step in acquiring religious identity, the stories of female martyrdom all point to a recurring confusion over the status of the female-body-made-male. The display of the naked female body during public execution, the martyrdom proper, solicited varied emotions from the gathered crowd, such as grief, excitement, disgust, as well as, Miles points out, 'voyeuristic glee' (Miles 1989: 57). The public denuding of women was one way of stripping them of dignity and power. Nevertheless, the display of the nude female body does not result in the disempowerment of the victim in all cases.

The stories of the female martyrs Perpetua and Thecla, together with the martyrdom of Blandina, served as my template. In all these martyrdoms, the ambiguous pleasures of looking at the female body are a recurring trait. In contrast to Thecla and Perpetua, Blandina's story is not well known. Eusebius, a bishop who is mostly remembered for his *History of the Church*, transmitted the account of her martyrdom. Blandina, a slave woman belonging to a Christian master and a converted Christian herself, was part of a group of Christians from Lyon and Vienne, two Christian communities in the South East of France. The group was arrested and subjected to the most horrible tortures, which Eusebius describes in painstaking detail (Van

Henten and Avemarie 2002: 98-100). Even though Blandina is admittedly one of the weaker members of the group, on account of being a woman, she withstands the torment gloriously. Eventually, she is the last martyr to die. Blandina's martyrdom exemplifies the display of the tortured body. After extensive torturing and attacks by wild beasts, her torn body is fixed to a stake for general exhibition. To evaluate this display as mere spectacle for the onlookers is a serious misapprehension. The opposition between the active gaze of the crowd and the passive to-be-looked-at-ness of the martyr does not do justice to the premium martyrdom places on bodily suffering. As van Henten remarks with regard to Blandina and her fellow martyrs, 'the battered body is evidence of the martyrs' triumph and their participation in Christ's suffering' (Van Henten and Avemarie 2002: 99-100). The display of the battered body proves the subject's martyrdom.

In contrast, the case of Thecla can be read as a story of voyeuristic delight and denial. Miles' reading of Thecla's trials proposes 'clothing and nakedness [as] leitmotifs' of the story (Miles 1989: 58). Contrary to Blandina, Thecla did not die a martyr, and the physical excesses Blandina endured do not befall her. However, Miles argues, Thecla's punishment is situated in her enforced public nakedness. The governor who orders Thecla's execution plays a crucial role in the seesaw of a voyeuristic desire thwarted and fulfilled. Initially, he orders Thecla to strip, only to be overwhelmed by the beauty of her body. In the arena, her naked body is miraculously clothed with a cloud of fire, which protects her from the stares of the crowd and from the animals meant to kill her.[11] After this unsuccessful execution, the governor orders Thecla to be clothed again. Thecla obeys, but stresses that only she herself and ultimately God have final control over whether she covers or strips her body. By linking the integrity of her body to her religious integrity and subjectivity, Thecla renders outside forces powerless. After her failed martyrdom, Thecla decides to hide the physical markers of her femininity. She cuts her hair and dresses in a masculine fashion. This reinforces the connection between physical and spiritual devoutness.

In the case of Perpetua, the means of execution is connected precisely to her femininity and sexuality. The execution of women was an unusual practice, and the authorities seized the opportunity to put on a grand spectacle for the crowd. Perpetua and Felicitas were to be killed by a wild beast. Interestingly, the beast was a heifer, a female cow, whereas a bull

---

11. Thecla's mode of execution displays strong parallels with the mid-second-century *Martyrdom of Polycarp*. Like Thecla, Polycarp was sentenced to the pile and yet is unharmed by the fire: 'The fire, making the appearance of a vault [...] made a wall round about the body of the martyr; and it was there in the midst, not like flesh burning, but like [...] gold and silver refined in a furnace'. Online source: the Internet Medieval Source Book: http://www.fordham.edu/halsall/basis/martyrdom-polycarp-lightfoot.html

would have been the customary choice. This, Salisbury asserts, points to a symbolic dimension of the execution. Whereas the use of a bull 'signaled [the] sexual dishonor' of the accused woman, the use of a heifer can be read as an indication of the even more serious nature of the offense. The deliberate choice of a female, instead of a male animal signals the women's sexual degradation (Salisbury 1997: 141). Perpetua and Felicitas were no mere adulterers; their crimes were of a more severe order. Salisbury, following Brent Shaw's reading of Perpetua, states that the women were suspected of being of a 'different sort of sexuality' (Salisbury 1997: 141). Shaw argues that their sexuality was mocked to such an extent that they were simply not 'real women' enough to be adulterers. 'After all', he remarks, 'where were their husbands?' (Shaw 1993: 7-8). It is safe to assume that the absence of Perpetua's husband was caused by her conversion to Christianity. She had either rejected him or he had rejected her.

In the execution of the two women, the aspect of female nakedness, again, plays a crucial role. The condemned are brought into the arena naked, only covered by a net.[12] Upon seeing the women, the crowd protests against the fact that the physicality of the two reveals them to be mothers. The sight of these young, vulnerable and, most notably, maternal bodies was too much for the onlookers. Or, as Salisbury speculates, 'the incongruity of lactating mothers shedding their blood in the arena' might have robbed the crowd of their viewing pleasure (Salisbury 1997: 142). Felicitas and Perpetua are dressed, brought back into the arena and killed. Salisbury underlines the incompatibility between the roles of martyr and mother: 'mothers made milk, martyrs blood' (Salisbury 1997: 142).[13]

In the descriptions of the three female classical martyrs, the recurring themes of female martyrdom have become evident. Crucial is their ability to transcend the limits of their female corporeality and its concomitant notions of femininity. As I have shown, female martyrs stretch the common assumptions about gender and gendered behavior. In their acts and behavior, they constitute a transgression of femininity to masculinity. In the story of Thecla, the physical integrity of her female body is coupled with a devout religious and mental attitude. The changes Thecla undergoes can be understood as mere changes in outward appearance; yet, such a reading would undercut the fact that her outer appearance and inner piety

12. The net apparently made it easier for the wild beast to attack its victim. As Shaw notes with respect to this method of execution, it appears to have been a typical form of shaming. Both Blandina and Thecla were subjected to this type of punishment (Shaw 1993: 8 n. 22).

13. A contemporary example, which contests this classical paradigm, is the way in which Palestinian women, the so-called 'mothers of the martyrs' combine the practice of maternal activism and sacrificial discourse. For a critical discussion on the empowering as well as the constraining effects of this image, see Julie Peteet (1997).

are strongly dependent on each other. Thecla's outward manifestation is an integral part of her mental state of mind. Blandina refutes common conceptions of the female as being the weaker sex. She is praised for her 'manly', understood as physical and mental steadfastness, behavior in her martyrdom. She is literally the last (wo)man standing in the martyrdom of Lyon and Vienne.

Finally, the story of Perpetua offers the most challenging and complex picture of female martyrdom. In her vision, she transgresses the physical boundaries of her femininity. Her dream of becoming male uncovers the discourse on courage as a masculine trait. Perpetua's unease with her martyrdom, expressed in her uncertainty about whether she will be brave enough to face it, is represented in that dream. It functions as an empowerment for her, despite the fact that, after she wakes from that dream, she is still very much a woman. Ultimately, Perpetua acts heroically in the arena. More importantly, though, is her renunciation of her motherhood. In the abandonment of her child, Perpetua goes beyond set female behavior.

Despite Perpetua's unfeminine act of child abandonment, the markers of femininity persist. In all three stories, the transgressive move toward masculinity, or a changed appearance of femininity, is cut short. The recurring elements of nakedness, submission, and the maternal reinstate the femininity of the classical martyr. In the second part of this chapter, I look at Ripley as a contemporary female martyr. In her martyrdom, the three elements of nakedness, submission, and maternity are configured differently. The first two are virtually absent, whereas the maternal, due to the absence of the nudity and submission, is invested with a different significance. Ripley's divergent femininity is constructed and visually represented as corporeal. This, strangely enough, empowers her, since she does not have to discard or transcend that physique in the way the classical martyrs were forced to do.

The Muscular Mother

The muscular Hollywood cinema of the 1980s and 1990s, characterized by male stars such as Bruce Willis, Sylvester Stallone, and Arnold Schwarzenegger, is the focus of Yvonne Tasker's study, *Spectacular Bodies*. Aware of the emergence of the female action hero as the center of the action narrative, Tasker decides to focus on the representation of masculinity and femininity in the genre. She focuses on representations that exceed the traditional representations of women in film. The advent of the female action hero, not unlike the female martyr, opens up and broadens traditional imagery. An important parallel between the values of the classical martyr and the contemporary action film hero must immediately be asserted. Both the martyrological and the cinematic discourse emphasize courage, steadfastness, determination, and physical strength as indispensable for its respective heroes. My readings of Jericho Cane in *End of Days* and Harry Stamper in *Armageddon* position the act of martyrdom as congruous within a larger discourse on masculinity. The case of Ripley, the prototypical female action hero, signals a transgression, or intrusion, of this domain of masculinity.

Yvonne Tasker's reading of *Alien* and *Aliens* focuses on the masculine, what she calls 'musculine' nature of the heroine Ripley. The term 'musculinity' Tasker argues, suggests the 'extent to which a physical definition of masculinity in terms of a developed musculature is not limited to the male body within representation' (Tasker 1993: 3). In certain cases, Tasker argues, female action heroes can be just as physically and mentally strong as their male counterparts. She concludes, 'musculinity indicates the way in which the signifiers of strength are not limited to male characters' (Tasker 1993: 149). This, I argue, enables the comparison between female martyrs and female action heroes. Tasker's concept of musculinity is indispensable for my discussion of female martyrs. It signifies the sliding scale between male and female aspects, as well the attendant notions of femininity and masculinity. As I have argued above, the classical female martyr transgresses and modifies gender categories. The contemporary female action hero does the same.

The musculine character of Ripley can be seen as a contemporary representation of the earlier paradigm set by Thecla and Perpetua. Ripley mirrors Thecla in the transformation of her outward appearance and her position within a group dominated by males and masculine values. She resembles Perpetua in her exceptional courage and the problematic function as a mother. Yet, despite the representation of a strong, gun-wielding woman in the film, Tasker rightfully, with a tinge of disappointment, remarks that these types of heroines are always at a certain point connected to configurations of motherhood. As she puts it, '[T]he ways in which image-makers have dealt with the 'problem' of the action heroine, [mobilizes] configurations of motherhood' (Tasker 1993: 15). The maternal is again a crucial element in the restriction of a femininity that attempts to go beyond its set limits. As a musculine heroine, Ripley transgresses the limitations of her gender, Tasker argues, but only to a certain point. In due course, the 'maternal bond' is invoked and Ripley is as much maternal as she is musculine (Tasker 1993: 152).[14] Tasker perceives Ripley's maternal characteristics as negative, whereas I argue that Ripley's transgressive potential resides in particular in the combination of the maternal and the musculine.

14. Tasker mentions the publicity shot for *Aliens* of Weaver 'clutching a child in one arm, weapon in another' (Tasker 1993: 151). This image perfectly encapsulates the ambiguity of the musculine action heroine. Unfortunately, Tasker does not expand on this. Instead, she emphasizes the vulnerability of the heroine and focuses on the threat of rape.

Maternity constitutes the outer boundary of the musculinity of female heroines such as Ripley. Consequently, the three concepts that I bring into play are musculinity, maternity, and martyrdom. If martyrdom in the classical estimation was open to women, it could only be achieved by letting go of typical feminine traits, most importantly motherhood. In the case of Ripley, the reverse picture seems to emerge: motherhood and martyrdom are knotted together. She embraces her motherhood at the very moment of her sacrificial death. This analysis points to a reconsideration of the martyrological discourse discussed so far, which construes maternity and martyrdom as mutually exclusive.

Joan Scott's seminal article on the concept of gender can be useful for the analysis of the ambivalent Ripley character. Scott provides a working definition of gender as an essential element of social relationships. Gender, according to Scott, consists of four interrelated elements. I focus on two of the elements she distinguishes. First, gender is represented in culturally available symbols. These symbols induce 'multiple (and often contradictory) representations' (Scott 1989: 94). Second, the analysis of these symbols is based on normative concepts that take the form of rigid binary thinking, grounded in notions of femininity and masculinity. As a result, the potentially open interpretation of a symbol is foreclosed and its possibilities constrained. Scott argues that adherence to this type of analysis results in 'the perpetual restoration of women's supposedly more authentic, traditional role' (Scott 1989: 94). Instead, Scott insists on the disruption of binary thinking 'to discover the nature of the debate or repression that leads to the appearance of timeless permanence in binary gender representation' (Scott 1989: 94).

In line with Scott's analysis, the pop culture icon Ripley offers a manifold image of gender and femininity. She has unmistakable transgressive qualities. This is what Tasker calls a symbolic and iconographic transgression, a physically and mentally strong woman at the narrative center of the action-adventure film (Tasker 1993: 15, 143). However, according to Tasker's analysis, Ripley's character balances her masculine side with a maternal one. Thus, this woman exhibits heroic qualities; she does so, however, without sacrificing her nurturing ones. By pitting the two qualities against each other, the normative one, the maternal, functions to reinforce the binary opposition, which was threatened with disruption. This line of argumentation effectively forecloses a deviant interpretation. The emphasis on Ripley's nurturing qualities at the end of *Aliens* restores her to the traditional female role of mother. When subjected to Scott's conception of gender, Tasker's final analysis of Ripley is a disappointing one. In *Alien3*, the femininity of Ripley takes center stage. More so than in the previous two films, it is represented as a dangerous aberration and her previously established maternal valor is tested.

De-sexing the Martyr's Body

In *Alien3*, the rejection and derision of femininity is strongly motivated by the film's plot. After her narrow escape at the end of *Aliens*, Ripley finds herself stranded on the planet Fiorina 161. The planet is an exclusively male prison colony for convicted rapists and murderers. With shaved heads and dressed in sackcloth, the men have taken a vow to have no contact with women. In addition, the prisoners have adopted an apocalyptic philosophy advocated by their spiritual leader, Dillon. The arrival of Ripley poses a threat to this closed and celibate community. The female outsider is viewed with a mixture of disgust and lust: she is repellent yet dangerously attractive to this group of rapists. Ripley's most visible sign of her femininity, her hair, is shaved off after her arrival, the prison complex is infested with lice, and the underwear she wore during her hypersleep is replaced by the standard sackcloth couture.[15] As Thomas Doherty argues in his essay on the *Alien* trilogy, despite these efforts to de-feminize Ripley, her presence in this all-male environment 'discombobulates the monastic social order' (Doherty 1996: 193).

The forced assimilation of Ripley into this community echoes the rituals of conversion to Christian life and, in particular, echoes the story of Thecla. Ripley, like Thecla, is rid of the external markers of her femininity in order to endure in an exclusively male environment. According to Castelli, conversion is 'constituted primarily as the practice of sexual renunciation' (Castelli 1991: 43). The fact that Ripley's hair is cut is no random act, but profoundly symbolic. As Castelli observes, the cutting of one's hair 'continues to this day as the bodily signifier for women taking religious orders' (Castelli 1991: 44). Furthermore, wearing men's clothing, which Castelli classifies as transvestism, is the more controversial sign of female piety and was regarded as 'a resistance to the proper order of nature/society' (Castelli 1991: 44). To travel freely and preach the gospel, Thecla renounced the common laws and practices of her society. Ripley's transformation echoes Thecla's; yet, a difference between the two women is apparent. In *Alien3*, the 'de-sexing' of Ripley is not a resistance to an established order. It is a forced act of submission to the status quo.

The gender ambiguity as a result of these practices is, Castelli argues, generally taken as a sign of 'special holiness' (Castelli 1991: 43). The film

---

15. The spectacle of a woman with a shaved head should not be underestimated: the publicity material of *Alien3* strongly capitalizes on the actress's baldhead. A large portion of the publicity shots show Sigourney Weaver lit from behind, thus placing extra emphasis on her baldness. The act of shaving her hair is, surprisingly enough, not shown in the film. In contrast, in *V for Vendetta* (USA: James McTeigue, 2005), the actual act of shaving is prominently featured. The actress Nathalie Portman, as the character Evey Hammond, is shaved in real time, in a long take that lasts several minutes.

certainly telegraphs, makes visually palpable the singularity of Ripley in practically every scene of the film. Yet, her nascent holiness is not enacted until the very end. Until her martyr's death, the de-sexualized, masculine and musculine Ripley is singular in an erotic way. In spite of her curbed femininity, she is alluring: a group of prisoners attempts to rape her.[16] An enraged Dillon manages to save her in the nick of time. Later in the film, the lethality of Ripley's deviant femininity is articulated in a love scene between Ripley and Clemens, the prison doctor who is also a prisoner (a slightly more privileged transgressor among transgressors). After they have made love, Clemens is punished for his offense and killed by an alien. Ripley's sexual ambiguity is coupled with the literal 'killing off' of the romantic subplot.[17] Perhaps the word 'romantic' is an ill-fitting adjective. As Doherty argues, 'in the only interhuman sex act of the series, she [Ripley] coolly propositions and mates with Clemens' (Doherty 1996: 196). These two instances of male sexual intrusion unto the female body, with its lethal consequences, indicate the increasingly 'untouchable' nature of the Ripley character.[18]

Ripley's physical transformation, with its markers of untouchable holiness, is completed with the act that concludes her conversion. Her death in the flames of the furnace is represented as a holy sacrifice, finishing the process of her becoming a holy woman or even a saint. The de-sexualized, masculine, musculine, holy body, still holds the physical allure of the female body. The second reading of the *Alien* series upon which I elaborate stresses the monstrously maternal side of Ripley.

16. This scene provides an interesting parallel with the Joan of Arc story: like Ripley, Joan was harassed and supposedly raped by her male guards while awaiting her final sentence. Again, Tasker's argument on the musculine woman's greater risk of being raped, as a punishment for her (tress)passing, reverberates in this scene of the film.

17. In her book *Female Masculinity*, Judith Halberstam offers an interesting reading of Ripley's masculinity. Halberstam argues that the transgressive potential of Ripley is undercut by her 'resolute heterosexuality' (Halberstam 1998: 28). Even though Halberstam discusses *Aliens*, her analysis is also very well applicable to *Alien3*. It is only when female masculinity is coupled with lesbian desire, which can be observed in *Alien: Resurrection*, that female masculinity is perceived as 'threatening and indeed 'alien'' (Halberstam 1998: 28).

18. The lethality of sex led several critics to the conclusion that the film can also be understood as a metaphor for AIDS. *Rolling Stone* film critic Peter Travers called it 'the first $50 million thriller that also functions as an AIDS allegory' (quoted in Swallow 2003: 59). Amy Taubin remarks that 'neither gay nor feminist press realized immediately that the film is all about the AIDS crisis' (Taubin 1993: 96). Taubin argues that AIDS is everywhere in the film, mostly in its central 'metaphor of a deadly organism attacking an all-male community' (Taubin 1993: 98).

The Monstrous Mother

In her book entitled *The Monstrous-Feminine*, Barbara Creed discusses various representations of women as abject in horror film. Vampires, witches, and the possessed woman, among others, constitute the appearance of the female monster or, as Creed calls it, the monstrous-feminine. The monstrous-feminine is not just a persistent character in horror films. It has a long history ranging from classic mythology and the Bible to Freud. The recurring trait of the manifestations of the female monster, as of stereotypes of the feminine in general, Creed argues, is that woman is defined in terms of her sexuality. Creed's main point is that 'when woman is represented as monstrous it is almost always in relation to her mothering and reproductive functions' (Creed 1993: 7). The abject in *Alien3* is connected with the monstrous act of childbearing. Ripley's act of voluntary death and the monstrous act of giving birth to the alien collide in the final scene of *Alien3*. The scene is a prime example of the tension between the female as strong and masculine, and the female reduced to a particular bodily function and typified as abject. Tasker's reading of Ripley stresses maternity as the outer border of female musculinity, the boundary that a heroic femininity may not cross. Motherhood saves Ripley from becoming too masculine, and restores her to the traditional maternal function. In Creed's reading, however, it is not so much gender transgression or ambivalence that is threatening, but the maternal itself that is disgusting or abject. As Creed asserts, 'woman's birth-giving function has provided the horror film with an important source of its most horrific images' (Creed 1993: 50). Creed is influenced by Julia Kristeva's theory of the abject and the maternal.

In her book *Powers of Horror: An Essay on Abjection*, Kristeva formulates the concept of the abject as that which does not 'respect borders, positions, rules' and 'disturbs identity, system, order' (Creed 1993: 8, Kristeva 1980: 4). The abject body, as opposed to the clean and proper body, is a body that has lost form and integrity. In Kristeva's view, the image of woman's body, because of its maternal functions, acknowledges its 'debt to nature' and consequently is more likely to signify the abject (Creed 1993: 11). 'The maternal womb', she argues, 'represents the utmost in abjection for it contains a new life form which will pass from inside to outside bringing with it traces of its contamination—blood, afterbirth, faeces' (quoted in Tasker 1993: 49).[19] This capacity to transgress the border between the body's inside and outside is what makes the maternal womb the site of the abject.

19. For a critique of the concept of abjection, and particularly its misogynistic connotations, see 'The Destiny of the *Informe*' by Rosalind Krauss (1997). The genealogy of the concept is traced back to the work of Georges Bataille, whose understanding of abjection is devoid of its later misogyny. As Krauss argues, it is through Kristeva's

The *Alien* films effectively use the associations of birth giving with the uncanny, the iconography of the intra-uterine, and the alien. The first two films explored the parallels between Ripley and the alien, yet *Alien3* takes the similarities between woman and monster to its logical conclusion. As I have mentioned, Ripley turns out to be impregnated by the alien.[20] She is carrying an alien queen, capable of giving birth to thousands of aliens, in her chest. The birth of the queen means the certain end of humanity. Ripley has no other option than to abort the alien fetus, the 'foreign tissue', which has invaded her body. The contours of Ripley's martyrdom are clear: she must sacrifice her life to kill the alien.[21]

As Creed remarks with regard to the final scene of *Alien3*:

> In possibly the most stunning sequence in the *Alien* trilogy, Ripley throws herself backwards into the fiery furnace. A close-up shot reveals an expression of ecstasy on her face as she plummets backwards into the void. At the same time, the alien bursts forth. Ripley brings her arms forward, enclosing the *infant* queen in an embrace both *maternal* and murderous—an embrace that ensures the alien will die alongside its surrogate *mother* (Creed 1993: 52, emphasis added).

Notice Creed's choice of words: 'infant', 'maternal', and 'mother'. In the context of Creed's analysis of this scene, with its emphasis on Ripley's maternal relationship to the alien, an important feature is finally integrated in the martyrdom discourse. The mutually exclusive concepts of martyrdom and maternity are forged together in Ripley's final act. The close, physical bond between Ripley and her monstrous offspring necessarily leads to the sacrificial ending of *Alien3*. The alien, emerging from Ripley's inmost parts, violently given birth to, is an irrevocable part of Ripley herself. The demarcation between human and monster is transgressed to the extent that

---

indebtedness to Jean-Paul Sartre's conceptualization of the *visqueux* (slimy) that her conception of the abject has become infused with the stereotype of 'female as degenerate'.

20. The act of impregnation is not shown, only suggested. In the opening sequence of *Alien3*, short shots of the escape pod which, besides Ripley, Newt, Hicks, and Bishop, also contains an alien, are interspersed with the credit roll. In the first scene of the film, it becomes clear that Ripley is the only survivor and that her fellow travelers all have fallen victim to the alien. The body of Hicks looks as though it was ripped open by a chestburster. Ripley's body is apparently unscarred. Yet, on the basis of the opening sequence, which contains x-ray shots depicting the strangulation mechanism of the so-called face hugger of one (or several) unidentified members of the crew, we can assume that Ripley was indeed attacked by an alien.

21. The sacrificial aspect of Ripley's death is abundantly clear; Creed even ventures to compare the scene with the death scene in Carl Dreyer's *The Passion of Joan of Arc* (USA: Carl Theodore Dreyer, 1928). Indeed, *Alien3* offers several instances of intertextuality, both on the level of the narrative as well as on the level of iconography.

killing, aborting, the monstrous infant does not suffice. Ripley's martyrdom resides in the perverse negation of the border between human and not-human/monster, reinforcing Kristeva's reading of the maternal as abject. Ripley has served as a fertile womb for a monstrous other.[22] The possibility that she may give birth to the alien, and thus become the 'mother' of a new breed of aliens, leaves her no other option than to kill the thing that is most intimate to her while also most radically different.

On the basis of Tasker and Creed's analysis of the *Alien* series, it seems to me that Ripley's transgressive potential resides in the permutation of two opposing elements, masculinity and femininity, here consistently figured as the monstrous maternal. On one hand, Ripley moves away from maternity in favor of a reconfigured masculinity, musculinity. Yet, as Tasker argues, maternity comes back to claim her as female. On the other, Ripley is too maternal. Or, as Creed would say, she is dangerous because of her maternal, reproductive potential. In a sense, both positions come down to the problematic, inevitable relationship between femininity and maternity. This relationship is essential as well as excessive. In her battle against the excessive manifestation of the maternal function, the alien fetus growing inside her, Ripley counters it by her own variety of equally lethal maternity. Her plunge into the lead, together with her monstrous offspring, locked in a deadly embrace, solidifies the connection between maternity and martyrdom. Unlike her previous encounters with the alien(s), where Ripley was simply trying to annihilate them and make sure she herself got away safely, the fact that she has given birth to one of them makes her involvement in its total destruction a matter of life and death. Her maternal and reproductive connection with this breed of aliens leaves her no option other than the chosen death of herself and her monstrous child. Thus, the significance of *Alien3* is located in the coupling of the mother and the martyr.

If the analysis of Ripley as a contemporary martyr were to end here, one could contend that the preposterous turn has been rewarding: the earlier discourse of the classical martyr stories serves as the template for the later

22. The horrendous scene of Ripley giving birth is certainly not unique in the *Alien* trilogy. The primal scene in this respect occurs in *Alien*. One of the male members of the crew, Kane, is orally raped. The tail of the alien penetrates his mouth in order to fertilize itself inside his stomach. After this rape, during which Kane is in a coma-like state and the alien grows inside him, the birth scene occurs quite unexpectedly when an apparently normal Kane and the rest of the crew are having dinner. In *Aliens*, the android Bishop becomes the host to the alien. In one of the final scenes of the film, he is literally ripped apart by the violent emergence of the monster. In this sense, it comes as no surprise that Ripley has to experience the same horror. Even more so, this death, a recurring trademark of the entire trilogy, seems a fitting way of dying for its heroine. The crucial difference between Kane and Bishop on one hand, and Ripley on the other is that Ripley is able to destroy the alien.

cinematic discourse of the *Alien* series. The juxtaposition alters the secular as well as the religious discourse: Ripley is imbued with intertextual and iconographical characteristics of Perpetua, Thecla, and Blandina, placing her in a line of female martyrs. The constellation of concepts that govern the construction of the female martyr; femininity, masculinity, and maternity are reconfigured in the Ripley character and her final act. In turn, the classical martyrs can be preposterously read as representations of gender crossing and, more specifically, displaying signs of musculinity. The maternal aspect of these classical martyrs, whether it is explicitly absent, as is the case with Thecla, or explicitly present, as is the case with Perpetua, is similar to Ripley's maternity and equally ambiguous. The classical conception of the coupling of martyrdom and maternity deemed the two mutually exclusive. The contemporary conception of the strong, masculine, yet maternal woman as hero and martyr, exemplified in the work of Tasker and Creed, turns out to be just as problematic. Either the masculine or musculine is eventually kept at bay through the maternal, as Tasker argues, or the maternal turned monstrous simply overshadows all other characteristics a woman may have, as Creed maintains.

My analysis of Ripley is positioned between the classical and the contemporary conceptions. Arguing against Tasker, I suggest that the maternal does not merely function as a device to curb too much musculinity, or put the transgressive woman back in her 'natural', nurturing position. Rather, the maternal enforces the musculine traits of Ripley. This is obvious in the musculine aspect of physical pain, the violent birth of the alien, which she has to endure. This ability to undergo pain resonates with the classical martyrdom stories, and with their secular counterparts too, as my analysis of Jericho's crucifixion in *End of Days* showed, which placed emphasis on the martyr's capacity to withstand pain. Arguing against Creed, I disagree with her emphasis of the monstrous maternal as all encompassing. This, to me, takes away the courageous nature of Ripley's humanitarian act. This act is performed to counter directly the lethal fertility principle of the alien. Ripley's martyrdom supersedes the one-sidedness of Tasker's and Creed's readings. She is positioned neither on the side of the masculine nor on the reductive side of the maternal. In the end, Ripley's act fuses the two opposing positions. My analysis, nevertheless, does not stop with this ending of *Alien3*. One more analytical turn must be made.

Preposterous Technology and Alternative Endings

The digital technology of the DVD has a major effect on the viewing and analysis of film. Films in a digital format, in contrast to celluloid, are capable of reversing the flow of spectatorship and academic analysis. This reversal of a flow is in itself preposterous. It challenges the common perception that films and analyses have a clear-cut beginning, middle, and end. Likewise, it undercuts the idea that films have stable endings and academic articles have logical conclusions. Endings, both in film as well as in academic writing, signal a definite stop to the processes of viewing and analyzing. The advent of digital film opens up the possibility of slowing down, speeding up, repeating, skipping, and viewing again the separate images that constitute the medium. Hence, a clear ending is never fully reached and can be postponed perpetually. The digital format not only allows for the interruption and the reversal of the flow of images, but also adds new textual streams to the already existing film text. With regard to *Alien3*, these two possibilities of the digital format, the reversal of the flow and the addition of new text, lead to a new analysis of the film. As I hope to show, the addition of an alternative ending to the existing film text fundamentally challenges previous analyses of the film, including my own.

At the time of the film's release in 1992, it was widely reported that the studio Twentieth Century Fox had taken *Alien3* out of director David Fincher's hands before its theatrical release, and re-edited the film without his consent. In 2003, the 'Alien Quadrilogy' DVD box set and special edition was released. This special edition contains the theatrical release as well as an alternative 'work print' cut of *Alien3*. This work print, previously unavailable, is the closest approximation of Fincher's original vision of the film.

The ending of the film was much discussed during production. The most important difference between the 1992 theatrical version (111 minutes long) and the 2003 special edition/work print (139 minutes) is the sacrificial ending. In the special edition version, the scene where Ripley falls into the molten lead—and this is the crucial difference—contains no shot of the alien (in *Alien* terminology called a 'chestburster') emerging from her body. The focus of the discussion was precisely whether the alien in Ripley's body should emerge at the end of the film. James Swallow, whose book on David Fincher charts the troubled production process of *Alien3*, claims there were no less than four different versions of the ending. In the first version, the alien emerges first, and then Ripley dives into the molten metal. In the second version, the alien does not emerge. Instead, a stigmata effect of blood blooming on Ripley's chest is shown, while she is falling down. This ending was discarded as being 'too religious [....] and vulgar' (Swallow 2003: 54-55). This second version appears to have been shot by Fincher but, so far, these outtakes are not available. The fact that these outtakes are not included in this particular special edition does not exclude the possibility of them surfacing in a later and 'improved' special edition of the film. As a result, the flow of analysis is extended, and a definitive, conclusive reading of the film is deferred once more. For now, my reading of the two endings of the film is based on the original, theatrical version and the alternative, work print version, available on the special edition DVD.

Before I compare the two endings in detail, I sketch the major difference between the versions. In the theatrical version (TV), the alien emerges during Ripley's fall. In contrast, the work print ending available on the special edition release of the film (SE), refrains from showing the alien altogether. In the SE version, the scene in which Ripley makes her final decision to drop into the lead is longer: she needs more time to build up her courage. The significance of this is addressed in detail below. The subsequent SE death scene consists of an alternate take: the alien does not burst forth from her body, Ripley seems more lifelike (in contrast to the obvious puppet used in the original shot), the fall is much shorter and takes place in slow motion, and Ripley's body can be seen to burn up just before it hits the lead.

Theatrical Version

The sequence lasts one minute and 32 seconds (92 seconds). Number of shots counted: 29. Average shot length: 3.1 seconds.

1. Pan right to Ripley lifting herself onto the platform
2. Close up of Ripley, looking over her right shoulder
3. Wide shot, establishing shot, of Ripley and helper on the platform
4. Bishop calls to Ripley
5. Re-establishing shot of Ripley on platform
6. Medium close-up of Bishop
7. Tilt of Ripley, walking toward the edge of the platform
8. Ripley positioned at the ledge of the platform, standing with her back toward the boiling lead
9. Close up of Ripley, she nods to Morse, her helper
10. Reverse shot of helper, moving the platform in the direction directly above the cauldron of lead
11. Close-up of Ripley
12 Pan of gathered scientists, looking at Ripley from a distance
13. Crane shot toward Ripley standing on the edge of the platform, she lets go of the railing
14. Close-up of Bishop, looking at Ripley and looking down at the lead
15. Point-of-view shot of Bishop on the lead
16. Sideways medium close-up of Ripley, positioned at the left of the frame
17, Crane shot (moving down) on Bishop saying to Ripley: 'What are you doing?'
18. Pulling focus shot through wired fence. [Possible point of view shot of Bishop]. Ripley, arms outstretched, falls backward
18. Crane shot (moving down) on Bishop, screaming: 'No!'
19. Continuation of shot 18, Ripley falling down

21. Medium close up of scientists, grabbing the fence to get a better look at the spectacle

22. Continuation of shots 18 and 20, Ripley continues to drop

23. Medium close-up of Ripley against the background of the hot lead. She opens her eyes and, at that moment, the alien bursts out of her chest

24. Close up of the screaming and squirming alien, Ripley's hands grab the creature and hold it tight to her chest

25. Close up of Ripley's face, eyes closed. [Soundtrack: the screaming alien]
26. Repeat of shot 24: Ripley's hand holding on to the alien

27. Wide shot, which serves as a re-establishing shot, of Ripley falling and then finally hitting and instantly disappearing (without a trace) into the lead

28. Wide shot of the prison complex industrial heat exhausts. The emerging heat changes color from bright yellow to orange, before it fades out and effectively stops
29. Shot of the planet Fiorina 161 which, up to that moment, was a dark planet, eclipsed by the sun. Now, the sun emerges, bringing (sun)light to the planet

Special Edition Version

The sequence lasts one minute and 51 seconds (111 seconds). Number of shots counted: 32. Average shot length: 3.4 seconds

1. The opening shot is identical to the one in the theatrical version (TV)
2. This shot corresponds to shot 3 in the TV
3. Medium close-up of Bishop
4. Close-up of Ripley, identical to shot 2 in TV
5. Wide shot of Bishop
6. Pan left of Ripley on platform, which serves as a re-establishing shot
7. Medium close-up of Bishop, imploring to Ripley: 'You must let me have it [the alien]'
8. Tilt of Ripley, reaching the end of the platform
9. Medium close-up of Bishop
10. High angle shot of member of scientist crew, equipped with video camera
11. Low angle of Bishop, shouting to scientist: 'No pictures!'
12. High angle reverse shot of scientist, who puts the camera away
13. Identical to shot 8 in TV
14. Identical to shot 9 in TV
15. Identical to shot 10 in TV
16. Identical to shot 11 in TV
17. Identical to shot 12 in TV
18. Identical to shot 13 in TV
19. Identical to shot 14 in TV
20. Identical to shot 15 in TV
21. Identical to shot 16 in TV
22. Close-up of Ripley, positioned at the right of frame. She swallows visibly, opens and closes her eyes and breathes hard. She whispers: 'You're crazy', which could be directed to Bishop or maybe she is talking to herself

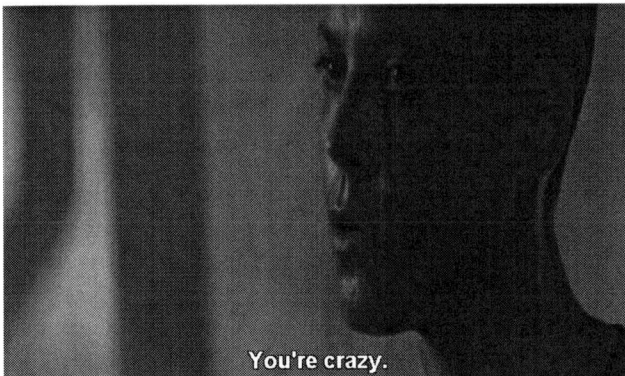

23. Identical to shot 17 in TV

24.   Close-up of Ripley, positioned at the right of the frame. She is still
        struggling, and pulls her head backward

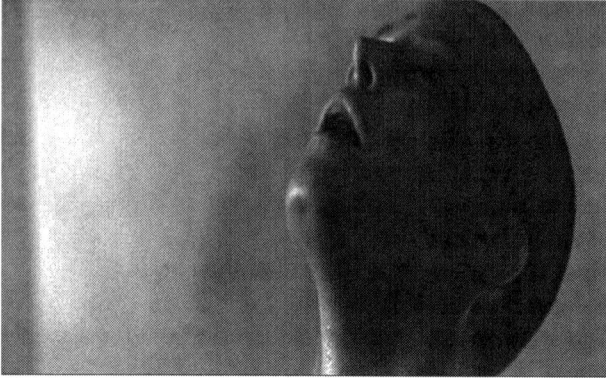

25.   Identical to shot 18 in TV
26.   Identical to shot 19 in TV
27.   Identical to shot 20 in TV
28.   Identical to shot 21 in TV
29.   Identical to shot 22 in TV
30.   Ripley falls from the platform, with arms outstretched. She disap-
        pears into the lead

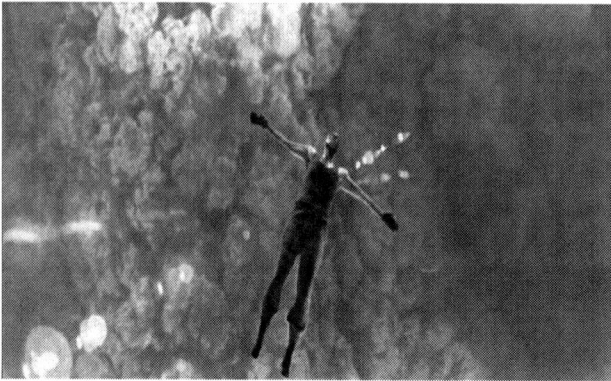

31.   Identical to shot 28 in TV
32.   Identical to shot 29 in TV

The comparison between these two endings demonstrates that the SE
version is largely based on material from the theatrical version. Roughly
speaking, over three-quarters of the footage from the theatrical version is
used in the SE version. Apart from my earlier remarks about the presence
or absence of the alien, to which I will return, on the basis of these shot lists
two other observations can be made. Since there is such a large overlap in
separate shots and sequences of shots between these versions, the crucial
differences are to be found in relatively small, singular shots.

The first difference resides in the dialogue between Ripley and Bishop. In the theatrical version, the halting conversation in which Bishop begs Ripley not to kill the alien is unfocused, that is to say, the dialogue is chopped up and dispersed. The importance of the Bishop character and his plea to Ripley is de-emphasized. By contrast, the SE version keeps the dialogue focused in the beginning of the sequence. The key shot here is shot seven. Bishop begs Ripley to let him and his crew take the alien out of her body alive. His final exclamation, 'you must let me have it', and Ripley's disregard of his plea signal her resolve. Rather than hand herself, and the alien inside her, over to Bishop, Ripley chooses to kill the alien and herself.

The remainder of the sequence in the SE version is also more balanced in the number of shots it assigns to Ripley's struggle of gathering courage for the drop. Shot 22 and shot 24 linger on this mental process for several seconds. Its equivalent in the theatrical version is shot 16, which fleetingly shows her face in medium close-up instead of the close-up in the SE. The difference between the use of a medium close-up and a close-up may seem insignificant, but it is not. The use of a close-up triggers a profoundly different effect. As Mulvey argues, the close-up provides 'a mechanism of delay', in the sense that the flow of narration is momentarily halted, and the spectator's attention is drawn to the human face, more specifically to the face of the film star (Mulvey 2006: 163-164).

The use of two close-ups in the SE version magnifies the importance of Ripley's decision to commit suicide. It is not just the difficulty of her decision that is emphasized; Ripley's death means a definite end to the *Alien* saga. As such, the close-up foreshadows the impeding end of Ripley's story. At the same time, since the close-up also highlights the star's face, the spectator takes a long, final look at Ripley/Sigourney Weaver. On this level, the close-up of the star also functions as a device to terminate the story, the film, and the *Alien* franchise as a whole. In hindsight, it is easy to assert that *Alien3*, as a planned ending to the film series, was never really the ultimate conclusion. Even though this ending did not leave future screenplay writers much space to maneuver, more improbable resurrections have taken place in Hollywood cinema.[23]

The second difference between these two versions is, again, tied to the decisive choice between showing and not showing the alien. Before I turn to that discussion, though, an iconographic consequence of this presence and absence must be noted. The fact that the alien bursts out in the theatrical

23. If the return of Ripley in itself was not improbable enough, Hollywood knowingly and unashamedly marketed this improbability. The tagline to *Alien: Resurrection* reads: 'Witness the Resurrection'. This tagline, almost casually, underscores and reiterates the Christ-like dimension of the Ripley character and the sacrificial nature of her death in *Alien3*.

version forces Ripley to struggle with it as she falls. She clutches the creature to her breast to prevent it from jumping away from her. This struggle is given prominence in shots 24 to 26. However, if we remember Creed's analysis of this particular part of the climax of *Alien3*, a different reading can be proposed. Creed perceives what I label a struggle not so much as a struggle, but instead reads this act in terms of maternal love, lethal love, but maternal love nonetheless.

In the SE version, Ripley neither wrestles nor cradles the alien, as it is absent altogether. This absence, however, produces a postural, physical difference in Ripley's death dive. She plummets into the fire with her arms outstretched. This signifies and underscores two connotations. First, the stretching of the arms is associated with the joy of deliberately jumping from great heights, such as in bungee jumping. The person jumping stretches out in order to experience the sensation of flight fully. As such, this gesture emphasizes the voluntary and conscious dimension of Ripley's act.[24] Second, the extending of both arms instantaneously triggers the iconographical association with Christ' crucifixion posture. Moreover, the combination of this pose and Ripley's demise in the fire activates the martyr text of Thecla, who struck the same pose while she was burnt at the stake (even though she survived miraculously).[25] Thus, in the SE version, the voluntary and martyr-like nature of Ripley's choice is accentuated because of the nonappearance of the alien. This absence causes the entire mother/maternal association to remain absent. In this version, Ripley is more martyr than mother. Moreover, the SE ending reaffirms and reiterates the classical discourse on female martyrdom, precisely because the maternal aspect to Ripley's martyrdom is totally absent. Instead, she is depicted as the strong, conscious, determined and, above all, active creator of her own destiny.

Now, I want to look in more detail at the consequence the presence or absence of the alien has for the reading of the martyrdom of Ripley. The first choice is whether or not the alien should burst out of Ripley's chest at all, thus giving the audience the paradigmatic thrill and satisfaction of the horror film's gory finale or not. The second decision is whether Ripley should dive *before* the manifestation of the beast or *after* it has revealed itself.

The chain of events is open to several variations and, accordingly, Ripley's act of martyrdom takes on different implications. Fincher was strongly in favor

---

24. As Taubin remarks with regard to this scene, Ripley's backward swan dive signifies her 'ecstatic abandonment to the inevitable' (Taubin 1993: 100).

25. The parallels between Ripley and Thecla do not end here. Similarly to Thecla, Ripley, or at least a part of her, also survives the fire. In *Alien: Resurrection*, genetic material in the form of a blood sample taken from Ripley on Fiorina 161 is used to clone several versions of Ripley. Furthermore, the martyrdom of Blandina mentions Blandina striking a similar, Christ-like pose while being erected on the stake.

of not showing the alien, simply because he thought it was not necessary. Additionally, Fincher was in support of Ripley's willfully, proactively, taking her life *before* the creature bursts out: 'If she gets ripped apart before she falls into the fire, that's not sacrifice, that's janitorial service. To knowingly step into the void carrying this thing inside her seemed to me to be more regal' (Swallow 2003: 55).

The essential word Fincher uses in his description of the significance and purpose of the final scene is 'sacrifice'. Ripley's death should be self-chosen and actively pursued. Her act of deliberately falling, arms outstretched, into the fire bestows her with the noble status of the martyr, instead of being a passive victim of a monster that is stronger than she. Thus, Ripley should demonstrate agency and self-mastery in destroying her body. The theatrical ending adheres to this scenario, yet at the same time grants the audience the spectacle of the chestburster: the creature emerges from Ripley's chest during her fall. This ending seems a perfect Hollywood compromise. However, as a result—and this can be observed in Creed's analysis of this scene—the theatrical ending activates the seemingly inevitable return to the archetype of the mother and child.[26] By comparing Ripley with the unfortunate mother of the monstrous child, the alien, Creed and the film effectively restore Ripley to the maternal function. In Creed's analysis, Ripley's monstrous maternity thus ultimately eclipses the sacrificial nature of her act.

Conclusion

In this chapter, I have read three examples of classical, Christian female martyrs in tandem with a contemporary, secular representation of female martyrdom. The classical discourse shows that women who wished to become martyrs had to renounce their femininity to some extent. The masculine role of martyr is available to women, but only when they renounce the most evident symbol of their femininity, maternity. Classical martyrs, I argued, lay bare a gendered continuum between masculinity and femininity. Nevertheless, in the end, I concluded that these martyrs are restored to their traditional, maternal role.

Subsequently, I read the action heroine Ripley as a contemporary example of a woman who accepts the role of martyr. Similar to her classical predecessors, Ripley is ambivalent in her expression of gender. Yvonne Tasker's concept of musculinity demonstrates Ripley's transgression of typical feminine qualities in favor of masculine ones. Similar to the classical martyrs, Ripley, in Tasker's appraisal, takes on the maternal role. The inescapability

26. Creed was not the only critic who observes the maternal connotations of Ripley's death dive. *Rolling Stone*'s Peter Travers describes the final scene as 'a war between her maternal and killer instincts' (Travers 1992).

of maternity takes on monstrous dimensions in Barbara Creed's analysis of Ripley. The monstrous mother, woman predetermined by her reproductive function, overshadows all other qualities. In the case of Ripley, Creed reads her sacrificial death as a derivative of her reproductive function. In my analysis, I positioned Ripley neither on the side of musculinity nor on the reductive side of the monstrous maternal.

Finally, I compared two versions of *Alien3*, the theatrical version and the special edition version. The difference between the two is the presence of the alien in the ending of the former, and the absence of it in the latter. This, I argued, has implications for Ripley's martyrdom. To conclude this chapter, I want to put forward a more ambivalent reading of the theatrical ending of the film. Contrary to the Special Edition ending, which reaffirms a classical martyr discourse, the maternity evoked in the theatrical version signals a preposterous vacillation between past and present representations of martyrdom. On one hand, this ending reconnects Ripley as a female heroine to motherliness which, according to both Tasker and Creed, is ideologically cumbersome. But on the other, and this is the point I wish to stress, Ripley's maternal aspects reconceive classical martyrdom discourse which presupposes that mothers cannot become martyrs, only women made male can. In this sense, a motherly martyr critically reconceives that older discourse: the mother and the martyr become newly related in distinction to the classical examples. Critically, Ripley's maternity does not take away from her martyr's act of self-sacrifice for humanity. As a consequence, the potential reduction of Ripley to her assigned gender position of the archetypal mother is effectively dislocated. In her sacrificial death, mother and martyr are not parted but imparted.

Chapter 4

A FAILED FINAL GIRL:
APOCALYPTIC MISOGYNY IN *THE RAPTURE*

The Apocalypse is not a tale for women.

Tina Pippin (Pippin 1992: 78).

Introduction

The provocative epigraph of this chapter is derived from the work of feminist theologian Tina Pippin. She demonstrates throughout her work that the story of the Apocalypse, in its different versions, cannot be understood as anything other than a misogynistic male vision about violence and power. I subscribe to Pippin's estimation, among others, of apocalyptic discourse as misogynistic. The root of apocalyptic misogyny resides in Revelation, particularly in its use of violent imagery directed at the female characters in the book. As I pointed out in the introduction to this study, the misogynistic streak of this core apocalyptic text is carried over into contemporary representations of disaster. The Hollywood version of the Apocalypse links femininity with catastrophe. In order to prevent catastrophe, femininity needs to be contained and subjugated. More than the previous chapters, this chapter is concerned with the representation of the Apocalypse proper. The film I analyze, *The Rapture* (USA: Michael Tolkin, 1991), endeavors to stage a cinematic enactment of the Apocalypse. The other main theme of this study, martyrdom, also figures in the film, but is signified differently than discussed so far. Contrary to the three previous chapters, the act of martyrdom, or rather, the attempt at becoming a martyr by the film's heroine, does not save the world from disaster. At best, the film represents an act of misunderstood, and therefore failed, martyrdom.

The main character of *The Rapture* Sharon, (played by Mimi Rogers), works as an operator at directory assistance. To compensate for her mundane daytime existence, Sharon cruises airport hotels at night together with a male sexual sidekick, Vic. They pick up other couples and engage in casual, anonymous sex. Sharon's routine, however, is interrupted when she overhears a coffee break conversation between several of her co-workers. They talk about 'a boy and a pearl'. After this, Sharon encounters the image of the pearl once again, this time in the form of a tattoo on the back of Vic's partner. The pearl indicates spiritual knowledge, bringing about a major change in Sharon's life. After another night of anonymous sex, Sharon breaks down, steals a gun from one of her lovers, and attempts to shoot herself. However, at the final moment, she is unable to pull the trigger.

This failed suicide attempt leads to Sharon's conversion. She gives up her old life and marries a former lover. Sharon and her new husband Randy (David Duchovny) have a daughter named Mary, and become active members of a Christian fundamentalist group. Their calm and settled life is disrupted when Randy is shot dead by an angry ex-employee. This tragic incident strengthens Sharon's nascent conviction that the so-called 'rapture', the end of time, is at hand. Sharon and her six-year-old daughter Mary flee into the desert to wait for God, expecting to be 'raptured', that is, taken into heaven together with the other chosen people. When God does not arrive, Sharon decides to kill both herself and her daughter, who pleads to be with the father they both believe to be waiting for them in heaven. After she has shot her daughter, Sharon once again finds it impossible to turn the gun on herself. She confesses the murder to police deputy Foster (Will Patton) and is sent to prison. While imprisoned, Sharon's wish for the end of the world is fulfilled. The signs of the Apocalypse, described in Revelation, such as the angel with the trumpet and the Four Horsemen, appear before Sharon's eyes. Finally, she meets God. Sharon stands between Heaven and Purgatory, as God makes His demand for love and total submission. Unwilling to meet this demand, Sharon is deprived of God's permission to traverse the divide into Heaven.

My argument in this chapter focuses on three aspects. First, I address the violent and misogynist characteristics of *The Rapture*. My reading is based on Tina Pippin's notion that biblical apocalypses are similar to cinematic sequels. The notion of the sequel functions as an interdisciplinary tool that facilitates a reading that situates itself between the biblical text and the cinematic text. I suggest that the film's protagonist and victim Sharon can be interpreted as what feminist film theorist Carol Clover describes as a 'Final Girl'. Designated as such because she is the sole survivor of murder and mayhem in the genre of horror, this character is the indispensable condition for the production of a sequel. Reading Sharon as a Final Girl enables me to substitute the film's malevolent ending with an alternative, perhaps less misogynistic, ending.

Second, I focus on the film's incorporation of fundamentalist ideas, especially the notion of the rapture. I argue that *The Rapture*'s cinematic depiction of the end is problematic. I compare *The Rapture* with Rex Ingram's 1921 silent film *The Four Horsemen of the Apocalypse*. The two films deploy the same photographical technique to represent the Apocalypse;

yet, the effect this technique invokes differs dramatically in each film. The comparison between these two films uncovers the limits of *The Rapture*'s literal depiction of Revelation's apocalypse. This literalness, I argue, resides in the film's direct translation of biblical words into cinematic images. In addition, I draw a tentative conclusion with regard to the representation of the Apocalypse in Hollywood cinema.

My third and final goal in this chapter is to offer a preposterous reading of *The Rapture*'s depiction of its female protagonist. This reading brings to light an alternative to the fate of Sharon. This requires, on one hand, to be attentive to a number of core elements in apocalyptic texts, in particular Revelation, that can be traced in *The Rapture*'s secular representation of the role of the woman in the Apocalypse, while it requires, on the other, being equally attentive to the preposterous nature of these historically older traits in their contemporary re-configuration. Familiar and unbending as these recurring traits may appear to be, their placement in a new context, the Hollywood film, opens up a possibility of reading them against their traditional and normative meanings. My preposterous reading is driven by a twofold conception of the metaphor of (sun)light. That is, 'light' and 'seeing the light' can be understood in the (religious) sense of a revelation of wisdom and belief. This metaphorical use of light is, I argue, concretely represented in the film's mise-en-scene, specifically in the lighting of several scenes. The question, then, is whether or not and, if so, to what extent, religious and cinematic 'illumination' establishes the same or similar sets of meanings. Thus, in the concept of light or lighting, religion and cinema come together.

The Critical Reception of The Rapture

At its release, *The Rapture* received mixed reviews. Although some critics, such as Janet Maslin of *The New York Times*, praised writer and director Michael Tolkin for the 'brazenness of making a mainstream film about religious faith', the majority of reviews were damning. The film was not a success at the box office.[1] Particularly the climax of the film, the literal depiction of the end of the world, was met with disapproval. The most common complaint was that the film lacked the necessary budget to pull off a realistic and credible depiction of the Apocalypse. The question of what constitutes a realistic, cinematic representation of the end of the world is addressed below.[2]

---

1.   According to the Internet Movie Database (IMDB), the film grossed less than $2 million at the US box office.

2.   Among those critics who did not condemn the ending of the film is America's most famous film critic, Roger Ebert. In his review, first published in the *Chicago Sunday*

Despite the film's limited budget, Tolkin pushed his film to its apocalyptic ending. Tolkin, a practicing Jew, has admitted a profound interest in the idea of the Apocalypse in several interviews. He was one of the nonacademic speakers at the Third Annual International Conference on Millennialism, held at Boston University in December 1998. In an interview with the Boston University newspaper, he introduced his idea that entertainment culture is akin to the Apocalypse: 'I think a strong case can be made that the culture of entertainment is a calamity of apocalyptic scale, tantamount to a comet or a tidal wave or God's final judgment'.[3]

Although Tolkin does not elaborate on this notion of 'entertainment-as-apocalypse', at least not in this particular interview, his apocalyptic mindset can also be found in one of his later screenplays, which became the basis for the film *Deep Impact* (USA: Mimi Leder, 1998). In this film, a comet heading toward Earth threatens to cause a tidal wave, which would destroy large parts of the globe.[4] In this film, in contrast to *The Rapture*, the destruction of Earth is not complete. Yet, a recurring aspect of these two films is the theme of salvation and escape from impending disaster. In *Deep Impact*, a small number of people is able to seek refuge in special shelters, making the odds of survival a matter of logistics, managed by the government of the United States. In *The Rapture*, however, the issue of who (and how many people) will be saved is treated in a different manner.

In this film, salvation is represented by the notion of the rapture. In the biblical conception of the term, the rapture is defined as 'the final assumption of Christians into heaven during the end-time according to Christian theology'.[5] Salvation will only be offered to those who believe in God and, even then, salvation may not be certain, as Sharon is to find out. This blatant depiction of God's cruel judgment of mankind, combined with a straightforward, what can be labeled a Christian fundamentalistic, interpretation of the biblical Apocalypse makes *The Rapture* an extraordinary and disturbing film. Tolkin's film could be seen as an early and partially, at

Times, he argues: 'It has been accurately observed that Tolkin's special effects in the closing sequences leave something to be desired. True, George Lucas or Ridley Scott could have done more with the River Styx, given several million dollars. But the budget necessary for those special effects would have compromised the film—no one would have risked that kind of money on a movie this daring. Besides, it isn't how the effects look that's really important, it's what they say' (Ebert 1991).

3.   Eric McHenry, 'Deep Impact screenwriter to speak about apocalypse as entertainment, and vice versa', in *B.U. Bridge* (McHenry 1998). For a report on the conference on millennial studies, see Sheila Gibson 1999.

4.   The similarities between *Deep Impact* and the other film about a comet hitting planet Earth released in 1998, *Armageddon*, are obvious. For a comparison between the two films, see King 2000: 164-73.

5.   This definition is taken from the Merriam-Webster online dictionary.

least financially, unsuccessful precursor to the unprecedented popularity the Rapture narrative has gained in the last decade. While Tolkin's film failed to deliver the notion of the rapture to the masses, the popular evangelical novel series *Left Behind* succeeded gloriously.[6]

Margaret Miles provides a relevant discussion of the film's depiction of Christian Fundamentalism in particular. The representation of fundamentalism in film is exceptional. Despite Tolkin's self-professed intentions, Miles argues, his efforts to tackle the subject of fundamentalist rapture belief are misguided. The film presents a distorted picture of fundamentalism. The main reason for this is located in the scene in which Sharon kills her daughter Mary, resulting in an 'implicit equation of fundamentalism with murderous insanity' (Miles 1996: 104). *The Rapture*'s depiction of religion's influence on behavior, Miles argues, can be summarized as follows: 'religious commitment motivates [...] pathological compulsiveness and murder' (Miles 1996: 103). In her overview of the negative reviews of *The Rapture*, Miles notes that only one reviewer picked up on the child murder. The film, in contrast to, for instance, Martin Scorsese's 1988 film *The Last Temptation of Christ*, which caused great controversy at the time of its release, was critically trashed and subsequently forgotten.

I re-examine this film, not because it should be redeemed, but because it represents the doomed position of a woman at the center of an apocalypse. Sharon's terrible fate echoes that of a biblical predecessor, the 'Woman Clothed with the Sun' from Revelation. In *The Rapture*'s representation of the Apocalypse, in contrast to *Alien3*, the woman does not fulfill a heroic and martyrlike function, which would enable her to escape victimization through the voluntary act of martyrdom. Sharon is a failed martyr at best. Instead, the film forcefully taps into the misogynist spirit of Revelation. I pursue a more nuanced account. My reading of *The Rapture* may ultimately

6. The *Left Behind* series, consisting of twelve books in total, is conceived by evangelical prophecy writer Timothy LaHaye and written by evangelical fiction writer Jerry Jenkins. The first book, entitled *Left Behind: A Novel of the Earth's Last Days*, was published in late 1995. This book opens with the crucial moment of Rapture: Jesus secretly returns to earth to gather his believers. The true believers are taken to heaven and the world they leave behind is plunged into chaos. In the remainder of the series, which spans a seven year period called the tribulation, the world suffers plagues, famine, and the emergence of the Antichrist (in the guise of a world leader). After this, Jesus triumphantly returns to earth, defeats the Antichrist and establishes his kingdom. An estimated 60 million books have been sold (estimates of the number of potential readers vary between 80 million and 120 million), making the series only second in popularity to the Bible itself. For a short review of the first two films based on the *Left Behind* book series and its connection to *The Rapture*, see Lucius Shephard's review (2003) in *Fantasy & Science Fiction*. In a study on the book series, Amy Johnson Frykholm argues that the rapture narrative is popular in both religious and secular circles and is thus 'a fluid part of the broader culture' (Frykholm 2004: 4).

not be capable of saving the heroine and her biblical counterpart from their poor destiny; yet, the issue of misogyny needs to be addressed.

Surviving the Apocalypse: The Final Girl

According to feminist theologians, the defining characteristic of apocalyptic discourses is their malignant representation of women. A particularly spiteful passage is Revelation 17.16: 'And the ten horns that you saw, they and the beast will hate the whore; they will make her desolate and naked; they will devour her flesh and burn her up with fire'.

In her evaluation of Revelation, Susan Garrett, in *The Women's Bible Commentary*, emphasizes that the book consistently uses metaphorical language based on feminine imagery (Garrett 1992: 377). With regard to the passage quoted above, Garrett writes that the author takes great pleasure in 'describing the gory destruction of the woman Babylon' (Garrett 1992: 381). There are three main female figures in Revelation: Jezebel, the Whore of Babylon, and the Woman clothed with the sun.[7] The first two are sexually impure, since they are no (longer) virgins. This unchecked sexuality is dangerous and must be constrained through the use of violence. The Woman clothed with the sun, is a stereotypical representation of feminine purity and virginity, despite the fact that she is pregnant. None of the three women, however, escapes physical or mental punishment.[8] The objection that Revelation deploys metaphors, and as such cannot be held responsible for its horrible depiction of femininity, is a fallacy, as Garrett points out. The text creates a problem for women readers, Garrett argues, and the 'dehumanizing way in which [John] phrased his message will remain deeply troubling' (Garrett 1992: 377).

Catherine Keller formulates it as follows: 'Here is the paradox for feminist meditation on 'the end of the world': while innumerable women have found means of private resistance and public voice in the symbols of

---

7.   All three figures are symbolic. Jezebel, however, is probably based on an actual historical figure, most likely a false prophet. See, Van Henten 2003: 745-59.

8.   For a close analysis of the basic female archetypes in Revelation, see Pippin 1992. The crucial exception to the negative feminist interpretation of Revelation is Elizabeth Schüssler-Fiorenza, whose work is characterized by attempts to redeem the text and (re) interpret it positively from a feminist perspective. This takes the form of a socio-historical reading of biblical texts, coupled with an attempt to undermine the patriarchal stance of the Bible. Schüssler-Fiorenza seeks to read biblical texts as useful guides for dealing with present, often political, situations involving inequality and injustice. Interestingly, Pippin's dissertation follows Schüssler-Fiorenza's proposed liberation hermeneutic. Pippin applies a Marxist hermeneutic to reveal the narrative of Revelation as 'resistance literature'. As she states: 'The Apocalypse was the literary equivalent to a book burning or a food riot or a violent revolutionary takeover' (Pippin 1987: 158).

the Apocalypse, overt or subvert, the *toxic misogyny* of much of its imagery cannot [...] be flushed out of the text or its tradition' (Keller 1996: 29, emphasis added).

The premise that apocalyptic discourses are violent, oppressive, and misogynistic supplies the motivation, for women in particular, to deal with these types of texts and representations. As Keller points out elsewhere, the cultural and religious grip apocalyptic discourse has on Christianity and Western culture should not be underestimated (Keller 1992: 183-95). Pippin displays a similar awareness, and endeavors to read the Apocalypse differently. I focus here on her study *Apocalyptic Bodies: The Biblical End of the World in Text and Image*. Crucial for Pippin's analysis of Revelation and related apocalyptic texts, ranging from Hollywood cinema to apocalyptic theme parks in the US, is the reading method she deploys, coupled with her unease about the issue of gender and sexuality that these apocalyptic texts convey. Pippin situates herself as a postmodern, interdisciplinary reader of texts (Pippin 1999: 118), albeit with a solid background in biblical studies. As Pippin states in her conclusion, in her work she is 'resisting the master (pun intended) narrative and the traditional reading strategies, not in order to set up yet another master narrative but to create another site/space for a resisting reading' (Pippin 1999: 118).

Pippin's 'resisting reading' takes into account strategies adopted from semiotics, Marxist feminist critical theories, and deconstruction. Taken together, her postmodern approach to biblical narrative engenders a reading 'unattainable by historically grounded biblical exegesis' (Pippin 1999: 118). Nevertheless, Pippin's starting point for her reading of the Apocalypse necessarily originates from the biblical texts.

I start with Pippin's interpretation of the several apocalyptic texts in the Bible and the ways in which these texts can be understood as *sequels*. According to Pippin, they should be read in relation to each other. Pippin's connection of Bible and film, via the idea of the sequel, leads to her reading of *The Rapture*. I will take that reading as the starting point of my own analysis of the representation of the end of the film.

In her introduction, Pippin puts forward the idea that the Apocalypse (or any Apocalypse, since the Bible contains more than one apocalyptic story) should be understood as a sequel. A sequel refers to 'a work which follows another work and can be complete in itself and seen in relation to the former and also what follows it' (Pippin 1999: 1). The use of this metaphor from contemporary cinema culture enables Pippin to address two important characteristics of the apocalyptic genre. First, if the Apocalypse is to be understood as a sequel, then what constitutes the predecessor of the Apocalypse? Where can one find the original, first apocalyptic story ever told? Pippin's answer is unequivocal: 'the chaos of apocalypse cannot be essentialized' (Pippin 1999: 1). The disorder found in the text mirrors its disorganized hermeneutical history. Pippin opts for an understanding of apocalyptic discourse as never-ending and open.

Yet, in a rhetorical move, Pippin departs from her anti-essentialist stance to outline the history of apocalyptic sequels that can be found in biblical as well as extra-biblical texts. This outline serves to bolster her contention that apocalypses adhere to the rule of the sequel, understood here in the frame of the sequel in cinema. Hence, Pippin reads the notion of the sequel preposterously: the contemporary, cinematic concept of the sequel is transposed onto an older, non-cinematic discourse, the Bible. This transposition gives the notion of the sequel its particular appropriateness. Sequels, for instance, those in the genre of the horror film, and the indeterminate sequence of biblical apocalypses, Pippin argues, share a common denominator: as a viewer, or reader, of those narratives, 'one expects [..] a replaying of the violence in a grander scale' (Pippin 1999: 3). She writes

> The Apocalypse of John is a sequel of the Hebrew Bible and Pseudepigrapha; its details of the end time violence are more extreme. Sequels only produce more horror. Much of the Apocalypse of John (like Mark 13) comes from Daniel and other Hebrew Bible apocalypses. New Testament apocalypses are thus sequels of sequels. Some of the apocalypses in early Christianity (sequels of the earlier apocalypses) are even more descriptive than the Apocalypse of John (Pippin 1999: 3).[9]

Pippin's historical sketch underlines her argument that apocalyptic discourse evades essentializing regulation and classification ('sequels of sequels').

I surmise that Pippin's inventory functions to denounce apocalypse as a genre. The phrase 'more descriptive' euphemistically points to the sliding scale of extremes the biblical and extra-biblical apocalypses display. Like the sequel of a horror film, which adheres to the unwritten rule that the sequel needs to have a higher body count than the previous installment(s), apocalypses tend to get bloodier and more violent.[10] Revelation, a text of

9.   Pippin opts to name what is generally known as the Book of Revelation, the Apocalypse of John instead. By doing so, both the nature of the narrative ('apocalypse' means 'revelation', but by naming it 'apocalypse' instead of the more euphemistical 'revelation', the violent connotations of the word 'apocalypse' are put to maximum use) and its authorial source (a man named John) take center stage.

10.   In another chapter, Pippin compares the Apocalypse to horror literature and remarks, 'the Apocalypse is less like the shower scene in *Psycho* than the all-out killing in *The Texas Chain Saw Massacre*' (Pippin 1999: 83). Both films have spurred an impressive list of sequels. In the case of *Psycho*, four sequels, a remake, and a television spin off. *The Texas Chainsaw Massacre* has three sequels, one prequel, and one recent remake. It should be noted that *Psycho* is generally regarded as the starting point of the 'slasher flick'. Moreover, there is an obvious intertextual connection between the two films. Both *Psycho* and *The Texas Chain Saw Massacre* are based upon the true story of serial killer Ed Gein.

horror, is the final chapter in a sequence of apocalypses. Incidentally, the phrase 'the final chapter' is often used as a subtitle of film titles.[11] The phrase is also explicitly used in marketing campaigns for film sequels: the last installment that will make all the previous ones seem trivial in comparison.

However, biblical apocalypses, particularly Revelation, also deviate from the cinematic template of the sequel. Unlike cinematic sequels, Revelation's biblical horror is absolute: 'nothing and no one survives on the earthly plane' (Pippin 1999: 2). Destruction is complete, as Pippin suggests with reference to Revelation 21.1: 'Then I saw a new heaven and a new earth; for the first heaven and the first earth had passed away, and the sea was no more'. Revelation is the equivalent of the final sequel in film, the one that will end all sequels. Because of Revelation's total destruction, an important prerequisite for a successful sequel as it functions within the context of cinema is missing: there are no survivors.

I want to expand on Pippin's observation on the absence of survivors. Although she mentions a few examples of 'postmodern horror [films where] the female protagonist survives' (Pippin 1999: 2), the full reference to this notion is missing. Carol Clover's 1992 study of gender in the horror film titled, *Men, Women, and Chain Saws*, argues that every horror film follows the same murderous pattern: a killer massacres a group of people, but one resourceful young woman, who Clover has famously typified as 'the Final Girl', is able to outsmart the killer and survive. The survival of this Final Girl is the narratological condition for one or more sequels, in which the killer returns to finish the job.[12] Pippin proceeds to delineate the apocalyptic logic and its 'no survivors' mentality'. The surviving 'winners' may suffer martyrdom on earth but gain eternal life in heaven. The losers survive in a sense, so they can suffer eternal torture' (Pippin 1999: 2).

Survival is to be experienced in either heaven or hell. The winners and losers are set apart by the strength of their belief in God. This apparently simple requirement for eternal life, a steadfast belief in God, proves to be difficult in the case of *The Rapture*'s Sharon. Pippin criticizes the 'us versus them' logic implicit in rapture belief. The notion of the chosen insider, the 'us', in opposition to the damned outsider, 'them', is represented in the ending of the film.

Pippin discusses the film's notorious ending briefly. Her observations serve as the springboard for my analysis of the character of Sharon and, particularly, the ending of the film. Sharon, according to Pippin, 'panics

11. For instance, *Friday the 13th: The Final Chapter* (USA: Joseph Zito, 1984) and *Puppet Master 5: The Final Chapter* (USA: Jeff Burr, 1994).
12. The classic example is *Halloween* (USA: John Carpenter, 1978) and its series of numerical sequels, *Halloween II* (1981) to *Halloween 5* (1989), plus three additional non-numerical sequels (released in 1995, 1998, and 2002 respectively).

at the end [the moment of rapture], refusing the grace of God and opting instead for hell' (Pippin 1999: 2). I take issue with this reading. Sharon might have panicked before, when she was unable to kill herself but, at the moment of rapture, she is anything but scared. Sharon does not 'refuse the grace' of God, as Pippin suggests. God's 'grace' is exemplified by his method of persuading Sharon to bear witness to her love for God and be raptured. He sends Sharon's deceased daughter Mary, and the six-year-old girl argues the case on behalf of God. Mary functions as a divine messenger and attempts to convince her mother to love God despite everything. God himself is conspicuously absent.

In the final scene of the film, Sharon resolutely declines being raptured, saying: 'No, I don't want to go'.[13] Mary begs her mother to confess her love for God, so she can join her in heaven. Although heaven can be glimpsed in the distance, the prospect does not change Sharon's mind. To the contrary, she persistently refuses God's instant grace: 'Why should I thank Him for so much suffering, Mary. So much pain on the earth that He created. Let me ask Him why'. In a final attempt to change Sharon's mind, Mary asks her: 'Do you know how long you'll have to stay here?' When Sharon answers, 'Forever', she has accepted her condemnation to solitude. The film leaves her standing alone. The closing shot of the film, in which the camera slowly tracks out before the screen fades to black, underscores Sharon's position as an apostate outsider.

In the apocalyptic logic of the chosen and the damned, Sharon's fall from grace is now complete. Recall how Sharon ended up in the desert to begin with: she was initially the only member of her congregation 'called' to go on account of the vision of her deceased husband Randy. This vision was so much an insider's vision that, when Sharon asked the other members to join her in the desert to await the Apocalypse, the answer was, 'We weren't invited'. Yet, when she denounces God for making her kill her own daughter, Sharon chooses apostasy over salvation. She shifts from being a privileged insider to an outsider and is left standing at the gate, presumably forever. The God of *The Rapture* is not merciful, but implacable in His final judgment. I cannot help but wonder: could Sharon be considered a Final Girl? Or, and this question I cannot shake off even after repeated viewings: Why can't she be a Final Girl?[14] The film leaves us with an image of her as

13. The film *Book of Life* (France/USA: Hal Hartley, 1998) deploys a similar scenario. Only here, it is Jesus Christ himself who gets cold feet and refuses to open the final seals of the Apocalypse. Instead of passing judgment on mankind by opening the book of life that contains the names of those who are saved, Jesus decides to give mankind another chance. The book of life, in this film cleverly represented as an Apple laptop computer, is kept closed for at least another thousand years.

14. When read according to Carol Clover's theory, the character of Sharon could never function as a Final Girl for the simple reason that Sharon is not a virgin. Strictly

the last woman standing, triggering the reflex of a possible cinematic sequel. According to Pippin, *The Rapture* has allowed no space for a possible way out for Sharon, or for her eventual triumphant return in a sequel. Biblical apocalypses have no Final Girl.[15]

Irreconcilable Endings

I contend this is so because the two discourses at work, apocalyptic and cinematic, and the narratives they formulate, are ultimately irreconcilable. A cinematic depiction of the end is impossible. Precisely because *The Rapture* unveils, in the truly apocalyptic sense of the *apocalypsis*, the uncovering, the revelation of a truth, a cinematic representation of the end, it is difficult to come to terms with that end. There is a discrepancy between the literal and fundamentalist apocalyptic discourse and a cinematic one. It is, of course, possible to believe in the divine fulfillment of God's judgment as it is written in Revelation. Yet, the concrete visualization of this judgment is impossible within the medium of cinema. The two discourses cannot be combined. This leads to the paradox that the technologically most advanced of all visual arts, cinema, is incapable of representing the most extreme event imaginable.

This incapacity, I argue, is expressed both on the level of narrative and on the level of the image. The film's ending exemplifies that cinema can

speaking, within Clover's model this would be unacceptable, yet she herself mentions Ellen Ripley from the *Alien* saga as an example of a Final Girl (Clover 1992: 46). I would, therefore, venture a slight broadening of the category of the Final Girl. The attribute of feminine virginal purity would still be an important, but not an exclusive trait. By enlarging the category, a memorable character such as Ripley can be included. Kristin Thompson also argues for the inclusion of Ripley into the Final Girl category, 'Ripley's final solitary escape from the ship and conflict with the alien in the shuttle may owe something to the travails of the Final Girl' (Thompson 1999: 386 n. 2).

15. According to Michael Tolkin, there was an alternative ending. In an interview with *Film Comment*, he explains, 'The original ending as written was, after the Seventh Call Sharon says, 'Oh, I get it now, it's all clear to me, how could I have been so stupid, please take me'. And Mary says, 'you can't come, you have to see it before the Last Call. Anyone can see Heaven after the Last Call. You have to take it on faith'. Every woman working on the film [...] came to me privately and had a long talk with me why she thought that if we kept that ending I was selling Sharon out and her entire life was a shaggy dog story and she had learned nothing, she was compromising at the moment when it was really important for her not to compromise. So I wrote another ending. And then when we shot the original ending, we shot something that was really beautiful using a very complicated special effect. A $ 100,000 later, the effects house scratched the negative, so we had to throw it out. [...] I came across some stills of it a couple of weeks ago and I was just crushed, because it was really great-looking' (Tolkin quoted in Smith 1994: 58-59).

only express the Apocalypse in a restricted manner. In the introduction to this study, I mentioned the paradox of apocalyptic anticipation followed by cancellation. This contradiction is the first reason why the completion of the end is impossible: it goes against the structural nature of these narratives.[16] The apocalyptic narrative desires and prophesizes an end, but thrives on the actual delay of that end. Hollywood's desire for the end does not so much suggest 'apocalypse now' as 'apocalypse never'. Or perhaps, 'apocalypse later', since the event is perpetually announced, yet perpetually postponed. Technically, and on the condition of a large enough budget, film should be able to visualize the Apocalypse. Yet, it seems that the story about the ultimate end is better told without that ultimate end included.[17]

The apocalyptic climax becomes more complicated when it is represented visually. The film stays true to its fundamentalist core, and portrays a literal depiction of the events that are prophesized in Revelation. Mick Broderick argues that precisely the literal depiction of the Apocalypse is unsettling: 'What is so discomforting and disconcerting about the film is its deliberate evasion of metaphor, allegory and allusion to signify the eschatological events, particularly since both Christian and Jewish apocalyptic is (un) ambiguously expressed in this manner' (Broderick 1994).

Refusing the symbolic realm, the film's ending is not just bewildering but, I think, also unconvincing. The problem lies in the literal depiction of biblical scenes, in the sharp transition between the realistic diegesis of *The Rapture* and the fantastic events of the Apocalypse. These apocalyptic images, which originate from text, words, are bluntly translated into image. The imagery of Revelation, when read, is complicated and fantastic. As

---

16. Schüssler-Fiorenza argues that a forward movement that is neither linear-logical nor linear-temporal characterizes Revelation (Schüssler-Fiorenza 1981, 1991). As such 'it can best be envisioned as a conic spiral moving from the present to the eschatological future' (Schüssler-Fiorenza 1981: 25-26). She rephrases this argument slightly in a later book, claiming 'the author's numerical interweaving of visions combines a cyclic form of repetition with a *continuous forward movement*' (Schüssler-Fiorenza 1991: 33, emphasis added). However, Schüssler-Fiorenza adds, 'paradoxically, this forward movement of the narrative leads not to a flight into a utopian future but anchors the reader in the present' (Schüssler-Fiorenza 35). Ultimately, after Revelation has disclosed its 'symbolic drama', the reader is '*returning* and goes back to the starting point' (Schüssler-Fiorenza 37, emphasis in text). This leads me to the conclusion that, even though Revelation is characterized by a cyclical, conical structure, which creates a forward movement, the end itself is never actually fully and conclusively reached.

17. In this sense, I cannot help but invoke Slavoj Zizek's suggestion (following Lacan) that the prime purpose of desire is not fulfilment, but the replication of desire itself: desire seeks not its consummation, but its eternal prolongation. The desire of desire is to remain unconsummated for, once it is sated, desire ceases. Besides, the object of desire, in this case the end, the apocalypse, is empty, a void. Therefore, the end remains unfulfilled, destined to repeat itself perpetually (Zizek 1991: 83-87).

Schüssler-Fiorenza argues, the strength of its imagery lies in the fact that it invites 'imaginative participation'. However, she adds: 'The symbolization and narrative movement of Revelation elicit emotions, feelings, and convictions that cannot, and should not, be fully conceptualized' (Schüssler-Fiorenza 1981: 18).

Expressing this imagery in a visual manner is not only nearly impossible, given that Revelation's bizarre images often affront logical-rational sensibilities, but also robs it of its persuasive power (Schüssler-Fiorenza 1981: 18, 31). Yet, despite Schüssler-Fiorenza's doubts about the representability of Revelation, the fact remains that the book has engendered countless works of visual art. One of the most famous examples of apocalyptic art, the woodcuts of Albrecht Dürer, is discussed below.

The literal visualization of Revelation is the weakness of *The Rapture*. Initially, the film situates the events prior to the Apocalypse in a realistic mode of representation, carefully maintaining the impression of reality. According to Elsaesser and Buckland, realism in film should be understood as 'nothing more than an effect of the successful positioning of the spectator into an imaginary relation to the image, a position which creates a sense that the film's space and diegesis is unified and harmonious' (Elsaesser and Buckland 2002: 202).

The realistic mode, which strives to uphold the logic of unity and harmony, is violated by the advent of the Apocalypse. Though the fantastic nature of the Apocalypse is initially represented in a realistic and non-metaphorical manner, conforming to the film's established impression of reality, for a viewer, *The Rapture*'s cinematic depiction of the Apocalypse does not convince. A shift occurs halfway through the apocalyptic sequence, which triggers this particular feeling.

The Rapture's treatment of the Apocalypse begins with the manifestation of Revelation's four horsemen.[18] They appear in the middle of the diegesis,

18. The relevant verses are Revelation 6.1-8. 'Then I saw the lamb open one of the seven seals, and I heard one of the four living creatures call out, as with a voice of thunder, "Come" I looked, and there was a white horse! Its rider had a bow; a crown was given to him, and he came out conquering and to conquer. When he opened the second seal, I heard the second living creature call out "Come!" And out came another horse, bright red; its rider was permitted to take peace from the earth, so that people would slaughter one another; and he was given a great sword. When he opened the third seal, I heard the third living creature call out,"Come!" I looked, and there was a black horse! Its rider held a pair of scales in his hand, and I heard what seemed to be a voice in the midst of the four living creatures saying, "A quart of wheat for a day's pay, and three quarts of barley for a day's pay, but do not damage the olive oil and the wine!" When he opened the fourth seal, I heard the voice of the fourth living creature call out "Come!" I looked and there was a pale green horse! Its rider's name was Death,

chasing Sharon and police deputy Foster down the road. Their sudden appearance in the diegesis is shocking, yet effective. The established realism is inter-penetrated by the supernatural. This intervention is seamless, and forfeits a gesture toward a symbolic representation. The human and divine characters unequivocally share the same frame. This part of the sequence is effective, because it capitalizes on this seamlessness: Revelation's third horseman, the one on a red horse carrying a huge sword, chases Sharon and Foster. Through the conventional methods of editing a chase, human and divine agents interact in the same frame.

In the second part of the sequence, however, incredibility takes over. The impression of reality is broken by the use of a special effect. A figure seated on a cow, holding a chandelier in his hand, appears in the sky. The representation is ineffective because the superimposed figure is hopelessly

out of scale in relation to the film frame. There are two types of special effects, invisible and visible. The first type simulates events in the actual world that are too expensive or inconvenient to produce. The visible special

and Hades followed with him; they were given authority over a fourth of the earth, to kill with sword, famine, and pestilence, and by the wild animals of the earth'.

effects simulate events that are impossible in the actual world. The crucial aesthetic point, Elsaesser and Buckland point out, is that, while this type of special effect is clearly visible, they 'attempt to hide behind an iconic appearance (or photographic credibility); that is, they are visible special effects masquerading as invisible effects' (Elsaesser and Buckland 2002: 210).

In other words, the visible special effects attempt to confer realism upon an object that does not exist in the actual world. In *The Rapture*, the appearance of a cow in the sky is created through superimposition, a technical process through which two separately filmed events are printed on the same strip of film. Elsaesser and Buckland discuss this particular type of visible special effect in detail. Theoretically, they argue, superimposition fabricates a 'spatio-temporal unity, giving the impression that the two separate events are taking place at the same diegetic space and time' (Elsaesser and Buckland 2002: 210). However, this process has technical shortcomings that are difficult to disguise. Apart from the disparity in scale, which I have mentioned above, there is another problem. The most common setback with superimposition, which can be observed in *The Rapture*, is the loss of resolution and grain. The image of the cow is noticeably 'softer' than the surrounding image. Furthermore, the lighting of the cow, which seems to come from above, does not match the lighting pattern of the landscape on top of which the cow materializes. As Elsaesser and Buckland conclude, even though superimposition may 'give the impression that two separate events share the same screen space, they eventually fall short in convincing the increasingly sophisticated spectator that the separate events occupy the same diegesis' (Elsaesser and Buckland 2002: 210-11).

The evaluation of superimposition as an unconvincing special effect is felt in the climax of *The Rapture*. Contrary to the beginning of the sequence, the chase, the second part of the sequence is unable to convince the spectator that the human and the divine characters share the same diegetic world. Consequently, the initial seamlessness is lost and, with that, the credibility of an emerging Apocalypse. For that reason, *The Rapture*'s representation of the Apocalypse, despite its use of sophisticated cinematic technology, falls flat. This strengthens my contention that, despite the medium's general technological prowess, representations of the Apocalypse are impossible.

The Rapture's depiction of the Apocalypse is exceptional. There is, however, an intriguing precedent. The silent film *The Four Horsemen of the Apocalypse* (USA: Rex Ingram, 1921) offers an intertextual connection with *The Rapture* on the levels of content matter as well as technology. Although *The Four Horsemen of the Apocalypse* is not a religiously themed but an anti-war film, the imagery of the Apocalypse is remarkably similar to *The Rapture*'s images of the four horsemen. I compare the two films' employment of a literal vision of Revelation. I argue that the earlier film, oddly enough, succeeds in its depiction of the Apocalypse, where the contemporary one fails.

The film, situated during the years preceding World War I, tells the epic tale of a family torn apart between nationalistic sentiments, as one part of it is French and the other is German. The main character Julio, played by Rudolph Valentino, is the protagonist. Unlike his two brothers-in-law, who choose to fight for the German and French armies, Julio just wants to dance the tango in the salons of Paris. His indifference is challenged when, on the eve of France's mobilization, he meets the mysterious character called 'the Stranger'. This man, who strongly resembles a Christ-like figure, opens a book and begins to prophesize: 'The Revelations of St. John as conceived by the great master—Albrecht Dürer'. When the stranger proclaims that the 'age of fulfillment' has begun, a shot of a female angel holding a scroll is shown.

I focus on the transition between the realistic and the fantastic in this scene. Contrary to *The Rapture*'s depiction, the arrival of the Apocalypse is framed through the narrating act of a character. Moreover, this act is embedded by the use of Dürer's woodcut. The use of the woodcut of the horsemen has a double effect. First, since this work is probably one of the most recognizable depictions of the Apocalypse, an immediate intertextual association is established. The woodcut signals the Apocalypse. The film

follows Dürer's representation faithfully. As Kovacs and Rowland point out, Dürer was the first artist to depict the four horsemen as a quartet. After that, many artists have closely linked all four horsemen (Kovacs and Rowland 2004: 93). In *The Four Horsemen of the Apocalypse*, the horsemen appear as a tightly knit quartet, strengthening the influence of Dürer's work on the cinematic rendering of the horsemen. Second, the woodcut serves as a transition between the realistic and the fantastic. The static insert of the woodcut temporarily breaks the flow of images and 'opens the door' to another dimension. The apocalyptic events do not break into the diegesis by themselves, but are mediated through the woodcuts of Dürer and the story of the stranger. The Apocalypse is a representation of the stranger's inner vision, a representation of his mental subjectivity. This is underscored by the editing, which emphasizes the narrator's point of view through the use of close-ups of his face as he tells the dreadful story of the four horsemen.

In a smooth transition, the film shifts from a mental representation to a literal one. After the stranger has concluded his story, he suddenly points out the window where, indeed, the four horsemen emerge riding in the sky. The presence of the four horsemen in the diegesis has now become literal. The stranger, Julio, and his servant look out the window and see the

horsemen. The four horsemen appear three more times at crucial moments in the film. The final scene of the film, which drives home its pacifist theme, shows the stranger at a massive burial site commemorating the countless dead soldiers of World War I. There the stranger again points to the sky to the retreating four horsemen.

I argue that a specific narrative device is responsible for the smooth shift between the realistic and fantastic realm. The narrator, who appears to be simultaneously of this world and of another, functions as mediator between the two modes of representation. In addition, on a stylistic level, one can argue that the film's black and white photography is effective as a way of portraying the fantastic.[19] The recurring shot of the four horsemen in the sky is an instance of trick photography, namely superimposition. The image of the galloping horsemen is laid over another, in this case an image of the sky, either by double exposure in the camera or in laboratory printing. Contrary to *The Rapture*'s similar use of superimposition, here the result is effective. The special effect does not disturb the tenuous balance between the film's established impression of reality and the unexpected, yet in this case credible, appearance of the fantastic.

The Rapture's discordant rupture of filmic reality gives the viewer an unconvincing encounter with the Apocalypse. The impossibility to render the events of the Apocalypse in a credible manner partly lies in *The Rapture*'s debatable artistic choices. Technical flaws further weaken these choices. Specifically when viewed alongside *The Four Horsemen of the Apocalypse*, *The Rapture* points to the manifest and relentless dichotomy between biblical words and images. Whereas *The Four Horsemen of the Apocalypse* manages to overcome this dichotomy by means of specific aesthetical choices, namely the use of black and white photography (which was, granted, a technological inevitability at the time) and a narratological device, the film's persistent use of a realistic mode of representation signals its cinematic collapse. *The Rapture*'s one-on-one translation of biblical words into cinematic images results in a materialized, yet disappointing, Apocalypse.

In spite of an Apocalypse fulfilled, *The Rapture* does not end in Apocalypse. As I argued above, what interests me most is what happens to the female protagonist *after* the Apocalypse has taken place. Reading the character of Sharon as a possible Final Girl has proven to be unproductive,

---

19. This is a tricky argument as a general claim on black and white film. The effect of black and white film is ambivalent, to say the least. In fiction films of a certain historical period, for instance German expressionism of the 1920s, it might lend itself to a more veritable depiction of the fantastic. At the same time, non-fiction films, such as newsreel footage of events from the two World Wars, are generally deemed more historically 'accurate', or realistic when shown in black and white. So, black and white film has a double effect, depending on context. Again, I would emphasize that particularly the latter claim perhaps only holds for the contemporary viewer.

despite the fact that she is the sole survivor. The survivor theme leads to an association with a female figure in Revelation, the woman clothed with the sun, whose predicament echoes Sharon's. They share another metaphorical characteristic: they are characters of light and wisdom. In what follows, these two female figures are subjected to a preposterous reading.

A Possible Sequel? The Woman Clothed with the Sun

The assessment of apocalyptic discourse by means of a preposterous analysis is paradoxical and warrants elaboration. Whereas the former, by definition, assumes teleology and a historical linearity that culminates in a final ending, the latter problematizes these aspects altogether. A preposterous approach is characterized by temporal loops, rather than causal linearity. Preposterous time is not linear, but presupposes time to be 'folded'. The concept of the fold works as a way of conceptualizing time as infinite and curvilinear.[20] Since the two conceptions of history, apocalyptic and preposterous, are driven by diametrically opposed conceptions of temporality, the coupling of the two seems problematic. Yet, a preposterous analysis of *The Rapture* can counter and reinterpret misogynist readings of the Apocalypse, exemplified by the fate of *The Rapture*'s female character Sharon.

I attempt one final encounter with the Apocalypse. In order to do so, I return to the source text, Revelation, and its problematic representation of female figures. The woman clothed with the sun is unmistakably a mother figure. In Revelation 12:5-6, her crucial role is spelled out: 'And she gave birth to a son, a male child, who is to rule all nations with a rod of iron. But her child was snatched away and taken to God and his throne; and the woman fled into the wilderness, where she has a place prepared by God, so that there she can be nourished for one thousand two hundred sixty days'.

In common interpretations of this passage, attention is focused on the figure of the son. Many scholars assume that the son should be identified as Jesus Christ. James Resseguie argues differently; he claims that the son should not be interpreted as Jesus Christ, but as a representation of 'those who remain faithful' (Resseguie 1998: 144).[21] The mother is thus the mother of the group of people who will be saved. After giving birth, a dragon, Satan, chases her but, through the protection of God, she manages to escape 'into the wilderness, to her place where she is nourished for a time, and times, and half a time' (Revelation 12.14). David Aune emphasizes that this flight 'into the wilderness', or rather, the flight from 'desert to desert, occurs in a

---

20. See Deleuze 1993: 3-13.

21. Compare Resseguie's interpretation with Aune, who states that the male child should be read as 'the Messiah of Jewish eschatological expectation' (Aune 1998: 688).

variety of apocalyptic contexts' (Aune 1998: 691). The desert should not be understood as a geographical place, but as a symbolic place of refuge.

The figure of the woman clothed with the sun can be read through the character of Sharon, making the former a preposterous manifestation of the latter figure. This reading focuses on the features that become observable when the woman clothed with the sun is considered though the character of Sharon. The film emphatically points out the connection between the two women. After Randy's death, Sharon receives a vision of her husband in the desert. This vision is conveyed to her through a photo-developing machine, which shows her photos of unknown people in a desert and the miraculous apparition of Randy on these pictures. On the soundtrack, functioning as a sound bridge, we hear the voice of the boy, the young prophet of Sharon's congregation. He reads Revelation 12.6: 'and the woman fled into the desert, where she had a place prepared for her by God'. The quotation serves as an explanation for the privileged knowledge and subsequent task Sharon has been assigned, possibly from God.

A comparison of the similarities between the two characters strengthens this reading. They give birth to a child who is endowed with specific powers, and both are incapable of raising that child, as it is taken away from them. The two texts share the motif of seizure (of the child), which leads to the apotheosis of the child of the woman clothed with the sun as well as Sharon's daughter Mary.[22] Apotheosis should be understood as the elevation of someone to a divine status, which is precisely what happens to Mary after Sharon shoots her. I understand Sharon's killing of her daughter as an act of supreme faith in God and, more importantly, as an act of faith ordered by God. At least, that is the way Sharon initially perceives it.

Like Abraham who almost sacrificed his son Isaac in order to prove his faith, so Sharon is willing to sacrifice her daughter. Sharon's unconditional faith in God and the imminent rapture enables her to grant her daughter's wish to be reunited with her father in heaven, though it means Sharon has to kill the person she loves the most. By shooting Mary, the little girl is instantly deified, taken up to God. In the remainder of the film, Mary returns twice to act as His messenger, urging Sharon to demonstrate her faith in God. Sadly, Sharon has lost her faith because of her supreme act of motherly love. The problematic concept of deadly, motherly love is represented differently than in the previous chapter on *Alien3*. In that film, the mother's infanticide results in her elevation to the ranks of the martyr.

Another similarity is the decrease of the women's role in the narrative with the birth of the child. As Pippin remarks with regard to the woman clothed with the sun: 'after her reproductive activity she is no longer useful'

---

22. Aune mentions this recurring motif in his commentary on Revelation 12.5 (Aune 1998: 689).

(Pippin 1992: 72). She gives birth to a son, who is immediately 'snatched away' and taken to God. After that, a dragon chases her to a place in the wilderness. There she is to remain for an amount of time. For her as a character, the part has ended. A similar diminishing in narrative importance happens to Sharon.[23] The first half of the film sets out to portray Sharon as a loose woman, a whore if you will, leading to the sequence where she begins to despair of the life she leads.[24] After her intensely desired conversion, the narrative takes a six-year jump, during which Sharon has married Randy and has given birth to Mary. Crucially, the event that disrupts Sharon's blissful life as a good Christian housewife is the violent death of Randy. This tragedy leads to Sharon's vision of Randy in the desert, which she interprets as a sign that she and Mary should flee to the desert to be reunited with him. Sharon is no longer an active agent in the narrative; to the contrary; she has handed over her agency to God (and, to a lesser extent, to Randy).

Both the woman clothed with the sun and Sharon are denied access to the realm of the chosen ones. At first, Resseguie remarks, the woman clothed with the sun is a source of light in the narrative but, after the Apocalypse, when the new heaven and the new earth are installed, 'her role of illuminating a darkened world is accomplished' (Resseguie 1998: 143). She is no longer needed. Compare this with Sharon's conversion and her role as a literal and metaphorical source of illumination and enlightenment. Immediately after her conversion, Sharon begins to spread the word of God: 'God made me an information operator for a reason. I'm in the position to spread His word to hundreds of people everyday, personally. One to one'. The film underscores Sharon's pure belief, visually expressed in the lighting of her character, rather bluntly. One critic observed that, after Sharon finds God, this faith is cinematically expressed in pronounced backlighting of her character, resulting in a kind of aureole.[25]

23. The marginalization of female characters recurs throughout the Bible, that is to say, it can be observed in the Old Testament, Hebrew Bible, and the New Testament. As Athalya Brenner remarks, 'In the Bible, in biblical interpretation and in theology, in religion and in religious texts, women and femininity and female sexuality may be loved; however, they are also and habitually marginalized into foreign Others' (Brenner 2001: 243).

24. Here Revelation's other female figure, the Whore of Babylon (Revelation 18), comes to mind. As such, one could argue that *The Rapture* charts the transformation of Sharon from a whore to a true believer (woman clothed with the sun) to an apostate, robbed of the light of belief.

25. This element of the mise-en-scène did not elude Caryn James of *The New York Times*, who somewhat cynically remarks with regard to Sharon's conversion, 'by now Sharon is usually seen with a halo of light around her head, which suggests the final message of *The Rapture*: Come the Apocalypse, there will be a lot of backlighting' (James 1991).

This reading of Sharon as a 'source of light' is strengthened by a close analysis of the mise-en-scène, principally the film's use of lighting. Indeed, the presence or absence of light is the key to understanding the character of Sharon. The mise-en-scene cues the spectator to take notice of and invest meaning in the evolving lighting patterns that surround Sharon. The scenes leading up to Sharon's conversion are situated in either the grey and blue setting of the workplace or various bedrooms at night. Obviously, the mise-en-scene suggests that, as a result of her sordid lifestyle, Sharon lives her life in (semi) darkness.

The conversion itself, preceded by the scene in which Sharon attempts to shoot herself, is almost comic in its literal deployment of the expression 'seeing the light'. When Sharon opens the Bible and begins to read, we first hear music, and then a light shines on her face. She has found God. From that moment on, Sharon constantly bathes in light, specifically sunlight. She is clothed with the sun. An example of this parallel between sunlight and religious belief is the scene where Sharon is sunbathing with a friend. Despite Sharon's fervent attempts at persuasion and conversion, this friend remains a skeptic. The scene's mise-en-scene is dominated by sunlight, which charts Sharon's development as a believer. Contrary to her skeptical friend, who does not wear a hat and is directly exposed to the sun, Sharon wears a sun hat. The presence of the hat could be interpreted as a metaphor: Sharon is a devout believer, but one who takes caution not to get sunstroke. In other words, at this moment, Sharon is not yet blinded by her belief.

When Sharon and Mary flee to the desert, the light metaphor becomes more pronounced and the sunlight takes on an increasingly ambivalent meaning. On one hand, it signifies Sharon's strong belief; on the other, the abundance of light is dangerous; it is now too strong. This is delicately accentuated by the fact that Sharon has forgotten to pack a sun hat. The strength of the desert light foretells the extent to which the light of belief becomes blinding and, ultimately, deadly. After the killing of Mary, Sharon has lost the light. She has killed the thing she loves the most, the light of her life, her daughter. Moreover, after the act, Sharon has lost her faith, her guiding as well as blinding light. It is no coincidence that she flees from the desert at night, while the signs of the Apocalypse emerge. From that moment on, the light of the sun is absent from the diegesis. Sharon is to await her fate in various shades of darkness.

In light of all this, I take a closer look at the final scene of the film and its play with light and darkness. This close analysis strengthens the connection between the biblical woman clothed with the sun and her secular counterpart, Sharon who, as I argued above, is also clothed with the sun. The sequence begins immediately after Sharon and police deputy Foster have been partly raptured. They find themselves in an undefined place, somewhere between earth and heaven.

The beginning and ending of this sequence mirror each other. The sequence starts with total darkness and ends with total darkness. However, the darkness at the beginning is significantly different from the darkness at the end. In the beginning, the darkness leads to an increasing amount of light, whereas the final darkness is irreversible. The extra-diegetic marker of the credit sequence, the most obvious sign that the film is over, emphasizes this permanent darkness. It functions as the way to terminate the narrative irrefutably. In general, the distribution of light across the frame and directed at the characters in the frame is even. In the realm of the rapture, each character supposedly has an equally strong belief, which is visually expressed in even lighting.

This sequence can be divided into two parts. The first part consists of thirteen shots.

1. Fade-in from a black frame. Long shot of Sharon's daughter Mary. The girl is emphatically lit from behind; the outline of her body is highly contrasted with the dark surrounding her

Mom?

2. Plan Américain of Sharon and Foster, who walk toward Mary. They are also lit from behind

Is this hell?

The first two shots parallel each other in lighting the characters from behind. As such, one could interpret these two shots as establishing a relationship of equality between the three characters. However, the fact that Mary is framed by herself in each shot, until the end of the sequence, hints at her singular status.

3.   Possible point-of-view shot of Mary by Sharon and Foster. This shot is subjective because, like Sharon and Foster, it is tracking in on Mary

4.   Medium close-up of Sharon and Foster, still approaching Mary

5.   Medium close-up of Mary. The background behind is slowly illuminated

Shot 5 is the first indication of a change in lighting: Mary, contrary to Sharon and Foster, is framed against an illuminated background.

The next five shots, 6 to 10, call attention to two points: first, they confirm Mary's special status and, second, by placing Sharon and Foster in the same frame, stress the latter two's shared situation, by means of the so-called same-frame heuristic. This widely used heuristic posits that, if characters appear in the same frame, they are united. Conversely, if cutting separates them, they are in conflict (Elsaesser and Buckland 2002: 89-90).

6.   Medium close-up of Sharon and Foster

7.   Medium close-up of Mary

8.   Repeat of shot 6
9.   Repeat of shot 7
10.   Repeat of shot 6
11.   Close-up of Mary

Shot 11 breaks the pattern. This is the first close-up of the sequence.

12.   Close-up of Foster, who declares his love for God and is instantly raptured

The next two shots, 12 and 13, ostensibly function as a reverse shot to shot eleven. They are balanced according to Hollywood narration, which dictates that close-ups are matched by close-ups and so forth, but the significance of shots 11 to 13 resides in the breaking up of the same-frame heuristic. Foster chooses God, Sharon does not.

13.   Close-up of Sharon, screaming 'No!'

Shot 13 is the closing shot of the first part of the final sequence.

14.   Sharon and Mary enter the frame left. Medium close-up of the two of them walking. Sharon gets down on her knees to talk to Mary

Between shot 13 and shot 14, which I mark as the beginning of the second part of the sequence, sits a peculiar transition. The editing does not skip a beat; yet, suddenly Sharon and Mary are walking. This shot is odd, because the previous shots were all static. Shot 14 is a so-called match-on-action shot, but the preceding shot that necessarily sets in motion the action, in this case walking, is missing. It is possible that between shots 13 and 14 an indeterminate amount of story time has elapsed, although this cannot be argued decisively. This strange transition signals the timelessness to the state of being raptured, which corresponds to the notion that, after the Apocalypse, human time no longer prevails.

15.   Close-up of Mary, frame left

If life is a gift...

16.   Close-up of Sharon, frame right

17.   Repeat of shot 15
18.   Repeat of shot 16
19.   Repeat of shot 15

Shots 15 to 19 are balanced shots, in which Mary still attempts to persuade Sharon to love God. The two characters are equally lighted and surrounded by darkness, implying equality in religious belief. Or, put differently, at this moment Sharon could still be saved. The climax of the sequence starts with shot 20. Despite Mary's ferocious arguing for God's case, Sharon refuses to choose God. Mary already knows that this means that the two of them can no longer be together and begins to say goodbye.

20.   Medium close-up of Mary, who embraces Sharon

21.   Frontal close-up of Sharon's face

I can't.

22.   Sideways close-up of Mary's face

you can't go to heaven.

23.   Repeat of shot 21

Shot 21 and its repeat shot 23 are forceful close ups of Sharon's face. These two shots favor Sharon's emotion over Mary's, hence the difference between a frontal close-up and sideways close-up. The use of close-ups aligns the spectator with Sharon and the difficult decision she is about to make.

24.   Medium close-up of Sharon and Mary still locked in their embrace.

They stand up and turn their backs to the camera, away from the viewer. They are facing the light of heaven

25.   Frontal medium close-up of Sharon and Mary. Mary disappears

Do you know how long
you have to stay here?

26.   Close-up of Sharon. She is lit sideways. As the camera tracks out slowly, the light fades and the screen turns to black

Forever.

In the final three shots of the sequence, the emphasis is again placed on the movement of the light. In their final moments together, shot 24 and 25, Sharon and Mary face the emerging light of heaven. Even this does not persuade Sharon to abandon her apostasy and only Mary disappears into heaven. The final shot is a frontal close up of Sharon, surrounded by darkness; she is dimly lit from behind and from the left side. The movement of the light matches the movement of the camera. The light as well as the camera retreat from Sharon and leave her alone in the dark. This final shot drives home the irrevocability of Sharon's fate: she is swallowed up by the darkness—a darkness that represents the loss of her belief, and with that the people she loves the most, her husband and her daughter.

The character of Sharon is preposterous in the sense that she illuminates a number of similarities between herself and the woman clothed with the sun. These features illuminate the woman clothed with the sun from the perspective of Sharon, the later character. Reading from the present back to the past uncovers connections between these two female characters that the older text in itself would not reveal. Unsettlingly for the contemporary figure, eventually the similarities are radically canceled. The film denies Sharon the possibility of an 'afterlife' in Heaven. Initially, she is endowed with the light of the sun and the light of belief, only to be progressively stripped of that light in the end. This is in contrast to the woman clothed with the sun, who is given an afterlife with God. *The Rapture* is a radical interpretation of Revelation. It denies its main protagonist such a reward, while almost sadistically presenting that denial as her own choice. Sharon's denial, her refusal to accept God, could be interpreted as an empowering act, yet the price she pays for this refusal is high. In the end, Sharon is the loser in a high stakes game with God. *The Rapture* closes the book indefinitely on both a possible sequel and a possible afterlife for Sharon, thus making it the most far-reaching Apocalypse imaginable.

Conclusion

In this chapter, I have drawn attention to two recurring aspects of apocalyptic narratives: the malevolent estimation of women and the narrative's need for an ending. I have attempted to challenge these persistent traits by under-taking three oppositional readings. The first reading attempted to counter the film's misogynistic disposition. I used the interdisciplinary concept of the sequel (and the affiliated idea of the Final Girl) to argue against the misogynistic fate of Sharon. I extended Pippin's idea that biblical apocalypses are governed by the cinematic concept of the sequel by arguing that Sharon, as a survivor of the Apocalypse in *The Rapture*, could be seen as an example of a Final Girl.

My second reading concerned the representation of the Apocalypse, spe-cifically the idea of the rapture. I argued that the film's treatment of the fundamentalist notion uncovers the difficulty of cinematically representing the Apocalypse. I compared *The Rapture* with *The Four Horsemen of the Apocalypse* on the basis of the photographic technique, superimposition, the two films use. Unexpectedly, the older film's use of superimposition results in a credible depiction of the Apocalypse, whereas *The Rapture*'s representation falls flat. I concluded that film in general is reluctant in representing the Apocalypse. The reason for this reluctance lies in the paradox that cinematic apocalypses strive to reach the end, only to have that end canceled at the last moment. The cinematic representation of the end is persistently deferred and, as the example of *The Rapture* shows, for good reason since the representation of the Apocalypse proves to be difficult. The question of what constitutes a realistic, cinematic representation of the end of the world, cannot be answered.

Finally, I added a third, preposterous reading of *The Rapture*'s female protagonist. This reading underscores *The Rapture*'s apocalyptic misogyny. This analysis focused on the notion of light and on lighting as an instance of interdisciplinarity between religion and film. In the shot analysis of the final sequence of the film, I emphasized that the presence and absence of light should be understood in both a biblical and a cinematic sense. By using light as a guiding principle, the likeness between the woman clothed with the sun and Sharon is uncovered. However, the similarities between them are ultimately ruled out in the contemporary manifestation. The cinematic use of lighting, which initially strengthened the connection between the historically older figure and the newer figure, renders the heroine powerless once it is stripped away. In my readings, I have tried to empower the female character of *The Rapture*. However, in the end, the Apocalypse is still not a tale for women.

Chapter 5

FEMALE VISIONARY:
APOCALYPTIC ANTICIPATION IN *THE SEVENTH SIGN*

For this reason, I now speak through a person who is not eloquent in the
Scriptures or taught by an earthly teacher; I Who Am speak through her
of new secrets and mystical truths, heretofore hidden in the books, like one
who mixes clay and then shapes it to any form he wishes.
        Hildegard von Bingen (Von Bingen 1990: Book 3, vision 11).

Introduction

Hildegard of Bingen (1098-1179) was an abbess and mystical visionary
whose writings are pervaded with apocalyptic imagery. Her book *Scivias* is a
report of twenty-five visions that sum up Christian doctrine on the history
of salvation. The notion of the vision is a recurring element in the present
study. It forms the primary characteristic of Revelation, which is generally
understood as the written account of the vision that John receives. The
vision also figures prominently in secular, popular manifestations of the
Apocalypse. In the films I have discussed so far, *End of Days*, *Armageddon*,
Alien3, and *The Rapture*, the visions are of crucial importance to the
martyrdom discourse, both past and present. The visionary segments of *The
Seventh Sign* (USA: Carl Schultz, 1988), the film under scrutiny in this
chapter, hint at the notion of a 'double reality', evoking a certain past in
the present, a common trait of apocalyptic narrative. The anti-linearity of
the vision can be connected to a preposterous perspective.

    In this chapter, I focus on visions in relation to gender. In *The Seventh
Sign*, the main character Abby, a self-confessed nonbeliever, receives a
series of mysterious and prophetic visions. This resonates with Hildegard's
epigraph, in which she positions herself as 'a person who is not eloquent
in the Scriptures'. I address the work of another female visionary, Anne
Catherine Emmerich, in relation to Abby. Abby's visions are a central
aspect of the narrative of *The Seventh Sign*. Her vision not only recurs
several times, increasing in both length and significance with each
occurrence, but is also emphatically marked as vision. This labels Abby's
visions as instances of self-conscious and self-reflexive cinematic narration.

The concept of vision resonates in a religious as well as cinematic sense. Both discourses incorporate it, though in diverging ways. Understood in a religious context, vision refers to the abstract: a thought, a religious belief, which is nevertheless rendered visually. Cinema *is* vision; its discourse centers on the visual, the image, the act of seeing and the power this act entails. In the martyr's vision, I will show, both discourses come together. In this chapter, then, vision functions as an interdisciplinary element that connects religion and film.

Cinematic vision unpacks a number of related issues. It adds another layer to the representation of female martyrdom, the female martyr as visionary. Abby's martyrdom resonates with the other examples of female martyrdom discussed so far, both religious and secular. In addition, the uncertainty of the temporal reality experienced during a vision provokes questions with regard to the status of the beginning and the end, a recurring issue in the apocalyptic discourse. The vision disrupts notions of linear time and, consequently, the unfolding of narrative. Time can be imagined as a loop, moving from past to present to future but, as *The Seventh Sign* illustrates, not necessarily in that order. A detailed analysis of the opening sequence of the film shows how the ending is already located in the beginning. Furthermore, the ending of the film, I argue, is emphatically an open ending. It refers back to the beginning. The film itself creates a perennial temporal loop. Finally, the film exemplifies the intimate link between motherhood and martyrdom, which I have signaled in the previous two chapters.

The film opens with several signs that forecast the Apocalypse. These are loose adaptations of the seven seals, signs, and bowls of judgment from the Book of Revelation. The messenger who unleashes them is the mysterious David (Jurgen Prochnow), an incarnation of the returned Jesus. Before long, David moves in as a lodger with pregnant Los Angeles housewife Abby (Demi Moore) and her lawyer husband, Michael (Michael Biehn).[1] The apocalyptic end, so David tells Abby, is set in motion and cannot be stopped. *The Seventh Sign*'s notion of the Apocalypse is informed by the ancient Jewish legend of the Guf, the hall of souls. It is the place where

1.   Many films represent Los Angeles as the place where the Apocalypse, or any other form of general mayhem and destruction, will enfold. For an overview of literary as well as cinematic examples of the annihilation of LA, see Mike Davis's *Ecology of Fear: Los Angeles and the Imagination of Disaster*. King notes that, 'favourite targets [of natural disaster and destruction] are the metropolises of New York and Los Angeles, [...] it is less common for the target to be rural' (King 2000: 146). Los Angeles, King remarks, 'stands as the ultimate signifier of decadence and "unreality".' As such, he argues, 'onto Los Angeles can be projected what are perceived to be the most decadent and deplored tendencies of modern American life, in an act of ritual sacrifice and displacement that implies, reassuringly, that much of the rest of the country remains essentially untainted' (King 2000: 148).

a finite number of souls are stored until they will inhabit the bodies of newborn babies. According to this legend, the Messiah will not arrive until the hall of souls is empty, that is to say, until the first child is born without a soul. Abby quickly realizes that her unborn child will be the first child born without a soul, and that his birth will usher in the Apocalypse.[2]

Abby questions David about possible ways of preventing this. He responds that the chain of signs can be broken, but that it would require hope, and that hope is what mankind has lost. Initially, Abby seems to have found an ally in the figure of father Lucci (Peter Friedman), a priest. However, his plans turn out to be diametrically opposed to those of Abby. One of the clients of Abby's husband, Jimmy (John Taylor), sentenced to death for killing his incestuous parents, plays a decisive role in father Lucci's schemes. For Jimmy's death is one of the seven signs that must occur before the Apocalypse can unfold. Amidst the chaos of the impending Apocalypse, Abby attempts to interrupt the sequence of apocalyptic signs. She is rushed to hospital where she gives birth to a son. The child, it appears, is stillborn. In an act of self-sacrifice, Abby gives her life so that her child can live. This act restores hope for humankind and the Apocalypse is forestalled.

I begin with the cinematic question of whether Abby suffers from dreams, flashbacks, or flashforwards. Whichever they are, these disruptions of causal temporality provide clues to Abby's destiny. This, I argue, can already be observed in the opening sequence of the film. My analysis of this sequence focuses on the enigma it invokes. The relationships among the three main characters are crucial for solving the film's enigma. Subsequently, I analyze the main characters as referential characters, part of an established frame of reference, adhering or deviating from it. In the next section, I analyze the maternal aspect of the martyrdom of Abby. I analyze the parallels and contrasts between Abby and the previous female martyrs. Finally, I return to the film's beginning through its ending and argue that the beginning and the ending of the narrative are preposterously condensed.

Glimpsing the Future Through the Past

The flashbacks or dreams that Abby experiences are the narratological and aesthetic entry point for my interpretation of the film. Their status is initially unclear. Are they recurring dreams? What is their temporal status? Do they pertain to the past, to the future, or maybe to both? The dreams or

---

2. The film's representation of hope, symbolized in the Hebrew legend of the Guf is addressed in detail by Conrad Ostwalt's reading of the film. As Ostwalt argues, the film 'provides the most explicit example [...] of contemporary apocalyptic vision through a creative combination of Christian and Jewish apocalyptic imagery and folk tradition'(Ostwalt 1995: 59). I return to Ostwalt's analysis of *The Seventh Sign* below.

flashbacks are familiar and ambivalent at the same time. Their familiarity lies in the way they are presented to the viewer, namely through conventional cinematic signs that signal the appearance of a dream or flashback. The first appearance of a dream or flashback is crucial in this respect, since it breaks the established diegetic world and introduces a different temporal and subjective register, establishing a template for the interruptions that follow. In *The Seventh Sign*, the first one is explicitly presented as Abby's *dream*. We recognize the school she visited earlier that day. Via a dark corridor, supposedly in the school, Abby ends up in a dark cave, where one man is beating another. Abby overhears the question, 'Will you die for him?' The signals that mark Abby's perceptions as dream are obvious: on the soundtrack, eerie music is heard, diegetic sound is deformed, and the action is shown in slow motion. The latter two characteristics are clear indications of her perception's subjective status. Then, Abby awakens startled and is comforted by Russell, who tells her that it was 'just a dream'. Yet, the most obvious and ambivalent aspect of the dream—which also hints at its status as a flashback—is the divergent temporal dimension in which it is staged. For it constitutes an abrupt break with the temporal setting of the diegesis, Los Angeles in the present time, and offers instead a nonspecific place in a distant past. The presence of Abby in both those time-worlds suggests a possible causal and temporal connection.[3]

The status of the first dream becomes more ambivalent after Abby follows David inside a synagogue. There, she recognizes a corridor as the one she has seen before in her dream, while she has never actually visited that synagogue before. The second occurrence of the dream takes place after David has revealed his true identity to Abby. After a whiteout of the screen, during which an unspecified amount of time transpires, Abby

3.   On the basis of the first vision, emphatically represented as a dream where we see Abby in a different historical period, it can be interpreted as a flashback. To be more precise, it could be an external flashback since it displays events that occur prior to the first event represented in the plot (Bordwell 1985: 78).

finds herself in hospital. In shock, she is administered a heavy sedative. As she loses consciousness, flashes of the earlier dream appear before her eyes. This time, however, the identity of the man who is beaten is revealed: David. The third time the dream occurs, Abby has not lost consciousness. This time, the identity of father Lucci is revealed. In addition, the dream shows Abby for the first time as part of a larger group of onlookers at the scene of the beating. In the final occurrence of the vision, Abby is fully conscious again, and she answers the persistent question, 'Will you die for him?' affirmatively. After that, she loses consciousness and dies.

On the basis of this pattern, I argue that Abby suffers neither from dreams nor experiences flashbacks. I propose to label them visions. Initially, the vision manifests itself while she is asleep, and can thus be coded as 'just a dream'. The other three times her perception takes place in front of her eyes, while she is, at least partially, conscious. This invalidates the category of the dream. The revelatory third vision comes to Abby when she is fully conscious. As Bal argues, 'memory is an act of 'vision' of the past but, as an act, situated in the present of the memory' (Bal 1997: 147). Elements of the past and the present are tangled and present themselves in an incongruent, associative fashion. Parts of the incident are revealed to her, but initially she is unable to make sense of them. Following Bal, I argue that what Abby suffers from can be compared to trauma, insofar as her memory of a certain event is disrupted. The kernel of the trauma is situated in the recollection of the question, 'Will you die for him?' Abby's engagement with, or her act of working-through, this question in the present makes closure possible.

Bal writes, 'memory is also the joint between time and space' (Bal 1997: 147). Bal discusses this aspect of memory with respect to postcolonial literature, where it is deployed as a means of countering the effects of colonizing acts such as mapping. Yet, her argument can pertain to other cases of time and space convergence as well (Bal 1997: 147-48). Abby's vision, shaped by a traumatic and faulty memory, uncovers the joint between first-century Jerusalem and present-day Los Angeles. Abby's vision is precisely a vision since it discloses secret knowledge about an event that took place in the past, which will be restaged in the imminent future. Time and place may be transposed and changeable, but the characters are not. In that sense, Abby is the receiver of a revelation as well as of a prophecy: her visions reveal something that happened in the past, while they also pertain to and prophesize the future.

This suggests the possibility that the visions are a kind of flashforward which, according to Bordwell, provides a glimpse of the outcome before all causal chains are understood. Flashforwards, understood within the context of classical narrative film, are generally problematic and uncommon. Narratologically, they exceed the set time span of the story. Stylistically, they are 'very hard to motivate realistically' (Bordwell 1985: 79). In rare cases, they are motivated as self-conscious acts of authorial intrusion, a characteristic of art cinema, not Hollywood cinema. The obvious reason why Abby's visions cannot be examples of flashforwards is the change in time and place between the present-day diegesis and the earlier, ancient setting of her visions. Abby's visions could have been flashforwards only, if they were also set in a hospital room in present-day Los Angeles.

Perhaps it is more productive to avoid the terms flashforward and flashback altogether, and focus on the tension between time and place in the visions as the key to understanding them. Abby's visions constitute a deviation of time and place. Though the visions are set in the past, the messages they convey are crucial for the future. Abby's visions provide glimpses of the future by way of the past. Bal has labeled this deviation of time 'anticipation within retroversion', a referring forward within a back-reference (Bal 1997: 98). When this notion of temporality is applied to Abby's visions, their significance becomes understandable. Retroversion means that the event present in the anachrony, here taken as the vision, lies in the past. This is the case in Abby's visions. Anticipation, Bal claims, often suggests 'a sense of fatalism, or predestination: nothing can be done, we can only watch the progression towards the final result' (Bal 1997: 95). Thus, anticipation within retroversion uncovers the importance of an act located in the past for another act located in the future. The visions imply that past and future are not only intricately bound to one another, as the latter replays, restages the former, but also are seemingly unalterable. This, then, is the significance of Abby's vision: it gives her privileged information on past and future events and her role in those events; yet, the outcome is already determined, or at least that seems to be the case.

However, a crucial aspect challenges this fatalistic, apocalyptic characteristic of the visions: the characters and their present incarnations. For, in order to alter her fixed destiny and those of the other characters, Abby and the spectator must understand what her destiny has been in the past. The opening sequence of the film offers clues about the past and future of Abby and the other main characters. An analysis of the sequence reveals repetitions and variations in time, place, and character development.

Beginnings: The Enigma as Catalyst

Unlike previous cases in this study, I will focus on the construction of the narrative and on the ways in which the narrative is presented through the plot.[4] To this end, I have divided the film into large narrative units

4. I follow Bordwell and Thompson's differentiation between plot and story. In a narrative film, plot is 'all the events that are directly presented to us, including their causal relations, chronological order, duration, frequency, and spatial locations'. This

or segments.⁵ According to Stephen Heath, the segmentation of a film 'operates at the level of the narrative signified according to the simple criteria of unity of action, unity of characters, unity of place; it has no analytic status other than that of allowing reference to the film as narrative' (Heath in Bellour 1976: 35).

The segmentation of a film into units serves a practical and analytical function. A segment, Bordwell notes, is not a sealed entity: 'spatially and temporally it is closed, but causally it is open' (Bordwell 1985: 158). This characteristic results in the forward thrust of the narrative, as each segment continues or sets off development. This progression is eventually terminated when a state of stasis is reached. Often, segments can be grouped together. In that case, they constitute what Bellour calls a 'sequence' (a suprasegment or macrosegment). Like a segment, a sequence often adheres to the classic rules of unity of time, place, and action.

The parallel and alternating storylines of *The Seventh Sign* are presented in the plot through crosscutting. This is a common type of editing, which emphasizes action in separate places and times.⁶ The technique of cross-cutting is the governing principle of the first large and expository sequence of the film, consisting of ten segments. Apart from introducing the main characters and locations, the editing suggests a connection between characters. The film is thus an example of the 'converging fates' device, which connects the several protagonists of a film. Bordwell remarks: 'When a multiple-protagonist plot brings strangers together, the more the narration emphasizes their separate lives, the more we expect significant encounters among them' (Bordwell 2006: 99). The link between Abby, David, and father Lucci is not disclosed in the first sequence of the film. Instead, the enigma serves as a catalyst for the narrative.

In this sense, *The Seventh Sign* adheres to the classic rule. As Elsaesser and Buckland argue, the opening should be regarded as a manual or meta-text for the film. The 'opening-as-a-manual' idea is strengthened by the initial

is opposed to story, which they define as 'the viewer's imaginary construction of all the events in the narrative' (Bordwell and Thompson 1997: 481).

5.   The film adheres to the classic three-act structure common in Hollywood story-telling. In this chapter, I analyze the opening, or exposition, in detail. As mentioned, this opening sequence takes place in the first ten segments of the film. The second act, the complication, takes place between segments eleven and twenty-eight. The third act, the climax, runs from segment twenty-nine to forty-one. It is clear that the three-act structure distributes and balances the number of segments dedicated to each act. The middle section takes up most of the film (nearly twenty segments), whereas the beginning and ending are balanced, with roughly ten segments each.

6.   The most famous example of this type of editing is D.W. Griffith's 1916 film *Intolerance*, which shifts between locations (as diverse as Babylon and France) and historical periods.

sequences' divergence at the level of style as well as content in relation to the rest of the film. The opening, Elsaesser and Buckland state, is 'separate from and yet part of the narrative, in that it usually establishes setting, place, and time, as well as introducing the main protagonist(s)' (Elsaesser and Buckland 2002: 47). In *The Seventh Sign*, the stylistic difference of the opening sequence is signaled by the use of crosscutting. Hence, the opening points to a possible reading of the film, or introduces 'the rules of the game' (Elsaesser and Buckland 2002: 47). These rules become clear when the opening sequence is analyzed.

My delineation of the segments that constitute the opening sequence, segment one to ten, needs to be motivated first. The main reason for imposing an end to the opening of the film after segment ten is the fact that the main characters have been introduced by then. The function of the opening lies in its creation of the enigma that fuels the film. The use of crosscutting between different locations and characters prompts the viewer to look for a possible connection. Immediately, one can observe formal repetitions between the segments. These repetitions set up an alternating rhythm among the segments.

The obvious repetition is found in the first three segments, which alternate between different locations and calendar dates. However, segment three, which functions as the introduction of Abby, displays a striking alteration. Though repetition is continued in the date and location information given to the viewer, variation is now added. For segment three opens with a prolonged close up of Abby. Dialogue reveals a major theme of the film: the character's troubled history of pregnancy. The following segment breaks with the previous pattern, since it does not return to the characters or the locations of the previous two segments. Instead, Abby's privileged position is stressed. Segment four opens with a subjective tracking shot that is attributed to Abby's point of view. The appearance of this subjective shot is unexpected and confusing but, as it turns out, crucial for the remainder of the film. Segments five and six continue to privilege Abby to the extent that a

separate character-based sequence can be isolated within the larger opening sequence. Segments five and six provide more information about Abby's life. The extreme close-up of the scars on Abby's wrists, the result of a failed suicide attempt, is followed by the first of a series of subjective segments.

Segment seven, the first appearance of the vision, is crucial. I discuss this segment, as well as its repetitions throughout the film, in greater detail below. Segment eight closes off what can be called the 'Abby sequence', and returns to the previously established pattern. However, segment nine once again shows a shift. Here, the minor character of Russell, Abby's husband, is presented. A client of Russell, Jimmy, is foregrounded. This segment is not only a disruption of the previous pattern, but also initially appears to be superfluous. Nevertheless, within the system of Hollywood narration, any information given, redundant as it may seem, will turn out to be essential to the story. The storyline of Russell and Jimmy is key to the unraveling of the mystery. The opening is closed in segment ten, the moment when David's identity is revealed and, more importantly, where the two central characters of the film, Abby being the other one, converge. This meeting will cause a disturbance of balance, a disturbance that pushes the narrative to the next level.

Thus, the opening sequence of the film functions in a number of ways. It introduces the main characters and provides their backgrounds. In *The Seventh Sign*, Abby takes center stage. The opening sets up a specific configuration among characters. Their relationship is, however, deliberately left patchy: some links are obvious, while others remain opaque. For instance, the character of Father Lucci is featured just once in the opening. His function in the narrative is purposely withheld. The configurative opening thus operates as enigma and catalyst for the film.

This obvious patchiness also points to a possible reading of the film. It can be interpreted as a rather impromptu dissemination of, literally, signs. The sign that takes on prime importance is the sealed letter, recurring in segments one, two, and eight. The letter with the broken seal functions as what Elsaesser and Buckland call 'a privileged image', or 'emblematic cluster': 'a condensation of the various narrative motifs', which implies 'a temporal structure of anticipation and foreshadowing' (Elsaesser and Buckland 2002: 51). Additionally, the sealed letters can also be read as a 'circulating object' among the main characters (Bordwell 2006: 97). David sets the circulation of the letters in motion, Father Lucci finds them along his journey, and Abby breaks one of the seals, unintentionally speeding up their circulation and thus the countdown to the Apocalypse, which will result in the confrontation among the three main characters.

The material letter itself is more than a sign: the letters literally release the apocalyptic signs. Their scattering initially appears to be devoid of system or structure, just as the locations at which the signs are released seem random.[7] Gradually, however, the system is revealed and the narrative is thrust forward by anticipation, more precisely by the countdown. Since each letter corresponds to one of Revelation's apocalyptic signs, the breaking of each seal brings the Apocalypse nearer. Time is running out. Abby's frantic attempts at bringing the signs to a halt will be futile, as David already explained to her early in the film. Desperate, Abby attempts to reverse the thrust by going back one sign in the chain. This is Revelation's fifth seal, which speaks of 'the souls of those who had been slaughtered for the word of God' (Revelation 6.9). As I will argue below, the film translates this seal as the death of the last martyr, Jimmy. However, Jimmy's death— he is sentenced to the gas chamber—cannot be averted. Unsurprisingly, the countdown is brought to a standstill at the last moment and by means of the greatest possible effort, the sacrifice of Abby. The unstoppable sequence of signs needs to be completed; its function in narrative terms needs to be exhausted, as it were. Only then, when there are no more signs that can be stopped or averted, the true destiny of Abby's character can be unveiled. The concluding act should close the causal openness of the narrative. Whether this is actually the case in *The Seventh Sign* is debatable.

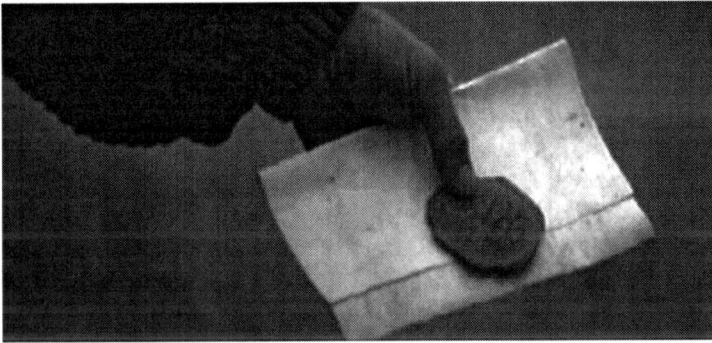

The film's initial enigma of the sealed letters is solved, yet replaced by another one, revolving on the relationship among the three main characters, David, Abby, and Father Lucci. The revelation of the purpose of each character as well as their shared historical connection, a culmination of their past, present, and possible future, takes place in Abby's recurring visions. The visions provide access to a different time and place, where the contemporary characters become visible in their previous incarnations.

7.   As Phil Hardy points out in his review of *The Seventh Sign* in the *Encyclopedia of Horror*, the film seems to suggest that God has pretty much the same foreign policy as, at the time of the film's release, US president Ronald Reagan. In short order, the film shows catastrophe strike Haiti, Iran, Iraq, and Nicaragua.

Referential Characters and Critical Re-Incarnations

Abby's visions are the key to unlocking the enigma of the film. One can argue that the film deals with the threat of the possible end of the world and with the ways in which the main character attempts to avert that end, an argument I will address when I discuss the nature of Abby's sacrifice and martyrdom. However, I argue that the film's narrative is driven by the constellation of the four main characters of the film. Each main character is a representation, or better, *incarnation* of another, historically older, (quasi-) biblical figure. Incarnation refers to the visual presence of imagery that is derived from religious tradition in a culture that defines itself as secular, and to the imagery of Christianity's central concept of (re-)incarnation. The (re)incarnation of predominantly Christian imagery in popular culture is structured by resemblance, resonance, and difference. Resemblance and resonance are deployed in a visual and thematic sense. The third, difference, is the potential analytical outcome of the first two terms and is, in itself, crucial in positioning and clarifying the incarnation in the present context.

As a contemporary visual production, the film reconfigures images, in this case characters, of a past biblical tradition. These contemporary reworkings of the characters could be labeled 'referential characters' (Bal 1997). They are part of an already established frame of reference and 'act according to the pattern that we are familiar with from other sources' (Ball 1997: 121). Or, as Bal is quick to add, they do *not* act according to expectation. Precisely the tension between expectation and realization is fascinating. The faithfulness or accuracy of the characters to their original source is only part of my analysis. Their deviation, hence re-incarnation, is what my analysis seeks to uncover.

The first two characters, Jimmy and David, are marked explicitly as re-incarnations of biblical characters. The latter two, Father Lucci and Abby, are amalgamates of several biblical and extrabiblical traits. Contrary to Jimmy and David, Father Lucci's and Abby's possible biblical intertext is not explicitly acknowledged in the film. Even though he is not a main character, Jimmy plays a pivotal role in the conflict of the film. He is explicitly positioned within the context of Revelation, albeit with an essential deviation. In her quest for the advancement of the seven signs, Abby quickly discovers, or rather interprets, that Jimmy's death represents the fifth seal of Revelation. In Abby's exegesis, Jimmy stands for the souls under the altar: 'When he opened the fifth seal, I saw under the altar the souls of those who had been slaughtered for the word of God and for the testimony they had given' (Revelation 6.9). The link between Bible and film is explicit in that Jimmy is repeatedly called the 'Word of God' killer. Jimmy finds justification for killing his incestuous parents in the Bible (in verses from Leviticus, to be precise).[8] However, the film also invests another meaning into this character. Abby, again based on her own exegesis, calls him 'the last martyr', which could adhere to the source text in that it signals the completion of a particular, yet unspecified, number of souls that will have to be martyred before the return of Christ: 'until the number would be complete' (Revelation 6.11). Yet, Revelation makes no mention of a particular, individual last martyr. The deviation can thus be located in the marked individuality of Jimmy against Revelation's unspecified 'number', a faceless group of martyrs.[9] In addition, the emphasis on Jimmy being the last martyr serves the deadline structure of the film. Unlike Revelation, which often couches its prophecy in shrouded terms, *The Seventh Sign* drives home the idea that the apocalyptic signs are unambiguous in their meaning and relentless in their unfolding.

David is the personification of a returned Christ. However, it takes well into the second act of the film before this is revealed. Until then, the narrative knowingly represents David as a character with dubious intentions. In the opening sequence of the film, the spectator is to infer that his character is in some way connected to the death and destruction he encounters everywhere he goes. Moreover, he has no dialogue, and the nondiegetic soundtrack provides his character with an eerie musical theme. In a crucial scene, he reveals his identity and divine mission to Abby. He cryptically refers to himself as 'the messenger', who was on earth before and now has returned. But an unequivocal statement follows: 'I came as the Lamb and I return a Lion'. This is a direct reference to Revelation: 'Do not weep. See, the Lion of the tribe of Judah, the Root of David, has conquered, so that he can open the scroll and its seven seals' (Revelation 5.5). The final part of this reference stresses David's connection to his biblical counterpart, as it is only David who can open the seals of the letters he disperses on earth. After David has revealed his identity, a panicked Abby tries to stab him but, instead of blood, David's body releases a bright light. He then proclaims: 'Now I am His wrath',

8. The film seems to waver between painting this character with respect and ridicule. What to make of the fact that Jimmy suffers from Down's syndrome? One could read this as an implicit debunking of religious people; that is to say, being a believer equals having a lower than average intelligence. Alternatively, one can read this character as possessing a kind of innocence: he is forthright in his acts and motivations.

9. The complete reference to the martyrs is as follows: 'When he opened the fifth seal, I saw under the altar the souls of those who had been slaughtered for the word of God and for the testimony they had given; they cried out with a loud voice, 'Sovereign Lord, holy and true, how long will it be before you judge and avenge our blood on the inhabitants of the earth?' They were each given a white robe and told to rest a little longer, until the number would be complete both of their fellow servants and of their brothers and sisters, who were soon to be killed as they themselves had been killed' (Rev.6.9-11).

which refers to Revelation 6.16: 'fall on us and hide us from the face of the one seated on the throne and from the wrath of the Lamb'.

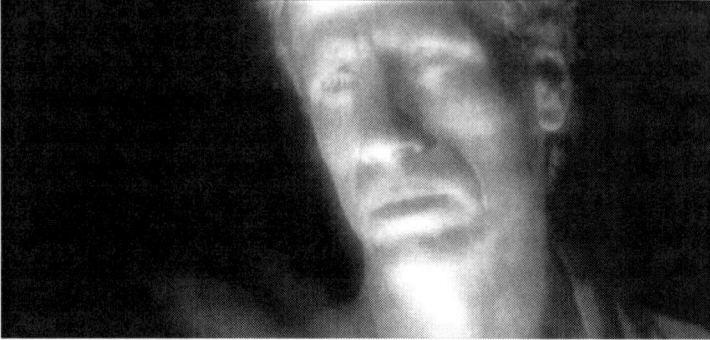

At that moment, a reversal takes place. Whereas in Revelation, the fierce lion turns out to be a lamb, in *The Seventh Sign*, the benevolent lamb is turned into a wrathful lion. In his earlier incarnation, witnessed by Abby in her vision, David functioned as the sacrificial lamb. In the present-day re-incarnation, he sheds his sacrificial cloak to reveal an enraged Christ persona. Crucially, David/Christ refuses to sacrifice his life for a second time and grant humankind another chance. In this resides the re-incarnation of his character: from a sacrificial to a non-sacrificial Christ. Given the fact that David is so emphatically represented as a referential character, Christ, the fact that in the end he does not act accordingly is one of the film's greatest upsets. The implications of this deviation become apparent in my discussion of Abby's martyrdom below.

The character of Father Lucci is another referential character, derived from the legend of the Wandering Jew, as well as a reworking of a biblical character, Cartaphilus, Pontius Pilate's gatekeeper. As Hasan-Rokem and Dundes explain, in the legend Jesus curses the Wandering Jew for his unwillingness to allow a weary, cross-bearing Jesus a moment's temporary respite. He will remain ageless which is why, in some versions of the legend, his name is Longinus, and he will walk the earth until the Second Coming, the return of Jesus (Hasan-Rokem and Dundes 1986: vii). Hasan-Rokem and Dundes also list the reasons for the sustained popularity and countless interpretations of the Wandering Jew legend. They argue that the legend is a 'pivotal reflection of the Jewish-Christian relationships' (Hasan-Rokem and Dundes 1986: vii). Though the story is not common in Jewish tradition, the legend holds an enduring appeal for Christians since it portrays the confrontation between Judaism and Christianity, a confrontation that, according to the Christian interpretation of the legend, results in Judaism voluntarily yielding to Christianity. The legend's apocalyptic undercurrent is important: the Second Coming, Jesus' triumphant return to earth, is the moment when the Wandering Jew's curse will be lifted.

This aspect of the legend is deftly deployed in the plot of *The Seventh Sign*: Father Lucci eagerly awaits the Apocalypse in order to be freed from his plight, and will therefore thwart Abby's attempts to stop the apocalyptic signs.[10] Lucci's earlier incarnation as a Roman officer of Pilate, revealed in Abby's visions, is derived from one particular version of the legend.[11] This version has a biblical source, namely the New Testament Gospel of John (18.19-24). It relates that one of the officers of the High Priest struck Jesus with the palm of his hand.[12] In the film, this particular scene is the climax of Abby's vision, as it reveals father Lucci's true identity by the ring he wears on his hand, as the officer who strikes Jesus/David.

Father Lucci acts as the antagonist, whose objectives are opposed to those of the protagonist, Abby. The question of whether the figure of the Wandering Jew in general should be perceived as 'a villain or a victim', as

10. The Lucci character is emphatically represented as the antagonist to the film's two protagonists, Abby and David. By extension, the Roman Catholic Church, to which Lucci belongs, is also pictured as a power-hungry organization, eagerly awaiting the Apocalypse. The representation of the Roman Catholic Church as an evil institution is a recurring trait of apocalyptic blockbuster cinema (for instance, *End of Days* which features a malevolent, obscure cult of Roman Catholic origin) as well as many interpretations of Revelation which attempt to read it as a blueprint for possible papal plots aimed at world domination. Or, even more bluntly, in common Protestant historicist interpretation, Revelation's Rome is read as a thinly veiled allusion to the Roman Catholic Church and/or the Pope, both of which are regarded as the Antichrist (Newport 2000: 10).

11. For several more detailed versions of the story, see George K. Anderson, *The Legend of the Wandering Jew* (Anderson 1965: 16-21).

12. 'Then the high priest questioned Jesus about his disciples and about his teaching. Jesus answered, 'I have spoken openly to the world; I have always taught in synagogues and in the temple, where all the Jews come together. I have said nothing in secret. Why do you ask me? Ask those who heard what I said to them; they know what I said'. When he had said this, one of the police standing nearby struck Jesus on the face saying, 'Is that how you answer the high priest?' Jesus answered, 'If I have spoken wrongly, testify to the wrong. But if I have spoken rightly, why do you strike me?' Then Annas sent him bound to Caiaphas the high priest'.

Hasan-Rokem and Dundes put it (Hasan-Rokem and Dundes 1986: viii), is not an issue in the film's deployment of this character. After the initial ambiguity of his character is cleared up, he represents the antagonistic force of the narrative. For a long time, the spectator expects father Lucci to be some kind of helper to Abby. That is the impression he gives her when they meet for the first time: 'A priest has come to help you and your baby'. But soon his intentions become clear. Abby merely functions as his deliverance: the birth of her son is the seventh and final sign necessary to bring about the Apocalypse. In his guise as consultant on apocalyptic affairs for the Vatican, a position that allows him to travel all over the world, Lucci deliberately lies to the Pontiff and his counsel about the nature of the occurring signs. Moreover, when an older priest recognizes father Lucci, he has no qualms about killing the man who might reveal his identity.

In this lies the important change the character of the Wandering Jew has undergone. Whereas several versions of the legend emphasize his meekness and his search for peace, patiently awaiting the Second Coming, father Lucci is an active agent in bringing about the return of Christ. This reversal from passive to active character is brought about by the specific context in which the re-incarnation of the Wandering Jew is resituated, namely Hollywood film. A central feature of classical Hollywood storytelling is the presence of protagonistic and antagonistic characters, good guys and bad guys, whose battle shapes the narrative. In *The Seventh Sign*, the spectator's attempt at character definition is constantly thwarted. Already in the opening sequence, the film deliberately suggests that David is the antagonist and father Lucci the helper for the protagonist. This proves to be wrong. Part of the appeal of father Lucci's character lies in this twist from helper to opponent.

The center around which the conflict between Father Lucci, the antagonist, and David, the protagonist, revolves is Abby. Her character is the most difficult one to read as a referential character, or as an incarnation of an earlier figure. In contrast to the other characters in the film, she is never explicitly marked as a biblical or extra-biblical figure. Nevertheless, I do think Abby's character is referential in nature; it is just that Abby's referential frame (or context) is less apparent. My assumption is that Abby is a contemporary manifestation of the extrabiblical character of Seraphia or, by another name, Veronica. This can only be inferred on the basis of the more clear-cut incarnations of the other main characters. The puzzle of Abby's character can only be solved once the other pieces of the puzzle, the other characters, are identified and brought together.

In order to understand the background and plausible inspiration for the Abby character, I turn to the work of the female stigmatic, visionary, and mystic Anne Catherine Emmerich (1774–1824). In his book on the practices of beatification by the Roman Catholic Church, Kenneth Woodward describes the case of Emmerich as particularly notorious. Initially, Woodward explains, Emmerich's life story displays the 'familiar pattern' of a number of female stigmatics. Already at an early age, Catherine experienced visions. After entering a convent, she also began to bleed from the head, hands, feet, and side. Bedridden, she passed much of her time in a state of ecstasy. It was during her ecstasies, however, that Catherine '*traveled back in time* to become a contemporary of Jesus […], experiencing the life and the passion of Jesus as if she were a participant-observer, filling in details not recorded in Sacred Scripture' (Woodward 1991: 180, emphasis added). The similarities between Catherine's visions and Abby's are striking: the element of time travel, their presence as observer during the passion of Jesus, and the additional details of their visions which are absent from canonical sources.

This last aspect requires elaboration. A German poet, Clemens Brentano, recorded Catherine's visions in a book entitled *The Dolorous Passion of Our Lord Jesus Christ after the Meditations of Anne Catherine Emmerich*. Brentano's work consisted of embellishing the visions, stylistically, which makes the visions highly readable to this day, as well as factually, by enhancing them with material taken from other sources such as maps and travel books of the Holy Land (Woodward 1991: 183). The notoriety of the visions stems not only from the obvious doctoring of the texts, resulting in, according to Woodward, 'bogus visions' (Woodward 1991: 184), but also from their fiercely anti-Semitic tenor.[13] Recently, Emmerich's work was the focal point of controversy again, as it was one of the principal sources, in addition to the four Gospels, for Mel Gibson's 2004 film *The Passion of the Christ*.[14] While the influence of Emmerich's visions on Gibson's film is widely known, in the case of *The Seventh Sign* it is more difficult to find support for the thesis that Emmerich's work has been an influence on the screenplay.[15] At best, I argue, its influence is circumstantial.

13. In Zev Garber's book on *The Passion of The Christ*, almost all essays address the malevolent influence of Emmerich's visions on Mel Gibson's film. Emmerich herself is described as 'a teacher of contempt' (Garber 2006: 8), whose visions are 'demented ravings' (Garber 2006: 125). In general, her work is judged as 'mean-spirited' (Garber 2006: 2).

14. The number of books and articles on the film is already enormous. For a good overview of the divergent critical responses the film evoked within an American context, see the article by Caroline Vander Stichele and Todd Penner. Zev Garber's edited volume of articles on the film also has a useful bibliography. In this volume, Penny Wheeler's contribution, 'Gibson at the Crossroads' (13-20), focuses specifically on Gibson's use of Emmerich's *Passion*. In Timothy K. Beal and Tod Linafelt's edited volume, Mark D. Jordan and Kent L. Brintnall note that Gibson's decision to take Emmerich's work as the basis for his film was a good one: 'Emmerich's visions of the Passion are cinematic' (Beal and Linafelt 2006: 81).

15. In fact, screenwriters Clifford and Ellen Green were unhappy with the treatment of their work by director Schultz and had their credits replaced with in-joke names

I focus on two short passages from Emmerich's work which, in my opinion, constitute a link with Abby's character in *The Seventh Sign*. The passages are taken from the thirty-fourth chapter of the Dolorous Passion entitled 'The Veil of Veronica'.[16] In this chapter, the character of Seraphia, who is later christened Veronica, makes her appearance. In the first passage, Seraphia approaches Jesus during his cross carrying procession through the streets of Jerusalem: 'Seraphia had prepared some excellent aromatic wine, which she piously intended to present to our Lord to refresh him on his dolorous way to Calvary' (Emmerich 2003: 162).

The film incorporates Seraphia's offering of wine into Abby's story. The first two visions Abby experiences end abruptly with the sound and image of a jug falling to the floor. The third vision discloses what happens before the jug is dropped. Abby is standing among a crowd of people, who appear to mock her, as she holds the jug. It is unclear what makes her drop the jug and, in the end, flee from the crowd. The following passage is crucial, since its cinematic reworking leads to the junction of the Seraphia story with the legend of the Wandering Jew: 'Both the Pharisees and the guards were greatly exasperated, not only by the sudden halt, but much more by the public testimony of veneration which was thus paid to Jesus, and they revenged themselves by striking and abusing him, while Seraphia returned in haste to her house' (Emmerich 2003: 163).

The film foregrounds the beating of Jesus and positions Cartaphilus/ Father Lucci as the one who strikes Jesus. In this scene, the two characters and the two different stories coalesce. By striking Jesus/David, in response to the momentary halt of the procession caused by Seraphia/Abby's offering of wine, Cartaphilus/Lucci will be cursed to walk the earth forever. The

taken from *North by Northwest* (USA: Alfred Hitchcock, 1959) and *How to Succeed in Business Without Really Trying* (USA: David Swift, 1967). Kim Newman 1988: 339-40.

16. There are numerous editions of *The Dolorous Passion of the Christ* available. I have consulted the 2003 edition. All editions are based on the original work in German, transcribed and edited by Clemens Maria Brentano.

actual enunciation of the curse, the decisive element in all versions of the Wandering Jew legend, is missing from this scene. The film adds a crucial line of dialogue. It is uttered by Cartaphilus as he addresses Seraphia, 'Will you die for him?' It can be interpreted as a threatening proposal: if Seraphia/Abby takes pity on Jesus, she might just as well take his place. The exchange suggests the possibility of Abby replacing Jesus as the one whose voluntary death will save humanity. The question bolsters the relationship between present-day Abby and Father Lucci. It also forms the impetus for the present-day conflict, as the question remained unanswered in the past. This threat, question, or proposition is not fully resolved, and functions as the reason for her traumatic vision of the past, until the present-day Abby decides to respond affirmatively and die to save humankind.

With Abby's self-sacrifice, the preordained future is averted. Her act of martyrdom gives her the agency that she was lacking throughout the film. Abby's initial dependency on the other characters, particularly David and Father Lucci, robbed her character of the agency with which a main character is typically endowed. Rather than actively setting the events in motion, Abby was caught in them. It takes her (and the viewer) some time to figure out what role she is intended to play. This lack of agency points to a paradox or tension between the narrative and the strategies of plot and visual style. As I pointed out in my analysis of the opening of the film, Abby is persistently visually marked as the main protagonist. Not only is she emphatically introduced via a prolonged close-up; she is also the only character to which the viewer has deep subjective access. This leads to the assumption that she will be a driving force in the narrative. Yet, as it turns out, her character is dependant on the other characters, particularly David and Father Lucci. Only at the last moment is she capable of bringing about the decisive turn of events. Her martyr death may not alter the past, but it does change the prophesized future.

Maternal Martyrdom Once More

In *The Seventh Sign*, the savior of humanity is not only fully human, but also female. Since Christ will not die a second time, fate rests with Abby, who is pregnant. The convergence of female martyrdom and maternity is a recurring theme in this study. *The Seventh Sign* offers a final case in point, illustrating the intimate, yet complicated connection between the two. Before I discuss Abby's act that saves the world in more detail, her status as savior of humanity warrants more explanation.

In 'Hollywood and Armageddon: Apocalyptic Themes in Recent Cinematic Representation', Conrad Ostwalt suggests the 'existence of a popular, apocalyptic imagination in contemporary society' (Ostwalt 1995: 55). To tackle this imagination in contemporary film, Ostwalt proposes to read a larger, yet unspecified, body of apocalyptic film along three separate strands: 'films that emphasize character, setting, or plot' (Ostwalt 1995: 56). On the basis of this reading, it is possible to isolate a number of basic *themes* of apocalyptic presentation in popular films.[17]

The fundamental theme Ostwalt unveils in *The Seventh Sign* is 'renewal of the world, yet avoidance of the apocalyptic cataclysm' (Ostwalt 1995: 59). This, Ostwalt argues, amounts to a rigorous rewriting of the traditional Jewish and Christian apocalyptic script, which favors annihilation rather than renewal.[18] In the Hollywood appropriation, the apocalypse is still

---

17. Ostwalt singles out three films for consideration. First, *Pale Rider* (USA: Clint Eastwood, 1985), representing the genre of the Western, is read as an apocalyptic film dominated by character and character development. Second, the Vietnam War film *Apocalypse Now* (USA: Francis Ford Coppola, 1979), Ostwalt argues, uses the apocalyptic setting of the Vietnamese jungle as a kind of Armageddon. Finally, Ostwalt singles out *The Seventh Sign* as an example of an apocalyptic film that emphasizes plot. This willfully separatist reading method, focusing on one particular aspect of a film, character, setting, or plot, strikes me as insufficient. Ostwalt espouses covert assumptions on genre, particularly the Western as the epitome of the conflict between good and evil, and the war film (and the nuclear disaster film) as representations of apocalyptic settings. These are faulty, because they fail to take into account the fact that the good versus evil theme is played out in most Hollywood films and in every genre. Most Hollywood films are mixtures of genres. This is where Ostwalt's categorization becomes problematic. A film such as *The Seventh Sign*, which determinedly eludes straightforward genre classification, is reduced to plot. More problematic is Ostwalt's self-imposed tunnel vision. The analysis of film as a visual medium involves strict attention not only to characters or plot, but also the relationship of characters to their setting. This type of analysis, mise-en-scene analysis, reads the tension or congruence between characters, setting, and the technologies of the filmic image. By intentionally separating the two, no more than a one-dimensional reading can be made.

18. In an article in the *Journal of Religion and Film*, Mary Ann Beavis analyses and classifies the ways in which the Bible has been used in horror film. The use of the Bible, specifically in horror films, she argues, should not surprise anyone, since the Bible is 'one of the great repositories of supernatural lore' (Beavis 2003). Yet, the connection between horror film and the Bible has not been subject to systematic study. The work of Adele Reinhartz is one of the few explorations of the role of biblical narrative in the plot structure of Hollywood film (2003). Beavis distinguishes five recurring manifestations of the Bible in horror film. The most important one is the use of the Bible as the source of apocalyptic plots. Beavis calls this the representation of the 'Bible as Horror' and states that, in the vast majority of this type of film, the Bible is 'the alleged source of lurid and horrific storylines'. Despite her own evident disapproval of apocalyptic film, mainly on the grounds of those films' incorrect or distorted use of scripture, she accurately observes the ways in which 'apocalyptic timetables derived from the prophetic and apocalyptic books of the Bible structure the plot'. *The Seventh Sign* is singled out by Beavis as a positive example of the apocalyptic genre. The film is 'creative and original in its use of the Bible, which is interpreted through the lens of Jewish folklore regarding the pre-existence of souls'. Unfortunately, Beavis' vital remark that the Bible structures this type of film is not

characterized by the destruction of evil forces; yet, the destruction of the world and the ensuing materialization of a new heaven and a new earth (Revelation 21.1) are preempted. As a result, the suspense of those films lies not so much in the impending end of the world itself as in the expectation that the end can be avoided. Another characteristic of this theme is that the power to deflect the end does not rest with God, but with an unlikely human agent.[19] As Ostwalt argues: 'The modern apocalyptic imagination removes the end of time from the sacred realm of the gods and places the apocalypse firmly in the grasp and control of humanity' (Ostwalt 1995: 63).

In the case of *The Seventh Sign*, a pregnant housewife from California represents humanity. It is up to her to stop the final countdown. In Abby's hands rests the responsibility to overcome the chaos of the Apocalypse and to ultimately stop the end. The transfer of divine power into human hands is, Ostwalt claims, what 'allows the apocalyptic message to remain meaningful for modern and secular society' (Ostwalt 1995: 63). To this I would add the importance of martyrdom to the contemporary reconfiguration of apocalyptic discourse. The shift of power from a celestial authority to a human agent is not enough; with that power comes the martyrlike commitment to die. The former is dependent on or even a condition of the latter. As all my cases make clear, saving the world comes at the cost of losing a life. One cannot save the world and get away with it unscathed, Hollywood seems to imply.

Abby's moment of martyrdom takes place in hospital, where she is not only suffering from a nearly lethal gunshot wound, but is also on the verge of giving birth to her much anticipated child. Here, contrary to *Alien3* and *The Rapture*, motherhood is fully and emphatically embraced. Abby giving birth to her son under extreme circumstances is the *condition sine qua non* for her martyrdom.[20] Her determination to fulfill the motherly task of giving birth

taken up in the remainder of her analysis. Perhaps part of the problem is the vagueness of the word 'structure' itself, which could pertain to thematic structure, as in the set of themes the film develops, narrative structure exemplified in, for instance, a three act structure, or even the aesthetic, visual structure of the film, which could be editing.

19. Hal Hartley's film *The Book of Life* (1998) presents Jesus as the human agent who has to bring about, rather than prevent, the Apocalypse. He displays a mixture of divine and human agency. He is sent to Earth by his father to perform the final judgment. However, Jesus has strong doubts about unleashing the Apocalypse. Finally, he decides to go against his father's divine will and grant humanity one more chance. God the father is relentless, whereas His son, the human representative Jesus, is all too human and, therefore, the film seems to suggest, unable and unwilling to judge mankind according to God's divine scheme.

20. Here it is useful to call to mind the relationship between childbirth and martyrdom in the story of Perpetua and Felicitas. First, according to Roman law, pregnant women could not be sentenced to death, hence to martyrdom. Both women gave birth to their children before they were martyred. Even more so, both women explicitly expressed their relief and gratitude for having given birth before their martyrdom. After this,

to a healthy and living child at all cost, even if it means she herself will not survive, constitutes her as a martyr.

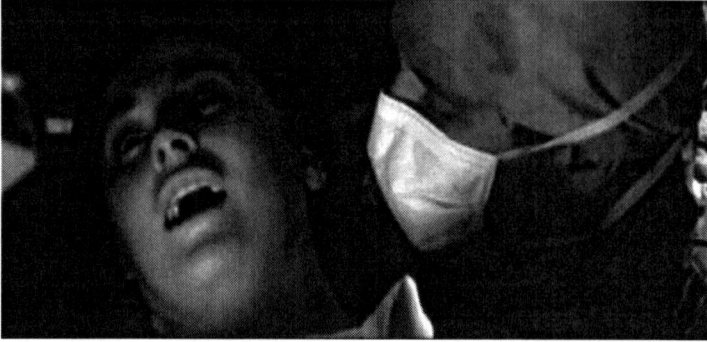

Abby's maternal martyrdom displays parallels with the other cases in this study, while adding new characteristics to female martyrdom. The figure of Revelation's woman clothed with the sun is the most evident source for Abby. Revelation 12.2 describes the physical state of the woman clothed with the sun: 'She was pregnant and was crying out in birthpangs, in the agony of giving birth'. Abby's troubled history of pregnancy and the pain she has to suffer during childbirth echoes the woman clothed with the sun's physical predicament. Revelation 12.5-6 speaks of the fate of both the child and its mother: 'And she gave birth to a son, a male child, who is to rule all the nations with a rod of iron. But her child was snatched away and taken to God and to his throne; and the woman fled into the wilderness, where she has a place prepared by God, so that there she can be nourished for one thousand and two hundred sixty days'.

In the previous chapter, I gave several interpretations of the woman clothed with the sun and read her through *The Rapture*'s Sharon. I concluded that both female figures share a number of characteristics. They give birth to a child who is taken away from them, their role in the narrative decreases after they have given birth to their children, and both are denied access to the realm of the chosen ones, yet ultimately, Sharon's fate, being denied an afterlife with God, is worse than that of the woman clothed with the sun. Similar to Sharon, I want to read Abby through the woman clothed with the sun. The similarities and differences between the two indicate Abby's specific maternal martyrdom.

nothing stood in their way to attaining martyrdom. As Castelli puts it: 'Her [Perpetua] relief when the baby is gone from the prison is double-edged—no longer required to claim the maternal role nor to worry over the well-being of the infant, she experiences the prison transformed for her into a palace [...]. Eventually, the renunciation of motherhood will liberate her, not only emotionally, but also physically from the ties that have bound her to her family, society, and the world' (Castelli 2004: 87).

I begin with the status of Abby's newborn son. Unlike its counterpart in Revelation, the boy is not 'snatched away' and taken to heaven. He is alive and well, and is handed over to his earthly father, Russell. This leads me to conclude that, again, unlike the child in Revelation, this child has no celestial status. Abby's son is not a Jesus figure reincarnated. As I argue below, this has consequences for Abby's role as a martyr. For Abby to become a martyr, she must sacrifice her life. This is the main difference between her and the woman clothed with the sun. Although the latter is literally chased from the text of Revelation, she does survive. Abby does not survive the agony of childbirth. Yet, it is death that grants her the status of a martyr. Moreover, as I will argue in the final section of this chapter, Abby's death is explicitly commemorated in a written text, which solidifies her martyrdom. This brief comparison between the woman clothed with the sun and Abby leads me to conclude that Abby's death during childbirth makes her a martyr, whereas the woman clothed with the sun's survival of a painful childbirth and persecution by Satan renders her powerless, relegated to the margins of the story.

The woman clothed with the sun is the template for Sharon as well as Abby; yet, where the woman clothed with the sun is relegated to the sidelines of Revelation and Sharon's ill-conceived martyrdom fails, Abby's martyrdom succeeds. Abby gives the world her only son. Significantly, his life signals a new hope. The film's inverted play on the divine Father and Son figures cannot be misread. Whereas Christ's *death* signals hope, in *The Seventh Sign*, it is the nameless boy's *life* that constitutes a new beginning. As I noted above, Christ, in the re-incarnation of David, refuses his sacrificial undertaking, a role that is taken over by Abby. The full implications of his refusal and her acceptance are now clear. Abby replaces Christ in his sacrificial death. She does not give birth to the new Christ, she herself is the new Christ. As such, she is a remarkable example of the classic martyr's ideal of *imitatio mortis Christi*.

Moreover, the sacrifice does not stop there: her martyrdom consists of giving up a life and giving (birth to) a life at the same time. Abby's death and her son's life are indivisible. In this sense, Abby's martyrdom is twofold. Not only does it constitute a selfless act of motherly love, but also the result of this act is beneficial to all mankind. It harbors no negative implications, contrary to both Ripley's act in *Alien3*, which results in the extermination of both human and alien, and Sharon's cruelly misguided infanticide in *The Rapture*. In this lies the purity and simplicity of Abby's act: it is a gift that keeps giving. Not only have the signs of the end been stopped, but also Abby's death has resulted in the filling up of the Hall of Souls, bringing about a second chance for humanity. In this respect, *The Seventh Sign* improves on its source text Revelation not unlike Jericho's martyrdom in *End of Days*, by granting the mother figure the status of martyr. Abby's death is not the end of the film. In a final twist, the film's ending refers back to the beginning.

Endings: The Suspension of The End

Ending a film, like beginning one, is an essential part of constructing a narrative. Simple as this may seem, when dealing with films influenced by apocalyptic imagery and end-of-the-world scenarios such as *Armageddon*, *The Rapture*, *End of Days*, and *The Seventh Sign*, an ending is never just an ending.[21] One of the major characteristics of Hollywood's reworking of apocalypse is the paradoxical desire to bring about the end while, at the same time, that apocalyptical end must be deferred at all cost. Abby saves mankind from extinction with a sacrificial act, which gives new hope. As such, *The Seventh Sign* is an excellent example of modern apocalypse, which removes the end of time from the holy realm of the gods and 'places the apocalypse firmly in the grasp and control of humanity' (Ostwalt 1995: 63).

However, there is something more to be said about the ending of the film. The self-reflexivity of the film is apparent in the final dialogue between David and Avi. The character of Avi has, by and large, gone unnoticed. Abby meets him when she visits a rabbi for help. Avi volunteers to help Abby with the translation of several of David's writings that she has stolen from his desk. It is possible that this character, similar to the others, stands for another, older character. Indeed, Avi can be read as an incarnation of John, the narrator/writer who has witnessed the Apocalypse and is urged by God to give witness and write it down. In the closing dialogue of the film, God, personified by David, tells Avi: 'Remember it all, write it down. Tell it. So people will use the chance she has given them'. Avi must provide the world with a record, which will function as a cautionary tale for future generations. Although David and Avi were witnesses to Abby's act of martyrdom, Avi is given the divine task of giving testimony to this act of self-sacrifice. In this sense, the film is self-conscious as a film text, as well as of its biblical source text, Revelation, which ends in a similar self-reflexive manner: 'Write this, for these words are trustworthy and true' (Revelation 21.5).

21. For a detailed account of the several degrees of closure in Hollywood cinema, see Richard Neupert's *The End: Narration and Closure in the Cinema*. According to Neupert's classification, *The Seventh Sign* is an example of the classical closed text film (Neupert 1995: 35-74), since it displays a secure ending and also satisfies conventional demands for unity and resolution. Moreover, the closed text film is characterized by an emphasis on character action and carefully limited time and space. Finally, the ending of a closed text film works toward a completion of the multiple, parallel plotlines.

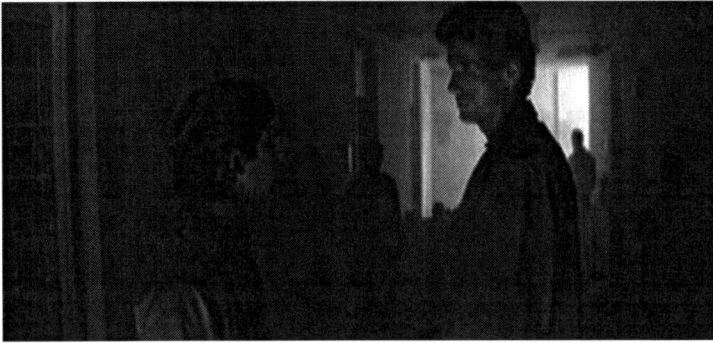

With this ending of the film in mind, I want to take one more look at the opening of the film and put forward the following hypothesis. The opening of the film can be interpreted as Avi's narration of the story. By positioning Avi in the role of narrator, the incongruous opening sequence can be explained. My analysis of the opening uncovered an emphasis placed on Abby. I argued that this emphasis is remarkable since, up to the final sequence of the film, this character has a limited amount of agency. Abby's actions and motivations are dependant on other characters, namely, David and Father Lucci. However, if we conceive Avi as the narrator, Abby's special status in the narration, via deep, subjective access, notably through her visions, can be interpreted differently. The narrator is 'omniscient': he knows of Abby's pivotal role in the narrative well before the spectator does. This knowledge is withheld; yet, the narration already hints at Abby's special status. The use of crosscutting and the superimposed markers of time and place exemplify omniscient, because retrospective, narration. If we imagine Avi to be the narrator, the opening sequence is cast in a different light. The film's perspective can be attributed to a concealed narrator, whose acts of structuring the narrative only become apparent at the end of the film. In this sense, the opening sequence shows that the ending of the film is already located in the beginning. Or, to understand the beginning, it must be seen in light of the end. The end influences the beginning, but this influence only becomes clear retrospectively. This element of *The Seventh Sign* as a retrospective narrative deserves more elaboration.

In his book, *Apocalypse Recalled: The Book of Revelation after Christendom*, Harry O. Maier discusses the narrative voice of Revelation. He argues that Revelation is a retrospective narrative: 'John stands at the end of his Apocalypse looking back' (Maier 2002: 18). This narration seems impossible, since it is retrospective; it is performed after the Apocalypse. The narrator tells the story from outside history. This retrospective stance gives the narrator complete mastery over the story. The narration can be slowed down, sped up, and it can leap forward and backward into time. This is what Maier calls 'John's games with time' (Maier 2002: 18). The retrospective perspective is, Maier emphasizes, not nostalgic or a 'trip down memory lane' (Maier 2002: 19). The narrative is driven by a sense of urgency; the recollection of the past not only invests this past with new significance and relevance, but also strives to make the past part of the present.

Avi, like John, tells the story retrospectively. As an omniscient narrator, he is able to play games with time—and this is what the film adds—with place. The visions of Abby, gradually presented, are the most intricate examples of this play on time and place. Here, similar to John's account of past events in Revelation, the emphasis is on the relevance of the past to the present. At the end, the narrator is revealed. The spectator catches up with him in a time closer to the present, when the narrator is given his divine task. This task, to remember the events and write them down, leads the story and its significance into the future, as a warning to future generations.

Ultimately, Maier argues, Revelation is not so much 'a tale of inevitable ending', but an account that situates both itself and its addressees in the present. The apocalyptic game played with the past and the future strives to invest the present with renewed significance. This optimistic assessment of apocalyptic narratives is preposterously foregrounded in *The Seventh Sign* which, in the end, propagates the notion of the restoration of hope, the new beginning, and the second chance mankind has been given.

Conclusion

In this chapter, I have taken the visions of Abby as the starting point of my analysis. The concept of the vision resonates in both a religious sense and a cinematic sense. In *The Seventh Sign*, the religious and the cinematic meaning of the vision come together. When viewed from a cinematic point of view, the visions are not straightforward, so I began my analysis with the question of how to label these disruptions of causal temporality. Initially, the vision manifests itself as a dream. Yet, this hypothesis turns out to be untenable, since Abby experiences a number of visions and several of them present themselves to her while she is fully conscious. Moreover, the content of the visions supersedes the dream: they are set in a time and a place in the distant past, while the message of the vision pertains to an unknown future.

An important aspect of Abby's visions is the presence of the film's other characters in them. In the second section of the chapter, I looked at the opening sequence of the film and to the way in which it introduces the characters and sets out the relationships among them. The purposely puzzling relationships and connections among the characters, stylistically conveyed through the use of crosscutting, provide the film with an enigma that sets the narrative in motion. The enigma of the film, I argued in the third section, is solved once we become aware of the fact that each character is an incarnation of a historically older, (quasi-) biblical figure. I deployed

Bal's notion of the referential character to read Jimmy, David, Father Lucci, and Abby. My analyses focused on evaluating to what extent the characters are faithful to their original source or, in contrast, re-envision this source. The ways in which they deviate from their established frame of reference, and are thus reworkings or re-incarnations, of the earlier source, leads to a more productive reading. In the case of Abby, a referential reading was the most difficult one to perform. Once I established that she can be considered a reworking of Seraphia, I inquired into the way in which Abby deviates from her template. The difference between Seraphia and Abby—the former was a bystander at the beating of Jesus, while Abby actively replaces Jesus—is played out in the final act of the film, where Abby's martyrdom takes place.

The Seventh Sign offers the final case of the connection between female martyrdom and maternity. I outlined Ostwalt's analysis of contemporary apocalyptic narratives, which postulates that the end of the world can be deflected by the sacrificial intervention of a human agent. Crucially, Abby can be the savior of humanity by virtue of, not despite, her femininity. Abby giving birth to her son constitutes the essence of her martyrdom. The motif of pregnancy exposed an obvious parallel between Abby and Revelation's woman clothed with sun. My reading of the woman clothed with the sun through her successor Abby confirmed this character's tragic fate. She gives birth to the savior, but is forgotten. Her contemporary reincarnation, Abby, conversely, succeeds where the precedent fails. Abby's act of childbirth saves humanity, but entails a heavy price. Remarkably, her death solidifies her commemoration as a martyr. Abby replaces Jesus, constituting a perfect *imitatio mortis Christi*. Moreover, the maternal facet of her martyrdom offers an additional benefit: she gives her own life while she gives a new life. This is a feat even Jesus was not able to pull off.

Finally, I addressed the ending of the film. *The Seventh Sign* adheres to the paradoxical paradigm established in Hollywood cinema, which dictates the advent of an ostensibly inevitable Apocalypse, only to have that Apocalypse averted at the last minute. I ventured a reading that posits the character of Avi as a reincarnation of John of Patmos, the assumed recipient of the revelation who wrote down his vision in the Book of Revelation. Reading the film as an act of retrospective narration sheds new light on the puzzling opening sequence of the film. Moreover, the shared narrative structure connects the film to its biblical predecessor. In the end, the film's message supersedes Revelation's tale of horror. In *The Seventh Sign*, the averted Apocalypse results in a restoration of hope. The birth of Abby's son signals renewal by the sacrificial act of giving, in both senses, instead of taking a life.

CONCLUSION

Understanding our past determines actively our ability to understand the present.

The Da Vinci Code (USA: Ron Howard, 2006).

Introduction

The central word in the epigraph of this conclusion is 'actively'. It points to the reciprocal relationship between the past and the present, and it demonstrates that to be an inexorable process. Because the present is in constant flux, the past is never stable either. To a certain extent, the quote illustrates the leading notion of my study, preposterous history. Yet here, the emphasis is still on the dominating influence of the past over the present, a notion that preposterous history seeks to undercut. I took this quote from a lecture by Professor Langdon, a fictional character. Tom Hanks plays the professor of religious symbology, who unwillingly becomes a hero in the blockbuster *The Da Vinci Code*, the film adaptation of Dan Brown's 2003 bestseller about the uncovering of Western culture's greatest mystery, the secret of the Holy Grail.

The film opens with Langdon's lecture on the language of symbols and how to read an image. Standing in front of a huge screen, which projects pictures of seemingly familiar symbols, Langdon quizzes his rapt audience, daring them to interpret them. He presents a detail, a close-up of a larger image, of a white mask and robe, which triggers the immediate response of 'racism' and 'Ku Klux Klan'. Zooming out, he reveals the men wearing the garments to be Spanish priests.

In this opening scene, the film conveys a number of issues that figure prominently in this study. In just under two minutes, Langdon's lecture teaches the audience a number of lessons. The interpretation of the symbol, the reading of the image, is dependent on many factors. The symbol is always situated in a particular context, often dependent on the person looking at the symbol. By zooming in or out, particular details are either revealed or obscured. Time plays a vital role in interpreting the image. Hence, one must trace back the influence of the past on the present. Most of all, Langdon impresses on us spectators that one should never be so arrogant as to assume that one knows for sure what one is looking at. The meaning of an image, the story it tells, is ever constructed and re-constructed. As Langdon puts it, 'As the saying goes, a picture says a thousand words, but which words?'

I subscribe to Langdon's observation. As I hope to have demonstrated, the powerful images that this study takes as its subject certainly cannot be conveyed in a mere thousand words. After four years of working on them, I am still not certain what these images signify. I do know that the context in which these images appear, Hollywood film, plays an important part in reading them. In what follows, I will briefly outline the most significant findings of this study.

Preposterous history seeks to escape the dominating influence of the past over the present. The past only partially determines our interpretation of an image or object. The present text is always an intervention in the earlier material and, hence, changes the preceding text. My reading of *End of Days* demonstrates history's ability to change the perception of the antecedent text. Revelation is the historical source for the film. However, the film transcends its status as a cinematic adaptation of Revelation. It actively affects Revelation as well. This reversal of influence is brought about by the presence of Arnold Schwarzenegger, whose character I have interpreted as a reincarnation of archangel Michael on one hand, and as a manifestation of Christ on the other. Whereas the juxtaposing of the images of Michael and Schwarzenegger results in an augmentation of the biblical figure, the preposterous collision between Schwarzenegger and Christ uncovers the uncompromising nature of the Christ figure in Revelation. The film improves on its source text by emphasizing the sacrificial nature of Schwarzenegger's martyrdom in favor of Revelation's vengeful violence.

The interpretive range of a preposterous approach to history is suggested by the two final chapters of this study. In these chapters, I understand their female protagonists, Sharon and Abby, in relation to the same biblical predecessor, the woman clothed with the sun. The results of both readings, though, differ dramatically. In *The Seventh Sign*, Abby emerges triumphant. Though she dies during childbirth, her death grants her the status of martyr. She will be actively commemorated, contrary to the woman clothed with the sun, who is relegated to the sidelines of the biblical text, and whose fate is uncertain. Sharon's fate, however, is even worse than that of the woman clothed with the sun. She is denied an afterlife with her loved ones in heaven. Using the same template, these two cases result in different contemporary reincarnations. Reading and viewing from the present back to the past not only uncovers numerous connections, but also indicates the influence of the present on our interpretation of the past. With regard to *The Rapture*, I argued that reading Sharon in tandem with the woman clothed with the sun resulted in a radical interpretation of Revelation. Whereas Revelation leaves open a possible afterlife for its female figure, the film closes the book indefinitely on a possible afterlife for Sharon.

My study attempted to be interdisciplinary in nature. I have emphasized that a mere encounter between two disciplines, film studies and religious studies, does not automatically turn this meeting into an interdisciplinary project. It takes more than the expansion of a certain topic or analytical tool to a neighboring discipline. At several points in this study, I have criticized existing studies that situate themselves between film and religion. From my position as a film scholar, I have critically assessed several studies by scholars of the Bible and religion into the field of film. My main contention was that these studies lack an engagement with the medium of film. Since, as a film studies specialist, I ventured into the field of religion studies, I was careful not to make the same mistake. I have tried to the best of my ability to engage with the biblical and extra-biblical sources that influence the images of this study. This engagement is expressed by taking them seriously as predecessors; yet, as preposterous history suggests, they should not be taken for granted as unchangeable sources. Given my background, the analysis of film has taken center stage. Yet, as I hoped to have shown, my engagement with religious studies has significantly enriched my analysis of the films. Conversely, I hope that my readings of the films, specifically in their themes of Apocalypse and martyrdom, add to the existing interpretations of these themes in religious studies. Before I deal with those themes in more detail, I want to point out the importance of shared concepts, which resonate in the encounter between film studies and religious studies.

The recurring concept of the vision interconnects the religious and cinematic discourses. The two come together in the vision of the martyr. Classic martyr stories almost invariably mention the occurrence of a vision before the death of the martyr. This detail is also consistently deployed in contemporary and secular representations of martyrdom. Jericho Cane in *End of Days* has a vision of his family in his moment of death. Harry Stamper's particular vision was the focal point of my analysis of the finale of *Armageddon*. In the case of Ripley, the occurrence of a vision is more difficult to determine. However, I have argued that the eventual death of Ripley was already foreshadowed in a vision or nightmare she had in the second part of the trilogy. In *The Rapture*, Sharon has a crucial vision, in which she sees her deceased husband Randy. This vision leads her and her daughter into the desert. Finally, the recurring visions of Abby in *The Seventh Sign* reveal the core of her martyrdom. The crucial difference between classic and contemporary martyr visions is that the classic vision usually pertains to the idea that the martyr will be united with God in heaven, as part of his or her reward. The contemporary vision concerns the reunion of the martyr with his or her family, not with God in heaven. The earthly family is favored over the divine, celestial one.

The Hollywood appropriation of martyrdom situates it in the larger context of the redemption of humankind. Rather than attest to his or her faith through death, the Hollywood martyr sacrifices his or her life in order to save the whole of humanity. However, if one looks more carefully, saving mankind only serves as a pretext for the redemption of the martyr's nearest family. Contrary to classical conceptions of martyrdom, which confine the act within the limited definition of a willingness to die for one's belief, Hollywood's reworking of martyrdom is connected to the reconciliation and continuation of the family.[1] The first aspect, reconciliation, is a more common motivation for martyrdom. As I have shown in my analysis of *End of Days*, the impetus as well as reward for Jericho Cane's death is the reunion with his deceased wife and daughter in the afterlife. For Harry Stamper's martyrdom in *Armageddon*, the continuation of the family is also an important feature of secular representations of martyrdom. The continuation of the family in the here and now, as opposed to the notion of reconciliation in the afterlife, figures prominently. Stamper takes on the role of a martyr to exempt his future son-in-law from this mission. As a result, the future of his daughter (and mankind, of course) is safeguarded. In *The Seventh Sign*, a similar motif comes to the fore: Abby dies so her child may live. Her death can be read as another example within this diverse arrangement of motivations for martyrdom. Her death seems close to Stamper's act in *Armageddon* in that it secures the future of her family. The bloodline of Abby is secured through the son. Moreover, it is not difficult to see Abby's sacrifice in relation to Ripley's fate, albeit with the opposite intention and result. Ripley's martyrdom in *Alien3* has the reverse objective: her death certifies that there is no survival of the alien to which she has given birth. This effectively cuts the bloodline and a potentially lethal miscegenation between human and non-human, alien other. The monstrous and lethal birth of the alien leads up to Ripley's self-sacrifice. The female function of pregnancy and childbirth uncovered a decisive difference between male and female martyrdom.

In addition, the act of the martyr leads to the redemption and confirmation of his or her individualism. Rather than demonstrating his loyalty to a particular group or collective, the Hollywood martyr is predominantly a heroic individual. The would-be martyrs are initially represented as improbable heroes, ranging from an alcoholic ex-cop to a pregnant housewife. Eventually, though, they overcome their assorted weaknesses and save the world. The crucial exception to this is Sharon. *The Rapture* offers a more extreme variation on the motif of dying for one's family. Sharon's, and more specifically Mary's, desire to join Randy in heaven lead

---

1. Perhaps not surprisingly, this motif can be read back to classical Greek literature, where it is an important theme. Van Henten gives the example of the *Heraclydae*, in which Euripides recounts how Heracles' daughter Macaria saves the lives of her brothers and sisters by her own death (Van Henten 1997: 158).

to Mary's death. Unfortunately, the reunion of the family is an incomplete one, since Sharon's sacrificial act results in her own apostasy. In the end, the film presents the viewer a bleak picture: Sharon stubbornly refuses to become a martyr, to surrender herself to God in order to be raptured and thus saved. What is more, Sharon refuses to save herself, let alone do what Hollywood expects its martyrs to do: save the world.

The films in this study deal with the martyr's act of self-sacrifice through which the Apocalypse is averted and the world is saved. The individual act of martyrdom prevents the Apocalypse. This is perhaps the most paradoxical result of this study, which so emphatically concerns itself with the representations of the Apocalypse: the end does not take place and remains unrepresented. As my choice of films suggests, the Apocalypse can come in many shapes and sizes. In the first film, *End of Days*, the potential reign of Satan will inaugurate the Apocalypse. In the following two films, *Armageddon* and *Alien3*, the Apocalypse takes on the shape of a natural threat in the guise of meteorite and the biological disaster of miscegenation. The final two films, *The Rapture* and *The Seventh Sign*, come closest to a representation of the apocalyptic signs and the Apocalypse as described in the Book of Revelation. But eventually, these films also refuse to render the ultimate end. Part of the reluctance to represent the Apocalypse, I suggest, lies in the impossibility of imagining such an event, let alone represent it cinematographically. Revelation speaks of the horrors of the Apocalypse in cryptic and elaborate language. *The Rapture* bravely attempts to offer a biblically accurate representation which is, paradoxically, hampered by a technical flaw in cinematography. This led me to conclude that the most technologically advanced medium of the visual arts is incongruously incompetent for representing the end of time.

Instead, these films use the narrative structure of Revelation, with its repetitive, serial structure of 'countdown' signs, as the catalyst and accelerator of their narratives. This is expressed in the deadline structure of these narratives. The films all thrive on the narrative of impending apocalypse, the dread that the end is near, only to have that end cancelled at the very last minute. I called this the paradox of apocalyptic anticipation followed by cancellation. The films desire and prophesize an end, but thrive on the postponement of that end. Hence, this study's central theme of the end can best be described as an evaded end, however eagerly anticipated it may be.

I want to end my conclusion with some remarks on the aspect of gender. In the introduction, I claimed I would deploy a critical gender approach as an analytical tool, as a lens through which the two themes would be read. Along the way, it became obvious to me that gender was more than an analytical or ideological stance; it became more and more prominent as a theme in its own right. The notion of female martyrdom, discussed in relation to *Alien3*, *The Rapture*, and *The Seventh Sign*, signaled the emergence of gender as a crucial theme in this study. Female martyrdom was distinguished from male martyrdom from the beginning of this study. I wanted to deal with male and female martyrs separately though, initially, I had no obvious reason to do so. Doing so, however, I was confronted with the effect of gender on discourses on martyrdom. Classic discourse suggests that men and women can both be martyrs; yet, the act of martyrdom is often described in masculine terms of physical and mental strength. It is no coincidence that the first two chapters on male martyrdom feature films in which arguably, Hollywood's most masculine men are the stars. As I argued, the representation of male martyrdom in the shape of Arnold Schwarzenegger and Bruce Willis, echoes the classic martyr stories of pain, strength, self-sacrifice, and endurance. Only when the focus is shifted toward female martyrdom, the discourse becomes unstable. The case of Ripley served as the turning point in my discussion. Her 'musculinity' actively questions and undercuts a straightforward dichotomy between masculinity and femininity.

The connection between gender and martyrdom is further expressed through the notion of motherly love. The three cases of female martyrdom in this study are intricately related to one another in their representation of motherly love. *The Seventh Sign* displays the purest representation of motherly love as a form of martyrdom. When compared to Ripley and Sharon, Abby's martyrdom holds no negative implications. The mother becomes a martyr precisely because she makes the ultimate maternal sacrifice: she dies so that her newborn child may live. This act constitutes the pinnacle of motherly love. Contrary to Ripley and Sharon, Abby is capable of embracing *both* motherhood and self-sacrificial martyrdom. Her martyrdom connects childbirth with hope. Instead of taking a life, Abby gives a life. This has implications for the larger martyrdom discourse. Martyrdom originates from the negative consequence of the act of giving, giving a life, sacrificing a life, meaning death. Yet here, the act is invested with positive connotations: Abby's death enables the emergence of a life and the forestalling of the Apocalypse.

My reading of Ripley in *Alien3* focused on the connection of this cinematic heroine to the early Christian martyr Perpetua. The link between these two figures is situated in their negation of motherhood. Their repudiation of the female reproductive function comes to serve as a condition for martyrdom. Their cases both point to the impossibility of taking on the role of the mother and the martyr simultaneously. Their martyrdom entails a decision: one can either be a mother or a martyr, but combining the two roles is impossible. Ripley also reaches the status of martyr by renouncing her motherly function, and thus effectively transcends her gender-based position.

Finally, Sharon's case in *The Rapture* is, again, more complicated. Her murder of her daughter should also be interpreted as an act of supreme motherly love, though it does not grant her the status of martyr, at least not in the eyes of God. Quite to the contrary, she becomes a failed martyr in that her act is not recognized as one of love and sacrifice. She, it could be argued, is neither a good mother nor a successful martyr. Infanticide is in no case a characteristic trait of motherhood and Sharon's subsequent desertion of her belief in God makes her unfit for martyrdom, despite her initial best intentions.

The Rapture has proven to be the exceptional case in my study. It consistently resisted the categories of Apocalypse and martyrdom I drew up. Sharon is a failed martyr precisely because she steadfastly refuses to surrender her belief. Her refusal would be a prime example of the martyr's will power. Unfortunately, her will power does not grant her access to the realm of the chosen ones. Her act goes unnoticed, she is left all alone, and her act goes unrewarded. *The Rapture* also breaks the rule of apocalyptic unrepresentability. Doing so, it not only shows the limits of a cinematic representation of the Apocalypse, but also it reveals, in a more general sense that, for the Apocalypse to enjoy enduring power, it must remain shrouded in the uncertainty of whether or not it will take place. In this sense, the film is an Apocalypse in itself: it unveils and reveals something that was hidden, or at least shrouded in mystery before. However, the effect of this *apokalyptein* is disappointing, the Apocalypse turns out to be little more than eternal darkness.

WORKS CITED

Allen, Robert C., and Douglas Gomery
    1985   *Film History: Theory and Practice* (New York: McGraw).
Altman, Rick
    1995   'A Semantic/Syntactic Approach to Film Genre', in *Film Genre Reader 2* (ed. Barry Keith Grant; Austin: University of Texas Press): 26-40.
    1999   *Film/Genre* (London: BFI).
Anderson, George K.
    1965   *The Legend of the Wandering Jew* (Providence: Brown University Press).
Andrews, Nigel
    2003   *True Myths: The Life and Times of Arnold Schwarzenegger* (New York: Bloomsbury).
Arroyo, José
    2000   *Action/Spectacle: A Sight and Sound Reader* (London: BFI).
Aune, David E.
    1986   'The Apocalypse of John and the Problem of Genre', *Semeia 36: Early Christian Apocalypticism: Genre and Social Setting*: 65-96.
    1998   'Revelation 6–16', *Word Biblical Commentary* 52b: 357-903.
Bal, Mieke
    1987   *Lethal Love: Feminist Literary Readings of Biblical Love Stories* (Bloomington: Indiana University Press).
    1988   *Murder and Difference: Gender, Genre, and Scholarship on Sisera's Death* (Bloomington: Indiana University Press).
    1997   *Narratology: Introduction to the Theory of the Narrative* (Toronto: University of Toronto Press, 2nd edn).
    1991a   *On Story-Telling: Essays in Narratology* (Sonoma: Polebridge Press).
    1991b   *Reading Rembrandt: Beyond the Word-Image Opposition* (Cambridge: Cambridge University Press).
    1999   *Quoting Caravaggio: Contemporary Art, Preposterous History* (Chicago: University of Chicago Press).
    2002   *Travelling Concepts in the Humanities: A Rough Guide* (Toronto: University of Toronto Press).
Barkun, Michael
    1994   *Religion and the Racist Right: The Origins of the Christian Identity Movement* (Chapel Hill: University of North Carolina Press).
    1997   'Racist Apocalypse: Millennialism on the Far Right', in *The Year 2000: Essays on The End* (ed. Charles B. Strozier and Michael Flynn; New York: New York University Press): 190-205.
Barr, David L. (ed.)
    2003   *Reading the Book of Revelation: A Resource for Students* (Atlanta: SBL).

Barthes, Roland
    1977   *Image, Music, Text* (New York: Hill & Wang).
Bauckham, Richard
    1993a   *The Climax of Prophecy: Studies on the Book of Revelation* (Edinburgh:
              T&T Clark).
    1993b   *The Theology of the Book of Revelation* (Cambridge: Cambridge University
              Press).
Baudrillard, Jean
    1993   *Symbolic Exchange and Death* (London: Sage).
    1994   *The Illusion of the End* (Cambridge: Polity Press).
Beal, Timothy K.
    2002   *Religion and Its Monsters* (New York: Routledge).
Beal, Timothy K., and Tod Linafelt
    2006   *Mel Gibson's Bible: Religion, Popular Culture, and The Passion of the Christ*
              (Chicago: University of Chicago Press).
Beavis, Mary Ann
    2003   '"Angels Carrying Savage Weapons": Uses of the Bible in Contemporary
              Horror Films', *Journal of Religion and Film* 7.2. June 2007
              <http://www.unomaha.edu/jrf/Vol7No2/angels.htm>.
Bell-Metereau, Rebecca
    1985   *Hollywood Androgyny* (New York: Columbia University Press).
Bellour, Raymond
    1976   'To Analyze, To Segment', *Quarterly Review of Film Studies* 1.3: 331-53.
    2000   *The Analysis of Film* (Bloomington: Indiana University Press).
Beqcuer, Marcos, and José Gatti
    1991   'Elements of Vogue', in *The Subcultures Reader* (eds. Ken Gelder and Sarah
              Thornton; London: Routledge): 445-53.
Bingen, Hildegard von
    1990   *Scivias* (eds. and trans. C. Hart and J. Bishop; New York: Paulist Press).
Bloom, Harold
    1993   *The American Religion: The Emergence of the Post-Christian Nation* (New
              York: Simon).
Bordwell, David
    1985   *Narration in the Fiction Film* (London: Routledge).
    1989   *Making Meaning: Inference and Rhetoric in the Interpretation of Cinema*
              (Cambridge: Harvard University Press).
    2006   *The Way Hollywood Tells It: Story and Style in Modern Movies* (Berkeley:
              University of California Press).
Bordwell, David, and Kristin Thompson
    1997   *Film Art: An Introduction* (New York: McGraw, 5th edn).
Boyarin, Daniel
    1999   *Dying for God: Martyrdom and the Making of Christianity and Judaism*
              (Stanford: Stanford University Press).
Boyer, Paul
    1992   *When Time Shall Be No More: Prophecy Belief in Modern American Culture*
              (Cambridge: Harvard University Press).
Bremmer, Jan N.
    1996   'Magic, Martyrdom and Women's Liberation in the Acts of Paul and

Thecla', in *The Apocryphal Acts of Paul and Thecla* (ed. Jan N. Bremmer; Kampen: Kok): 36-59.

Brenner, Athalya (ed.)
2001   *Prophets and Daniel: A Feminist Companion to the Bible* (Sheffield: Continuum).

Broderick, Mick
1994   'The Rupture of The Rapture: Recent Film Narratives of Apocalypse'. February 2007 <http://wwwmcc.murdoch.edu.au/%7Emickbrod/postmodm/m/text/rupture.html>.

Brooks, Peter
1984   *Reading for the Plot: Design and Intention in Narrative* (Oxford: Clarendon Press).

Bundtzen, Linda K.
2000   'Monstrous Mothers: Medusa, Grendel, and now Alien' in *The Gendered Cyborg* (ed. Gill Kirkup; London: Routledge): 101-109.

Campbell, Joseph
2008   *The Hero with a Thousand Faces* (Novato: New World Library).

Camus, Albert
1956   *The Fall* (New York: A Vintage Book).

Carroll, Noël
1998   *Interpreting the Moving Image* (Cambridge: Cambridge University Press).

Castelli, Elizabeth A.
1991   '"I Will Make Mary Male": Pieties of the Body and Gender Transformation of Christian Women in Late Antiquity', in *Body Guards: The Cultural Politics of Gender Ambiguity* (eds. Julia Epstein and Kristina Straub; New York: Routledge): 29-49.
1998   'Visions and Victims', *Women's Review of Books* 15.6: 14-15.

Castelli, Elizabeth A.
2004   *Martyrdom and Memory: Early Christian Culture Making* (New York: Columbia University Press).

Chion, Michel
1994   *Audio-Vision: Sound on Screen* (New York: Columbia University Press).

Clover, Carol J.
1992   *Men, Women, and Chain Saws: Gender in the Modern Horror Film* (Princeton: Princeton University Press).

Cohn, Norman
1993   *Cosmos, Chaos and the World to Come: The Ancient Roots of Apocalyptic Faith* (New Haven: Yale University Press).

Collins, John J.
1979   'Introduction: Towards the Morphology of a Genre', *Semeia 14: Apocalypse: The Morphology of a Genre*: 1-20.
1984   *The Apocalyptic Imagination: An Introduction to the Jewish Matrix of Christianity* (New York: Crossroad).

Corrington, Gail Paterson
1992   *Her Image of Salvation: Female Saviors and Formative Christianity* (Louisville: Westminster/Knox Press).

Corrington Streete, Gail
1999   'Women as Sources of Redemption and Knowledge in Early Christian

Traditions', in *Women & Christian Origins* (eds. Ross Shepard Kramer and Mary Rose D'Angelo; New York: Oxford University Press): 330-54.

Creed, Barbara

 1993   *The Monstrous-Feminine: Film, Feminism, Psychoanalysis* (London: Routledge).

 2000   'Alien and the Monstrous-Feminine', in *The Gendered Cyborg: A Reader* (eds. Gill Kirkup, Linda Janes, Kathryn Woodward and Fiona Hovenden; London: Routledge): 124-35. First published in *Alien Zone* (1990). Excerpted from Creed's 'Horror and the Monstrous-Feminine: An Imaginary Abjection', *Screen* 28.2 (1987).

Culler, Jonathan

 1982   *On Deconstruction: Theory and Criticism after Structuralism* (London: Routledge and Kegan).

 2002   *The Pursuit of Signs: Semiotics, Literature, Deconstruction* (Ithaca: Cornell University Press).

Cunneen, Joseph

 1993   'Film and the Sacred', *Cross Currents* 43.1: 92-104.

Davis, Mike

 1998   *Ecology of Fear: Los Angeles and the Imagination of Disaster* (New York: Vintage).

Deleuze, Gilles

 1993   *The Fold: Leibniz and the Baroque* (Minneapolis: University of Minnesota Press).

DeSilva, David A.

 1998   *4 Maccabees* (Sheffield: Sheffield Academic Press).

Dickinson, Kay

 2003   'Pop, Speed, Teenagers and the MTV Aesthetic', in *Movie Music, The Film Reader* (ed. Kay Dickinson; London: Routledge): 143-51.

Doherty, Thomas

 1996   'Genre, Gender and the *Aliens* Trilogy', in *The Dread of Difference: Gender and the Horror Film* (ed. Barry Keith Grant; Austin: University of Texas Press): 181-99.

Droge, Arthur J., and James D. Tabor

 1992   *A Noble Death: Suicide and Martyrdom among Christians and Jews in the Antiquity* (San Francisco: Harper).

Dyer, Richard.

 1979   *Stars* (London: BFI).

 1997   *White* (London: Routledge).

 2004   *Heavenly Bodies: Film Stars and Society* (London: Routledge).

Ebert, Roger

 1991   'The Rapture', *Chicago Sunday Times* 27 October.

Eliot, T.S.

 1950   *The Sacred Wood: Essays on Poetry and Criticism* (London: Methuen).

Ellis, John

 1982   *Visible Fictions: Cinema, Television, Video* (London: Routledge).

Elsaesser, Thomas, and Warren Buckland

 2002   *Studying Contemporary American Film: A Guide to Movie Analysis* (London: Arnold).

Emmerich, Anne Catherine
    2003   *The Dolorous Passion of Our Lord Jesus Christ* (El Sobrante: North Bay).

Fiske, John
    1995   *Television Culture* (London: Routledge).

Fleming, Charles
    1998   *High Concept: Don Simpson and the Hollywood Culture of Excess* (New York: Doubleday).

Frye, Northrop
    1982   *The Great Code: The Bible and Literature* (Toronto: Academic Press).

Frykholm, Amy Johnson
    2004   *Rapture Culture: Left Behind in Evangelical America* (Oxford: Oxford University Press).

Fukuyama, Francis
    1992   *The End of History and the Last Man* (London: Penguin).

Fuller, Robert
    1995   *Naming the Antichrist: The History of an American Obsession* (Oxford: Oxford University Press).

Garber, Zev
    2006   *Mel Gibson's Passion: The Film, The Controversy and its Implications* (Ashland: Purdue University Press).

Garrett, Susan R.
    1992   'Revelation', in *The Women's Bible Commentary* (eds. Carol A. Newsom and Sharon H. Ringe; Louisville: Westminster/Knox Press): 377-82.

Gibson, Sheila
    1999   'Something to Crow About', *Skeptic* 7.3: 20-22.

Gould, Stephen Jay
    1997   *Questioning the Millennium: A Rationalist's Guide to a Precisely Arbitrary Countdown* (New York: Harmony).

Halberstam, Judith
    1998   *Female Masculinity* (Durham: Duke University Press).

Hardy, Phil
    1993   'Review of The Seventh Sign', in *The Encyclopedia of Horror* (London: Aurum).

Hasan-Rokem, Galit
    2000   *Web of Life: Folklore and Midrash in Rabbinic Literature* (Stanford: Stanford University Press).
    2003   'Martyr vs. Martyr: The Sacred Language of Violence', *Ethnologia Europaea* 33.2: 99-104.

Hasan-Rokem, Galit, and Alan Dundes (eds.)
    1986   *The Wandering Jew: Essays in the Interpretation of a Christian Legend* (Bloomington: Indiana University Press).

Heath, Stephen
    1981   *Questions of Cinema* (London: MacMillan).

Henten, Jan Willem van
    1997   *The Maccabean Martyrs as Saviours of the Jewish People: A Study of 2 and 4 Maccabees* (Leiden: Brill).
    2003a   'De Openbaring van Johannes', in *De Bijbel Literair: Opbouw en gedachtegang van de bijbelse geschriften en hun onderlinge relaties* (eds.

J. Fokkelman and W.J.C. Weren; Zoetermeer/Kapellen: Meinema/
Pelckmans): 745-59.

2003b   'Internet Martyrs and Violence: Victims and/or Perpetrators?', in *Sanctified Aggression: Legacies of Biblical and Post Biblical Vocabularies of Violence* (eds. Jonneke Bekkenkamp and Yvonne Sherwood; London: Continuum).

2004   'Jewish and Christian Martyrs', in *Holy Persons in Judaism and Christianity* (eds. Marcel Poorthuis and Joshua Schwartz; Leiden: Brill).

2008   'Balaam in Revelation 2:14' in *The Prestige of the Pagan Prophet Balaam in Judaism, Early Christianity and Islam: Themes in Biblical Narrative* (eds. George H. van Kooten and Jacques van Ruiten; Leiden: Brill): 247-63.

Henten, Jan Willem van, and Friedrich Avemarie
2002   *Martyrdom and Noble Death: Selected Texts from Graeco-Roman and Christian Antiquity* (London: Routledge).

Henten, Jan Willem van, and Osger Mellink (eds.)
1998   *Visioenen aangaande het einde: Apocalyptische geschriften en bewegingen door de eeuwen heen* (Zoetermeer: Uitgeverij Meinema).

The Internet Medieval Source Book. <http://www.fordham.edu/halsall/source/perpetua.html>

The Internet Movie Database. <http://www.imdb.com>

James, Caryn
1991   'Film View: Zeitgeist Isn't a Snap to Capture', *New York Times* 13 October. February 2011 < http://www.nytimes.com/1991/10/13/movies/film-view-zeitgeist-isn-t-a-snap-to-capture.html?src=pm.

Juergensmeyer, Mark
2003   *Terror in the Mind of God: The Global Rise of Religious Violence* (Berkeley: University of California Press).

Keane, Stephen
2001   *Disaster Movies: The Cinema of Catastrophe* (London: Wallflower).

Keller, Catherine
1992   'Why Apocalypse, Now?', *Theology Today* 49.2: 183-95.
1996   *Apocalypse Now and Then: A Feminist Guide to the End of the World* (Boston: Beacon).
2003   *Face of the Deep: A Theology of Becoming* (London: Routledge).
2005   *God and Power: Counter-Apocalyptic Journeys* (Minneapolis: Fortress).

Kermode, Frank
1967   *The Sense of an Ending: Studies in the Theory of Fiction* (New York: Oxford University Press).

King, Geoff
2000   *Spectacular Narratives: Hollywood in the Age of the Blockbuster* (London: Tauris).

Kohlberg, E.
2004   'Shahid', in *The Encyclopaedia of Islam* (eds. C.E. Bosworth *et al.*; Leiden: Brill): 203-207.

Kovacs, Judith, and Christopher Rowland
2004   *Revelation: The Apocalypse of Jesus Christ* (Oxford: Blackwell).

Krauss, Rosalind E.
1997   'The Destiny of the *Informe*', in *Formless: A User's Guide* (eds. Yve-Alain Bois and Rosalind E. Krauss; New York: Zone): 235-52.

Kristeva, Julia
   1980   *Desire in Language: A Semiotic Approach to Literature and Art* (New York: Columbia University Press).
   1982   *Powers of Horror: An Essay on Abjection* (New York: Columbia University Press).
LaHaye, Timothy, and Jerry Jenkins
   1995   *Left Behind: A Novel of the Earth's Last Days* (Wheaton, IL: Tyndale).
Lawrence, John Shelton, and Robert Jewett
   2002   *The Myth of the American Superhero* (Grand Rapids: Eerdmans).
Lefkowitz, Mary R.
   1976   'The Motivations for St. Perpetua's Martyrdom', *Journal of the American Academy of Religion* 44.3: 417-21.
Lewinstein, Keith.
   2002   "The Revaluation of Martyrdom in Early Islam', in *Sacrificing the Self: Perspectives on Martyrdom and Religion* (ed. Margaret Cormack; Oxford: Oxford University Press).
Maier, Harry O.
   2002   *Apocalypse Recalled: The Book of Revelation after Christendom* (Minneapolis: Fortress Press).
Martin, Joel W.
   2000   'Anti-feminism in Recent Apocalyptic Film', *The Journal of Religion and Film* 4.1. August 2005 <http://www.unomaha.edu/jrf/antifem.htm>.
Martin, Joel W., and Conrad E. Ostwalt, Jr. (eds.)
   1995   *Screening the Sacred: Religion, Myth, and Ideology in Popular American Film* (Boulder: Westview).
Maslin, Janet
   1991   'Review/Film Festival: Religion Taken to the Breaking Point', *New York Times* 30 September. February 2011
            <http://movies.nytimes.com/movie/review?res=9D0CE7D71339F933A05 75AC0A967958260> .
McCarthy, Todd
   1998   'Armageddon', *Variety* June 23. February 2011
            <http://www.variety.com/review/VE1117477644?refcatid=31>.
McDonald, Paul
   2000   *The Star System: Hollywood's Production of Popular Identities* (London: Wallflower).
McEver, Matthew
   1998   'The Messianic Figure in Film: Christology Beyond the Biblical Epic,' *The Journal of Religion and Film* 2.2. October online version <http:// avalon.unomaha.edu/jrf/McEverMessiah.htm>
McHenry, Eric
   1998   'Deep Impact Screenwriter to Speak about Apocalypse as Entertainment, and Vice Versa', *B.U. Bridge* II.16. February 2011 <http://www.bu.edu/ bridge/archive/1998/12-04/features1.html>.
Merriam-Webster Online Dictionary <http://www.m-w.com/dictionary/vision>.
Miles, Margaret R.
   1989   '"Becoming Male": Women Martyrs and Ascetics', in *Carnal Knowing: Female Nakedness and Religious Meaning in the Christian West* (New York: Vintage): 53-77.

1996   *Seeing and Believing: Religion and Values in the Movies* (Boston: Beacon Press).

Mitchell, Jolyon P., and S. Brent Plate
2007   *The Religion and Film Reader* (New York: Routledge).

Moore, Stephen D.
2001   *God's Beauty Parlor and Other Queer Spaces In and Around the Bible* (Stanford: Stanford University Press).

Moore, Stephen D., and Janice Capel Anderson
1998   'Taking It Like a Man: Masculinity in 4 Maccabees', *The Journal of Biblical Literature* 117.2: 249-73.

Mulvey, Laura
2006   *Death 24x a Second: Stillness and the Moving Image* (London: Reaktion).

Neupert, Richard
1995   *The End: Narration and Closure in the Cinema* (Detroit: Wayne State University Press).

Newman, Kim
1988   'The Rapture', *Monthly Film Bulletin* 55.658: 339-40.

Newport, Kenneth G.C.
2000   *Apocalypse and Millennium: Studies in Biblical Eisegesis* (Cambridge: Cambridge University Press).

Newton, Judith
1980   'Feminism and Anxiety in Alien,' *Science Fiction Studies* 7.3. Rpt. in *Alien Zone: Cultural Theory and Contemporary Science Fiction Cinema* (ed. Annette Kuhn; London: Verso): 82-87.

Nolan, Steve
1998   'The Books of the Films: Trends in Religious Film Analysis', *Literature and Theology* 23.1: 1-15.

Ostwalt, Conrad E.
2000   'Armageddon at the Millennial Dawn', *The Journal of Religion and Film* 4.1. June 2008 <http://www.unomaha.edu/jrf/armagedd.htm>.

Ostwalt, Conrad E., Jr.
1995   'Hollywood and Armageddon: Apocalyptic Themes in Recent Cinematic Representation', in *Screening the Sacred: Religion, Myth, and Ideology in Popular American Film* (eds. Joel W. Martin and Conrad E. Ostwalt, Jr.; Boulder: Westview): 55-63.

Panofsky, Erwin
1967   *Studies in Iconology: Humanistic Themes in the Art of the Renaissance* (New York: Harper).

Papastergiadis, Nikos
1997   'Tracing Hybridity in Theory,' in *Debating Cultural Hybridity: Multicultural Identities and the Politics of Anti-Racism* (eds. Pnina Werbner and Tariq Modood; London: Zed): 257-81.

Paulien, Jon
2003   'The Lion/Lamb King: Reading the Apocalypse from Popular Culture', in *Reading the Book of Revelation: A Resource for Students* (ed. David L. Barr; Atlanta: SBL): 151-61.

Penner, Todd, and Caroline Vander Stichele
2003   'The Tyranny of the Martyr: Violence and Victimization in Martyrdom Discourse and the Movies of Lars von Trier', in *Sanctified Aggression:*

Legacies of Biblical and Post Biblical Vocabularies of Violence (eds. Jonneke Bekkenkamp and Yvonne Sherwood; London: Continuum): 175-92.

Peteet, Julie
 1997 'Icons and Militants: Mothering in the Danger Zone', *Signs* 23.1: 103-29.

Pippin, Tina
 1987 *Political Reality and the Liberating Vision: The Context of the Book of Revelation* (Southern Baptist Theological Seminary).
 1992 'The Heroine and the Whore: Fantasy and the Female in the Apocalypse of John', *Semeia* 60 (Philadelphia: Fortress): 67-82.
 1999 *Apocalyptic Bodies: The Biblical End of the World in Text and Image* (London: Routledge).

Plate, S. Brent (ed.)
 2004 *Re-Viewing The Passion: Mel Gibson's Film and Its Critics* (New York: Palgrave Macmillan).

Quinby, Lee
 1994 *Anti-Apocalypse: Exercises in Genealogical Criticism* (Minneapolis: University of Minnesota Press).

Reinhartz, Adele
 1999 'Scripture on the Silver Screen,' *Journal of Religion and Film* 3.1. July 2007 <http://www.unomaha.edu/jrf/scripture.htm>.
 2003 *Scripture on the Silver Screen* (Louisville: Westminster/Knox Press).
 2007 *Jesus of Hollywood* (Oxford: Oxford University Press).

Resseguie, James L.
 1998 *Revelation Unsealed: A Narrative Critical Approach to John's Apocalypse* (Leiden: Brill).

Ryan, Michael, and Douglas Kellner
 1988 *Camera Politica: The Politics and Ideology of Contemporary Hollywood Film* (Bloomington: Indiana University Press).

Salisbury, Joyce
 1997 *Perpetua's Passion: The Death and Memory of a Young Roman Woman* (New York: Routledge).

Salt, Barry
 1992 *Film Style and Technology: History and Analysis* (London: Starword).

Schneider, Karen
 1999 'With Violence if Necessary,' *Journal of Popular Film and Television* 27.1: 2-11.

Schüssler-Fiorenza, Elisabeth
 1981 *Invitation to the Book of Revelation: A Commentary on the Apocalypse with Complete Text from the Jerusalem Bible* (New York: Image).
 1991 *Revelation: Vision of a Just World* (Minneapolis: Fortress Press).

Scott, Joan
 1989 'Gender: A Useful Category of Historical Analysis', in *Coming to Terms: Feminism, Theory, Politics* (ed. Elizabeth Weed; New York: Routledge): 81-100.

Shaw, Brent D.
 1993 'The Passion of Perpetua', *Past and Present* 193: 3-45.

Shepard, Lucius
 2003 'Onward Christian Movies', *Fantasy & Science Fiction* 104.6: 120-25.

Shewring, W.H. (trans.)
  1931   *The Passion of Perpetua and Felicity* (London: Sheed and Ward).
Smith, Gavin
  1994   'We Fabricate Our Lives: Michael Tolkin interviewed by Gavin Smith',
          Film Comment 30.5: 54-59.
Strauven, Wanda (ed.)
  2006   *The Cinema of Attractions Reloaded* (Amsterdam: Amsterdam University
          Press).
Strozier, Charles
  1994   *Apocalypse: On the Psychology of Fundamentalism in America* (Boston:
          Beacon Press).
Swallow, James
  2003   *Dark Eye: The Films of David Fincher* (London: Reynolds and Hearn).
Tasker, Yvonne
  1993   *Spectacular Bodies: Gender, Genre and the Action Cinema* (London:
          Routledge).
Tatum, W. Barnes
  1997   *Jesus at the Movies: A Guide to the First Hundred Years* (Santa Rosa:
          Polebridge Press).
Taubin, Amy
  1993   'The "Alien" Trilogy: From Feminism to Aids', in *Women and Film: A
          Sight and Sound Reader* (eds. Pam Cook and Philip Dodd; Philadelphia:
          Temple University Press): 93-100.
Thompson, Kristin
  1999   *Storytelling in the New Hollywood: Understanding Classical Narrative
          Technique* (Cambridge: Harvard University Press).
Thompson, Leonard L.
  1990   *The Book of Revelation: Apocalypse and Empire* (New York: Oxford
          University Press).
Travers, Peter
  1992   'Alien3', *Rolling Stone* September 9. February 2011
          <http://www.rollingstone.com/movies/reviews/alien-3-19920909>.
Vander Stichele, Caroline, and Todd Penner
  2006   'Passion for (the) Real? The Passion of the Christ and its Critics,' in
          Biblical Interpretation, 1-2.14 (Leiden: Brill): 18-36.
Walsh, Richard
  2002   'On Finding a Non-American Revelation,' in *Screening Scripture:
          Intertextual Connections Between Scripture and Film* (eds. George Aichele
          and Richard Walsh; Harrisburg: Trinity Press).
  2003   *Reading the Gospels in the Dark: Portrayals of Jesus in Film* (Harrisburg:
          Trinity Press).
Watts, Pauline Moffitt
  1985   'Prophecy and Discovery: On the Spiritual Origins of Christopher
          Columbus's "Enterprise of the Indies"', *The American Historical Review*
          173-102.
Weber, Timothy P.
  1987   *Living in the Shadow of the Second Coming: American Premillennialism
          1875-1982* (Chicago: Chicago University Press).

Wojcik, Daniel
    1997   *The End of the World as We Know It: Faith, Fatalism, and Apocalypse in America* (New York: New York University Press).

Woodward, Kenneth
    1991   *Making Saints. Inside the Vatican: Who Become Saints, Who Do Not, and Why…* (London: Chatto & Windus).

Wright, Melanie J.
    2007   'Religion and Film', *The Religion and Film Reader* (eds. Jolyon Mitchell and S. Brent Plate; New York: Routledge): 438-44.

Wyatt, Justin
    1994   *High Concept: Movies and Marketing in Hollywood* (Austin: University of Texas Press).

Yacowar, Maurice
    1976   'The Bug in the Rug: Notes on the Disaster Genre', in *Film Genre: Theory and Criticism* (ed. Barry K. Grant; New Jersey: Scarecrow): 90-107.

Zizek, Slavoj
    1991   *Looking Awry: An Introduction to Jacques Lacan Through Popular Culture* (Cambridge: MIT).

INDEX

Lightning Source UK Ltd.
Milton Keynes UK
UKOW031249080212

186899UK00003B/2/P

9 781907 534249